REVISED EDITION

THE
ᴺᴱᵂ
BUSINESS
ᴼᶠ
BANKING

Transforming Challenges
Into Opportunities
in Today's
Financial Services
Marketplace

GEORGE M. BOLLENBACHER

A BankLine Publication

IRWIN
Professional Publishing®

1333 Burr Ridge Parkway
Burr Ridge, IL 60521
(800) 634-3966

BANK**LINE**™
A BankLine Publication

ISBN 1-55738-771-6

Printed in the United States of America

BB

1 2 3 4 5 6 7 8 9 0

JB

Table of Contents

Preface

In the publishing business, three years seems to be the half-life of the average book. After about that amount of time, a book is usually near the end of its natural life, and is either retired or relaunched. It has been three years since the first edition of this book came out, and I feel very fortunate that the Richard D. Irwin Company was positive enough about it that they decided to issue a revised edition.

In the banking business, on the other hand, three years can either be the blink of an eye or a lifetime. When I finished the first edition of this book at the end of 1991, the banking business was coming to the end of a very bad stretch. Profit levels had been depressed for at least three years, loan loss provisions were averaging above 1.2 percent of assets, and the press were freely predicting the demise of the industry as we knew it.

As I finished this revised edition at the end of 1994, things couldn't have been more different. The banking industry had enjoyed three years of extraordinary prosperity. Returns on equity had doubled, from around 8 percent to around 16 percent; loan loss provisions had been halved, from around 1.2 percent of assets to under .6 percent, and Congress was apparently planning to remove, at long last, the outdated provisions of the Glass-Steagall Act.

But, as the French saying goes, *plus cá change, plus cá meme chose.* The more things change, the more they stay the same. By the beginnings of 1995, there were plenty of signs that, as much as things weren't as bad as they looked in 1991, they weren't as good as they looked in 1994. Market forces were already pushing net interest margins down, noninterest expenses were creeping back up, and trading losses had begun to replace commercial real estate losses as the risk boomerang *du jour.*

The fact is that under the surface the business of banking was still very much as it was in 1991. As I looked at this book to see what needed revising, I found that much of it was still very relevant. The first chapter had to be completely rewritten, to reflect the new conditions of the banking marketplace. And I added a section at the end, about managing in a changing environment, with chapters on productivity and power, employee enhancement, and utilizing the branch as an engine of business.

In addition, my research over the last three years has led me to identify four imperatives for the banking business as it prepares for the twenty-first century. They are:

❑ Banks must regain lost market share--both in terms of customers and share of wallet.

❑ Banks must differentiate themselves from their bank and nonbank competitors.

❑ Banks must operate their businesses more efficiently--creating higher levels of revenue from the same or lower resources.

❑ Banks must manage the risks of their business, by watching for the pitfalls of the future instead of the pitfalls of the past.

However, it is important to understand that even these imperatives are not brand new; they have actually been around for years. They are the constant undercurrent of the banking business, only obscured by the shifting kaleidoscope of daily events and demands. And, at their core they depend on one common capability, the ability of bank management to combine employees and information in creative and effective ways.

It is this combination of well-motivated, -trained, and -equipped employees with useful, accurate, and available information that will create value for both customers and stockholders. It is this combination which will distance the winners from the rest of the pack. Some banks, and some bankers, have already grasped this thinking and, whether they are large or small, these are the banks which will dominate their markets.

In another three years, when this edition will have worn out its welcome, I can assure you that the business of banking will again be different from what it is today. In all likelihood, interest margins will be narrower, noninterest revenue sources will be both more plentiful and more important, and loan loss provisions will be higher. But the formula for success will still be the same: smart, motivated employees under inspired leadership delivering quality service at fair price. If this book can help you achieve that formula, I will have done my job.

I | The Fundamentals of the Business

When you are involved in the day-to-day struggles of the business world, and when things are going badly, it is hard to see the signs of a turnaround—the leading indicators that begin improving before the business as a whole does. And when things are going well, it is tempting to not look for the indicators of the next downturn.

But good businessmen and women, like good sailors, always keep an eye on the horizon. Is that cloud formation over there an interlude or a storm on the way? Is that breath of wind on your cheek going to fill your sails or rip them to shreds? Are we headed into a tropical sunset or the Bermuda Triangle? The secret is to look behind the appearances that satisfy most observers and find the real causes.

Good businessmen, like good sailors, know that experience is the best teacher, and that there is no substitute for time at the helm. Experience teaches us the patterns of the business, and it teaches us to distinguish the important from the spectacular. But even experience begins somewhere, and in business it begins with the fundamentals.

The fundamentals of the finance business can be divided into three parts. The first, which might be called research, answers the question, What is the status of the industry, and what is its future? The second answers the question, How do we build a winning strategy? And the third answers the question, What are the business practices we need to follow to have a good business foundation? Part I of this book will answer these questions.

1

1 | The Status of the Financial Services Industry

It is probably fair to say that every business is cyclical, and that almost every cycle follows a familiar pattern. Whatever the business, when its products find a ready market the business prospers. Increased demand leads to increased profits and increased production, which leads to a larger work force and increased wages and salaries. The larger work force and the larger production capacity lead to more need for control, which leads to an army of controllers and accountants, as well as a larger marketing force, all of which results in a larger overhead. In this ebullient environment, almost no one thinks about stagnation and contraction.

However, stagnation eventually comes to every business. As markets become saturated and more competitors enter the picture, margins shrink and profits sometimes disappear. The large production machinery that was once so necessary is now obese and must undergo a strenuous diet. In a stagnant market, the accumulated overhead which kept everything humming as demand grew suddenly reveals itself to be an unproductive and expensive luxury, which must be pruned for the business to regain its health. In this environment, almost no one thinks about recovery and growth.

But, quite often, the business does recover. New versions of the product spark new demand, and, even if the old versions have razor-thin margins, the new versions have healthier margins. New versions also appeal to new markets, which require new marketing efforts and resurgent production. Having gone through the painful slimming-down process, businesses start from a healthier base and reap the benefits of increased productivity as demand grows.

For a while, all those benefits of recovery accrue to the business, but gradually many of the old problems creep back in. Increases in production stop leading to increases in productivity, more requirements for control lead to bigger overhead, more competitors start eating into the market, and the storm clouds gather on the horizon again.

At any point in time, there are businesses in all stages of these cycles. Some, like the software business, seem to forever be in the up part of the cycle. Others, like the airlines or the steel industry, seem always to be in the down part. For those who read the business press, and are close observers of the business scene, there are literally hundreds of these stories going on all the time.

Every once in a while, many of the cycles seem to come together, in either the up or down part. At that point we have a business cycle, where each of the individual cycles reinforces the whole. As the 1980s came to an end and the 1990s began, we had such an event on the downside virtually everywhere in the industrialized world. A wide range of businesses entered a period of intensified competition, with shrinking margins, a wave of consolidations, and round after round of layoffs. Whether this event was caused by a decade of corporate leverage, or whether the leverage simply sparked a contraction which was destined to happen sooner or later, there is no doubt that the leverage made the contraction sharper and deeper.

At the very center of that leverage, and at the center of the recession, were America's banks. The role they played isn't necessarily well understood, but we will need to understand it to understand the new business of banking.

Since the first wealthy merchants began storing their customers' gold in their counting houses, and lending out the idle balances, banks have played a central part in all economies. Because that role is so important to the economy, bankers have viewed their business as primarily one of taking deposits in one window, and lending them out another. This was the oldest function of a bank, and it is still the central one in many countries. In fact, this function, called intermediation, has been absolutely essential for economic development. The industrial revolution in Europe in the eighteenth century, and in the United States after the Civil War, was only possible because banks channeled savings into the massive investments necessary for the industrialization.

With such an important role came many trappings, such as wealth and power. Bankers have sat within the circles of power in many countries, next to the politicians and businessmen they financed. Some, like the Rothschilds, Mellons, or Schiffs, have played a role in the rise and fall of kings, governments, industries, and companies, turning their control of the purse into financial advice, financial control, and sometimes outright ownership.

Given such a history, it is easy to see why bankers, and everyone else for that matter, would come to believe that banks had a protected position in the economic scheme. There is no doubt that the functions that banks traditionally perform are essential to any economy, but just what are those functions in today's world?

1. *Storing value.* By holding money and making it available, banks allow people and businesses to concentrate on other functions and operate more efficiently. However, as businesses and people become more efficient, they move from using currency to pay for goods and services to using bank instruments to pay for things. At this point, the bulk of the money in any country isn't paper and coins, it is what banks owe their depositors. In other words, what everyone else thinks of as an asset, banks think of as a liability.

2. *Processing payments.* When so much of a country's money consists of bank deposits, people and businesses will soon figure out a way to pay for things by instructing banks to make accounting entries instead of by handing over currency. Old fashioned ways of issuing instructions involve using paper, like checks or debit memos, but much more efficient electronic methods now exist. However, because the banking systems in some countries haven't priced out the inefficiencies of paper-based payments, they are still popular there. One of those countries is the United States.

3. *Making loans.* Because banks have been for hundreds of years the primary holders of public funds, they have also been the primary makers and holders of loans, to both individuals and businesses. Choosing to whom to lend, and overseeing the process of lending and being repaid, have long been regarded as a special expertise of bankers. The interest spread between what banks pay on deposits and what they charge for loans has long been the primary source of revenue for banks.

The importance of these three functions has led bankers, regulators, legislators, and the public in general to think of the business of banking in these terms. As a result, the business of banking has largely been defined as a balance-sheet and payment-processing business, and the kinds of expertise that are required of bankers have been thought of as balance-sheet and payment-processing expertise.

Everywhere one looks one sees evidence of this narrow view of banking. Call reports, which banks file quarterly with their regulators, show a heavy concentration on these balance-sheet businesses. When Congress looks at banks it tends to see balance-sheet businesses. And bankers themselves still tend to think of their business in terms of deposits, loans, and payment processing.

Unfortunately, balance-sheet based banking puts banks right in the heart of the business cycle. When banks depend on their balance sheets for the bulk of their revenue, they are incented to find loan categories where they can generate both large volumes and high spreads. Those loan categories also contain lots of risk. In the up part of the business cycle, banks congregate in certain industries where loan volumes and spreads can be manufactured. With so many banks looking to lend in the same industries, competition drives banks to take ever higher risk, financing ever more speculative ventures. Whether it is loans to less-developed countries, loans for leveraged acquisitions, or loans to finance commercial real estate, money in search of projects always leads to unserviceable debt.

Then, when economic reality finally sets in, banks often overreact in the opposite direction. After seeming to lend to any borrower who comes in the door, banks suddenly revert to not lending to anyone, no matter how good a credit risk. Saddled with a heavy load of nonperforming loans, banks often treat all borrowers in those industries as if they were in default. Not only does this reaction make the recession worse, it often makes the banks' position worse, because borrowers with unfinished projects often lose access to credit and must default.

Such a dark time existed for banks in the United States from 1988 to 1991, as the country grappled with a persistent recession. With the overriding impact of credit losses during that period, banks and banking observers were distracted from the larger picture of what was happening to their industry.

Looking at the Numbers

By 1992, both the economy and the banking industry were recovering, and that recovery was continuing through the middle of 1994. The recovery showed itself most obviously in banking profitability. In 1991, the average return on equity (ROE) for an American bank holding company was about 8 percent, in 1992, it was about 11.5 percent, and in 1993, it was about 15 percent. Incomplete reports for the first half of 1994 show that the ROE improvement was leveling off at around 16 percent.

These earnings improvements, coupled with some continuing consolidation in the industry, allowed many banks to report record earnings in 1993 (measured in absolute dollars), and in the first half of 1994. Regulators, bankers, Congress, and some of the business press took these improvements to mean that the banking business was healthy again, and that most of the banking industry's problems of the last ten years were behind us. In particular, it looked like the painful consolidation process the industry had been going through was finally paying off.

But a closer look at the profits and their make-up tells quite a different story. Using Sheshunoff call report data available through a OneSource CD-ROM, I looked at bank holding company performance in the United States from several viewpoints. First, I broke banking's return on assets (ROA) into its four main components: net interest margin (NIM), noninterest revenue (Nonint), noninterest expense (Ovhd), and loan loss provision (LLP), and calculated these components per dollar of average assets. I graphed ROA and those four components for all U. S. bank holding companies for 1992 and 1993 (Figure 1.1).

Figure 1.1
Bank Holding Company Performance, 1992-1993

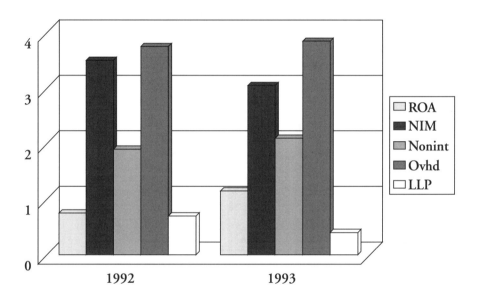

Source: Sheshunoff & Co.

The graph shows that ROA did indeed improve from 1992 to 1993, but that its improvement masked two negative developments over those two years. The first negative development was the erosion of NIM after two years of increases. The second was the increase in noninterest expense. These two negative developments were overshadowed by an increase in noninterest revenue and a drop in loan loss provision. We must keep in mind, though, that the two negatives outweighed the increase in noninterest revenue by itself, so ROA would have fallen without the boost from LLP. The problem is that banks cannot continue reducing their LLP every year, so, if NIM and overhead continue the way they are going, bank ROAs will have to begin falling soon.

Most bankers believe that one sure way around this earnings squeeze is consolidation—thinking that with larger size comes more efficiency. To test that hypothesis, I divided bank holding companies in the United States into five size classifications: very large (over $25 billion in assets), large ($10 – $25 billion), medium ($2 – $10 billion), small ($500 million – $2 billion), and very small ($50 – $500 million). First, I compared these categories on earnings for 1992 and 1993 (Figure 1.2). Because there was a significant incidence of extraordinary items for some categories and not others, I compared operating ROAs.

Figure 1.2
Bank Holding Company Performance, by Size 1992-1993

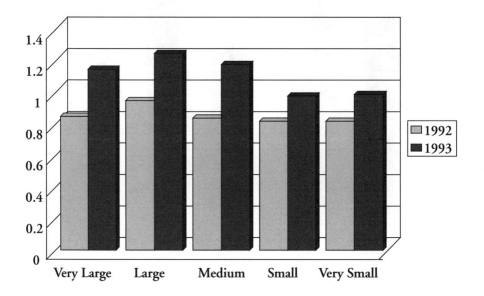

Source: Sheshunoff & Co.

The graph shows a surprising pattern for both years. Operating ROA rises as size increases in both years, until we reach the *very large* category, where it falls back. In fact, the *very large* category's ROA was roughly equal to the *medium* category's, meaning that there was little, if any, performance value to going all the way from, say, $5 billion to $50 billion in assets. The graph does indicate that there was some performance value in getting to $10 billion or so in assets.

I then categorized earnings by both size and income component for both 1992 and 1993 (Figures 1.3 and 1.4). The graphs for both years look almost the same, and they tell an interesting story about the banking business in the United States. All four components display distinct patterns across the size spectrum.

NIM decreases as size increases, slowly at first and then more rapidly. In one sense, NIM is a measure of the balance sheet's ability to generate income, so this

Figure 1.3
Bank Holding Company Income Components Full Year 1992

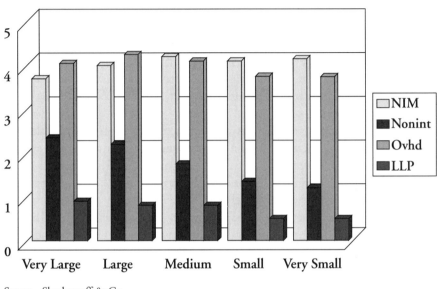

Source: Sheshunoff & Co.

Figure 1.4
Bank Holding Company Income Components Full Year 1993

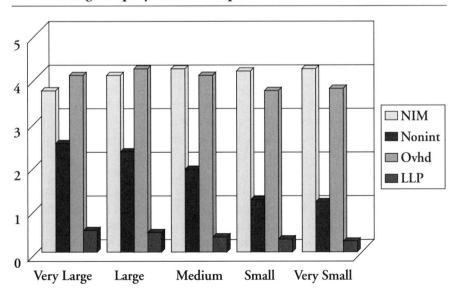

Source: Sheshunoff & Co.

comparison could be telling us that the larger the balance sheet is, the less efficient it is as an income generator. We could also read into this component something about competitive positioning, since smaller banks tend to be in less competitive environments, but the fact is that many small banks coexist in the same markets as big banks. Thus, there is a more signficant message in this pattern. The components of NIM are also reflections of the quality of an institution's customer relationships: how much the institution has to pay customers to keep their deposits and what it can charge them on loans. This pattern shows us that smaller banks have better relationships with their customers than large banks do, and that is one of their competitive weapons.

The exact opposite trend exists for noninterest revenue (Nonint). Here the level increases as size increases. Noninterest revenue stays fairly flat, just above 1 percent of assets, until we reach the *medium* category ($2 to $10 billion). It shows a big jump there, and continues increasing through the *very large* category, where it reaches approximately twice the level of the smaller banks.

Noninterest revenue comes from selling services, not space on the balance sheet. Although it is clear that some noninterest revenue is related to balance-sheet activities, like deposit-account fees, much of it, particularly in the larger banks, is not. Some of this revenue comes from processing business for others, like trade finance or securities safekeeping, while other revenues come from selling expertise, like cash-management services or mutual-fund sales. The implication here is that the larger banks are better at doing those things outside the confines of taking deposits and making loans, even if they don't have as good a customer relationship as smaller banks.

The trends for noninterest expense (Ovhd) are different from either NIM or Nonint. Overhead increases as size increases, until we reach the *very large* category, where it falls back. The first thing we should notice about overhead is that economies of scale do not appear to work in banking, with the exception of very large banks. At first this may appear counterintuitive, until we realize that banking is a service business, and that economies of scale are much less achievable in services, especially "knowledge-based" services, than in manufacturing. For example, there is a saying in the software industry that, if it takes one programmer one year to write a program, it will take two programmers two years to write it.

However, economies of scale do seem to work when we exceed $25 billion in assets. Unfortunately, they do not translate into increased profits. In fact, if we overlay the overhead graph from Figures 1.3 or 1.4 onto the operating earnings graph from Figure 1.2, we see that they show the same pattern—as overhead rises, so do earnings, and when overhead falls, so do earnings. This is also counterintuitive to bankers, who are used to the idea that one sure way to boost the bottom line is a round of cost cutting. This evidence suggests that there is a real danger in that approach.

So far, we have something of a dilemma, particularly in comparing the *very large* category to the *small* and *very small*. If the giant banks' NIM is somewhat lower, and their overhead is somewhat higher, and their noninterest income is significantly higher, why are their earnings lower? The answer lies in the last income component, loan loss provision (LLP), where the very large category is almost twice as high as the smaller banks. In 1992, when all categories had higher LLPs, this difference was more pronounced.

There are two main reasons why LLP rises as balance-sheet size rises. The first has to do with the quality of customer relationships, which appear to suffer as the category grows. Asset-quality management is really a function of knowing your borrower, not just at the time a loan is made, but throughout its life. When bankers go from having a first-name relationship with customers to thinking of them as numbers on a computer printout, their ability to track asset quality is bound to suffer.

But the primary reason is that large balance sheets are always hungry, requiring the very large institutions to generate lots of assets all the time. This voracious appetite, coupled with competitive pressures on NIM, lead lenders and the megabanks to put on a certain amount of lower-quality assets. Then, their distance from the customers makes it more difficult for them to monitor asset performance or do anything about the quality if something goes wrong.

When we look at the graphs in Figures 1.3 and 1.4 as portraits of banking, we can see that the business changes radically across the size spectrum. For one thing, at the small end NIM exceeds Ovhd, while at the large end Ovhd exceeds NIM. Small banks can afford to live off their balance sheets, if just barely, and big banks cannot. This is an absolutely fundamental difference between large and small banks, and one which will become more important as time goes by. It is also why we mostly hear small-town bankers talking about sticking to the basics of the business, while their big-city colleagues talk about remaking their bank in a different image.

Another crucial part of the portrait is the impact of asset quality as bank size increases. Loan losses are certainly the bane of a banker's existence, but they are also the major contributor to the volatility of bank earnings. Just as bankers play follow-the-leader in their lending practices, they play follow-the-leader in having to reserve for bad debts. Because large banks have such volatile loan losses, they have more volatile earnings than smaller banks do. Earnings volatility is the enemy of stock price, so it shouldn't surprise us that big banks tend to have a lower price/earnings multiple than smaller banks do.

Looking beyond the Numbers

These graphs and financial results can give us a good picture of *what* was happening, but not of *why* it was happening. To find out some of the whys, in 1992 Unisys Corporation commissioned a survey of about 300 banking executives at about 250 of the largest banks and thrift institutions in the United States. Our interviewers asked a series of questions about what bankers felt was important to their employers and themselves, and a series of questions about how well their banks were able to compete and satisfy their customers. Some of the results, which were reported in the *American Banker* in March, 1994, were eye-opening.

We began with a series of questions about banking in general. We asked bankers what were the most important developments in the industry, and their most common answer was consolidation. That answer was interesting in its own right, but it was even more interesting as a clue to why banks and bankers have found it so difficult to adapt to change.

Although consolidation is indeed a constant process in the banking business, and may be very important to those facing job-security issues because of it, it is a *derived* factor, not a causal factor. As long as bankers focus most of their attention on derived factors instead of causal factors, they will continue to play catch-up instead of getting in front of the curve of change.

So, what are the causal factors? One possibility was recognized by a significant minority of the bankers—the continual erosion of banks' market position, which was often expressed as increased competition from nonbank entities. A great deal of research has shown that, on both sides of the balance sheet, and in virtually all of their traditional product lines, banks have been losing market share for years. Two exceptions where banks have been gaining market share are mutual fund sales and insurance sales—areas which I will cover later in Chapter 4, Maximizing Noninterest Income. But what has caused this erosion? Is this just another derived factor, perhaps at a lower level?

There were several more basic causal factors which came out of our research, one of which became clear to me as I read the results, but was apparently not clear to the bankers who were interviewed. One of our questions was, "Overall, what is the most rewarding part of your job?" The three most popular responses were: 1) contributing to the bank's performance and making positive changes in their company and industry, 2) helping employees meet their career goals and building a team environment, and 3) helping customers get what they want.

Our researchers concluded from these answers that bank employees are particularly motivated by the activity of working together as a team, one that gets results in three critical areas: corporate performance, personal performance, and customer satisfaction. When we look at it, that is an impeccable recipe for success in any business. The fact is, there is nothing wrong with the motivations of most of the people who work in this industry.

Our next question was, "What would you say is the most frustrating part of your job?" By far the biggest frustration faced by these relatively senior bankers was the bureaucracy and political nature of the banking work place. In other words, the good motivations and desires of these bankers were being consumed by their own corporate culture, and, although they wanted very much to change the culture, they believed that they were powerless to do so, even though they are perceived within their own organizations as wielding most of the power. This dichotomy is found in most large businesses, and it is a major contributor in the inertia that afflicts many of them. I will address it in more detail in Chapter 15, Productivity[2] and Power in a Changing Bank.

Another basic causal factor surfaced from two other questions that we asked. Because of the order in which they were asked, most of the respondents didn't see the significance of the relationship between the questions. I will present them in the reverse order, so that their impact becomes more obvious.

The second of the two questions was, "What are the primary things that your customers tell you they want from you?" Over half the respondents said that their customers were asking for more personalized service from more knowledgeable employees. Of all the things we learned in this survey, this has the most far-reaching import. What these bankers were telling us was that, according to their customers, their primary differentiator was not their branch locations, or their ATMs, or their "Super-Saver CDs," or their interest rates, or their convenient hours, but their employees.

The first of the two questions was, "What changes have increased competition precipitated at your bank?" The three main responses, in order of frequency were:

Developing and offering new products
Doing more with less, often by reducing staff
More cross-selling and better understanding of the customer

There is an obvious disconnect here, one which was not immediately apparent to the bankers themselves. The only mention of employees in these responses was to indicate that they were a declining part of the equation. If customer retention is the key to higher profitability, as most bankers think it is, and customers place the highest value on employee interaction, then why are most bankers focusing their efforts in areas which customers tell them are less important, and essentially ignoring areas in which customers place a high value?

Drawing Some Conclusions

All of this information comes together to lead us to some conclusions about the banking business.

Continued consolidation is inevitable, but its impact on banking profits is not likely to be beneficial. With the recent passage of the interstate banking bill, it looks very much like the constant, albeit slow, process of banking consolidation will continue, and probably accelerate. There is some indication that much of the consolidation will consist of mergers of equals between smaller institutions instead of acquisitions of small institutions by bigger ones, but all the evidence I can find leads me to the conclusion that such a concentration in the industry will not lead to higher returns, and will probably lead to lower ones.

That is not to say that banking profits cannot continue at current levels, although I do not expect that. It is to say that the forces unleashed by consolidation contain more negatives for bank earnings than positives. Whether I look at large versus small banks in the United States, or at banking industries around the world, I see evidence that consolidation may reduce noninterest expenses, but it will reduce net-interest income twice as fast. In addition, although larger banks are better at generating noninterest revenue than smaller ones, they have much more trouble with asset quality, and that makes their earnings lower on average and more volatile. Consolidation is inevitable, but it is not the answer to banks' earnings troubles; in fact it may add to them.

Although bank earnings are currently better than they have been for many years, the trends in bank earnings are not encouraging. Most bank holding company annual reports for 1992 and 1993 trumpet their record earnings, particularly if the banks balance sheet has grown over the same time period. However, a look inside those earnings shows quite a different picture. Returns on both equity and assets had begun to level off by the second half of 1993, and had further leveled by the first half of 1994.

The most unsettling news, though, is the make-up of those earnings improvements. Beginning in late 1992, and continuing through early 1994, net interest margins have been dropping after two years of increases and overhead has been rising, both of which are negative trends. While noninterest income has been rising, it hasn't improved enough to overcome these two negatives. The real kicker in recent earnings is the reductions in loan loss provisions, which are now under 50 basis points for the industry as a whole. Not only can banks no longer rely on reductions in LLP for earnings, but the drop in NIM will probably prompt banks to take on riskier assets, which can only lead to higher LLPs later. Overall, the prognosis for further increases in bank earnings is not favorable, and the stock market is reflecting that perception.

Although banks have fixed their earnings problems, at least for now, they have apparently not found a remedy for their market-share erosion. In their zeal to attend to credit and cost issues for the last several years, banks have largely let the service-quality issue slide. As a result, the erosion of banks' market position, particularly with the high-net-worth customer, continues unabated. Mutual fund companies and securities firms continue to eat into the liability side of bank balance sheets, and mortgage bankers and nonbank credit card issuers eat into the asset side. More and more, banks are left with the less-profitable customer, and the less-profitable part of their remaining customers' business.

The erosion of market share is the most serious long-term threat the banking industry faces. Because bankers view themselves as a necessary ingredient in a healthy economy, they appear not to recognize the critical nature of this threat. What they seem not to be aware of is that Ed Furash, of the banking consulting firm, Furash and Co., made the observation that it is possible to have a banking system without having banks. Unless banks wake up to the market-share issue, they may suffer the same fate as the dinosaurs, who were extinct before they realized that they were in danger.

The key to regaining market share is differentiation, and the key to differentiation is the bank's employees. Increasing market share means displacing a competitor; it means taking a competitor's customers away. When it comes to banking relationships, this means differentiating yourself from those competitors. In spite of the importance of differentiation in this regard, most bankers know very little about it.

Most bankers, particularly those at large institutions, try to differentiate themselves through such things as branch location, product features, advertising, or cost. But our research indicates that the primary differentiator, in the mind of the customer, is personalized service from a knowledgeable employee. In spite of this fact, bank managements continue to de-emphasize the employee in many ways. Customer-contact employees, like tellers, customer-service representatives, and telephone-center employees, tend to be at the bottom of the corporate ladder, in compensation as well as position. Banks still regard products as their primary offerings, instead of personalized service. And banks continue to regard most contact with a customer as a cost-driven event instead of a revenue-driven one.

In order to regain market share and maintain profitability, banks and bankers will have to look at their business in an entirely new way. In 1991, I began the first edition of this book by telling bankers that their business wasn't as bad as it appeared. In 1994, I must begin the second edition by telling banks and bankers that their business isn't as good as it appears. But one message remains the same—*in order to succeed, bankers will have to approach banking in an entirely new way.*

Bankers will have to stop thinking of their business as balance-sheet driven. They will have to think of products as something other than loans and deposits. They will have to view their employees as engines of new business, and even as partners in the success of the business. They will have to challenge themselves and their employees as they have never been challenged before. They will have to use every resource at their disposal, learn from other industries, and embrace change as a competitive weapon. In short, they will have to become topnotch businessmen and women.

Not all bankers will embrace this new business, but those who do will achieve a great deal. They will satisfy their customers and attract new ones. They will enrich their stockholders, which will allow them to acquire other financial institutions. And they will motivate their employees to achieve great heights, enriching themselves and their institution in the process.

So how do we get into this new business? We begin with the fundamentals, as any business professional would.

2 | Building a Winning Strategy

Wanting to Win

The first step in building a winning strategy is wanting to win. On its face, that may seem a ludicrous statement. Of course, every institution wants to win; that's what it's in business for, you might say. But winning is not the same as making money, and the finance industry operates under a special set of circumstances. Even though the industry has been making more money over the past two years than ever in its history, the specter of consolidation hangs over it. Because of this ongoing consolidation, the issue is really one of survival. The choice is either win or disappear.

The surviving institutions will not only have to want to win, they will have to want it more than their competitors do. For all the improvement that banking has made in the last two years, acquisition is still a heartbeat away for many institutions. In fact, the current situation in the industry has been described as "Darwinian banking," but that term implies a gradual, evolutionary process. Natural selection happens over thousands, if not millions of years, with each generation blissfully unaware that its species is headed for either supremacy or extinction. Although some bankers seem to evidence the same kind of blissful ignorance that the dinosaurs had, theirs is, in fact, a very different kind of struggle.

It might better be called "gladiatorial banking." At the height of the Roman Empire, gladiators were sent into the arena to engage in a struggle to the death, and they knew what they were in for. That knowledge made them fight all the harder, and it gave the Roman crowds good entertainment, if not good sport. Gladiatorial banking will add a little additional spice to that formula because the audience will be in the arena with the competitors, not watching from the stands.

Winning in Sports

This sports analogy might be a good place to start our search for a winning strategy, because certain sports teams have managed to achieve enviable winning records; for example, Pennsylvania State University in football, Brazil in soccer, The West Indies in cricket, Iowa State University in wrestling, and the Montreal Canadiennes in professional hockey. If there are common denominators among these teams, they should give us some clues, or a place to start.

There are three common denominators among perennially strong sports franchises. They are:

1. *They recruit quality people, and those people keep improving.* In sports the players, not the coaches or the strategy, win the games. And it isn't enough to recruit good players, they must get better all the time. Good teams start with good players, who have not only the talent but the work habits to be winners. These people hate to lose, and they will go the extra mile, year after year, to stay on top. What we can also infer from recent events in various professional sports is that such people do not come cheap. It is up to management to ensure that the company gets its money's worth from them.

2. *They play with an intensity that their competitors can't match.* In every game, tournament, or meet, there comes a point when one team wants the victory more, and both they and their competitors sense it. One team's heads start to droop, and the other team's rise just a bit. At that point, the outcome has been decided, and the teams are just playing for the score. In banking, employee intensity is sometimes regarded as unwelcome, but managing that intensity is another of management's challenges.

3. *They pay attention to detail.* In the heat of competition, the little things that go wrong decide the outcome. Making the right blocks on a long drive in the fourth quarter, always seeing the off-side trap in the making, hitting free throws down the stretch, keeping your form at the end of the 1500 meter free-style—these all require countless hours of practice when lesser teams have gone home. In the corporate world, staying late is often regarded by both employees and management as de rigeur, but the real question is whether all those hours of overtime are investments in the future or make-work.

Now, business isn't sports, and these sports ingredients aren't necessarily the business answer. They do, however, give us a jumping-off point. Building a winning strategy in business depends on a three-legged approach: strategies about the institution itself, about the institution's competitors, and about its marketplace.

The First Leg: The Institution Itself

This business is about people. This is probably the closest parallel to the sports analogy. Success in business, especially service businesses, is not about production machinery or financial statements, but about people. That idea is, in itself, not so revolutionary, but its implications are.

A business that is about people is about all the people in the business. Not just the chairman of the board, but every employee. *In a service business there are no unimportant people, because the people are the real engines of the business, its most important asset.* That means that every person in the institution must be the best he or she can be, and must keep improving throughout his or her career. Constant improvement requires constant effort, and constant effort is foreign to basic human nature. Thus the institution must foster constant effort, even though the industry itself appears to be doing very well.

This constant effort requires an environment I think of as "self-selection." All of your employees must feel that there is both the opportunity and the incentive to improve their position by improving their performance. But the political realities are that institutions are often populated by people who are quite comfortable in their present positions, who have no burning desire to make an extra effort, and who feel threatened by those, especially those subordinate to them, who are on the march and on the rise. I will address this subject in more detail in Chapter 15 on Productivity[2] and Power in a Changing Bank.

Of course, this political reality applies to all businesses, and may well be the bane of corporate America, but it is particularly a problem in financial services. Getting and keeping the best people at all levels of the institution will require that top management be seen by everyone as being actively involved in the development of all the employees. If an institution's survival is at stake, nothing can stand in the way of its employees' development. I will address this subject in more detail in Chapter 16, Employee Enhancement as a Competitive Differentiator.

The institution must be focused. This is another parallel to the sports analogy. Even good people, constantly improving, will be ineffective if they are laboring toward different goals. The reality of the modern finance industry is that pockets of competence will not win, focused teams will. There must be a business plan that serves as the guiding light, complete with objectives and responsibilities, generated with the input and support of all parts of the institution.

But there are two points to be made here. First, no plan is cast in stone, so being focused doesn't mean being rigid. Midcourse corrections are essential to winning, and top management must encourage all employees to sound the alarm if they see the ship headed for the rocks. And no excuse, not even a lot of money spent on a strategy, is a sufficient reason to continue pursuing a wrong or unattainable objective.

The second point is that fostering a team spirit in business is often a matter of going against the established practices in compensation packages. The recent trend in corporate America has been toward "accountability," where individual compensation had been a function of individual or departmental performance. That system fosters internal competition, which often leads to a lack of cooperation, fractured marketing, and poor customer service. Accountability is most often a substitute for good executive leadership, and the winning institutions will have to institute shared compensation packages, where people will receive incentives to make other parts of their organization successful. This goes against the corporate grain, but it is the wave of the future.

But having a business plan and an incentive program is only part of keeping an institution focused. Another part is keeping every part of the institution focused on the same things, all pulling toward the same goal. Here management must not only be an example, it must set priorities and resolve conflicts. I will deal with this issue in more detail in Chapter 12, Strategic Alignment.

The institution must be obsessed with quality. With the startling reversal of Japanese products from a low- to a high-quality image, and with the institution of the Malcom Baldrige National Quality Award, the concept of making quality part of a company's product may sound old hat. There are those who say that this quality fixation has often been counterproductive, focusing too much attention on "warm fuzzies" instead of realizable benefits. But the quality fixation has largely been confined to the manufacturing sector of the economy. The services sector is somewhat down the quality learning curve, and financial services even further down the curve.

There is some confusion about what, exactly, constitutes quality. Valerie Zeithaml, A. A. Parasuraman, and Leonard Berry have authored an important book, *Delivering Quality Service,* which says a great deal about the subject, and which should be required reading in its entirety for management in winning financial institutions. For our purposes, I will make a few brief observations here.

The final arbiter of quality in financial services is the customer. Many quality programs at financial institutions are almost entirely internal in nature. "Quality circles" are made up of employees, quality meetings and task groups are attended entirely by bank personnel or outside consultants, and the definitions of quality come from the institution itself. But only the customer knows what he or she wants, expects, and will be satisfied with. No matter how high a quality the institution thinks its services are, its opinion is meaningless next to the customers'.

The only way to determine what the customer wants is to ask. It is never easy to ask a customer, What do you think of our service? What are we doing that we could do better? What are we not doing that we should? But those questions, asked of customers regularly, serve not only to sharpen the institution's focus, but to communicate to the customer that the institution is serious about delivering quality service.

The customer's perception of the quality of service is dependent, in no small measure, on his or her expectations, and therein lies a potential problem. In a competitive environment, it is all too easy to try to attract customers and gain competitive advantage by making lavish promises of quality service. Such promises can raise the customer's expectations to a level that no institution can satisfy. What is necessary instead is to determine what kinds of service are important to the customer, what levels of quality are attainable in those services, and to explain to the customer what the institution will deliver in those areas, and then ensure that it does.

Everyone in the institution must buy into the quality agenda. In services, where the people are the product, quality in services depends on the performance of people—all of the people, all of the time. Customers must have a way of expressing dissatisfaction with service quality, as well as expressing satisfaction. Employees who come up short in the quality spectrum must be corrected, and those who excel must be rewarded. Expectations of quality performance must be expressed, not just for clerical and staff employees, but for high-level executives—only the service is different, not the quality expectations.

The Second Leg: The Institution's Competitors

The essence of winning is beating competitors, so no winning strategy can exist, much less succeed, without a thorough understanding of one's competitors. Not only does *competitor analysis* give the institution a picture of the "other guy," it gives the institution a much clearer picture of itself. Many institutions pay lip service to competitor analysis, which they often call *competitive analysis,* but they are often just going through the motions of listing the "SWOT," or strengths, weaknesses, opportunities, and threats.

The problem with the SWOT list is that it is an invitation to recite the current mythology, about both the institution and its competitors. Mythological recitations tend to yield artificial pictures, the kind that people in an institution think their managers and executives want to see. But artificial pictures mislead the institution, causing poor strategy selection and poor performance.

A very useful method, although it takes more work, is one put forward by Professor Liam Fahey of Babson College (Figure 2.1). Like the SWOT analysis, Professor Fahey's framework has four sectors, but these sectors concentrate on the foundations of the institution's competitive ability, not the symptoms. Professor Fahey regards the factors on the horizontal axis as indicators of what a competitor is capable of doing, and the vertical factors as indicators of what it is likely to do.

Figure 2.1
Liam Fahey's Competitor Analysis

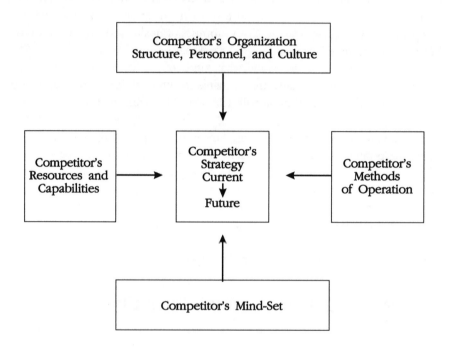

Resources and Capabilities

Let's begin with the most objective of the factors, the resources and capabilities. Professor Fahey defines resources as the wherewithal at the competitor's disposal. The first resource category most financial institutions think of is financial, in the usual forms of capital, liquidity, and cash flow. Because of the special nature of financial institutions, the most important and scarcest financial resource is capital.

But Professor Fahey points out that other kinds of resources are much more important, because they are harder to amass. For financial institutions, these resources can be categorized as physical, intangible, and human. Physical resources exist mostly as real estate, particularly owned office buildings which may have appreciated well above book value, and data centers. In the past, institutions have raised regulatory capital by turning those physical assets into financial ones through selling them and arranging to lease them back, but that practice has waned in the last year or so.

Intangible resources are the opposite of intangible assets, at least in the accounting sense. Intangible assets usually represent money spent for things the accountants can't put their hands on, and are the accounting equivalent of thin air. Intangible resources are things that aren't on the institution's balance sheet, so they are not acknowledged by the accountants, but are of definite value in the institution's business. Some intangible resources are data, technological breakthroughs, and state or federal charters. One intangible which banks often refer to but which may not be a resource is image or reputation. Too often, financial institutions overestimate the value of both their and their competitors' images. Most institutions are better off assuming that customers make decisions on the basis of service and value, not image and reputation.

In the end, though, human resources are probably the most important ones, as far as competitor analysis is concerned. Unfortunately, they are the hardest to evaluate. People are easy to count, but such things as their skill levels and enthusiasm are harder to pin down. I will discuss this topic in more detail in Chapter 16. In this area, competitor analysis is reduced to a subjective assessment of the other key ingredient, *capabilities.*

Capabilities refer to what an institution and its people do well. The capabilities of real interest are the unique ones, which the institution's employees do better than anyone else. Those capabilities, when skillfully combined with the institution's resources, give it a powerful competitive position in a market or product segment. Combining capabilities and resources is discussed in more detail in Chapter 12.

In financial services, as in most services, capabilities are often expressed in terms of product areas, since the real product in services is the capabilities of the people performing the service. We think of capabilities in terms of the product areas that our people are skilled in. Some institutions attract people who are good at the processing businesses, so those institutions tend to emphasize such businesses as custody or asset servicing. Others attract people who are good at principal businesses, and those institutions tend to emphasize trading or lending. Finally, there are those who attract expert advice-givers, and they emphasize things like money management or financial engineering.

But the key to winning is the right combination of capabilities. No institution can expect to survive and grow with only one area of competence, or with only one kind of resource. One of the marks of good management in finance is its ability to attract and blend people with a wide variety of capabilities, and that may be the most important capability of all.

Methods of Operation

This part of the analysis looks at how the competitor does business. It answers questions concerning, What market segments does the institution attempt to serve? What products does it offer to the market? How does it interact with its customers? How does it price its offerings?

Professor Fahey's analysis incorporates the "value chain" concept first introduced about 20 years ago, and most recently embellished by Professor Michael Porter of Harvard University. The value chain was originally designed for, and is best suited to, manufacturing companies, but it is a widely-used concept, and may have some appeal here. It divides the operations of a company into eight distinct operations:

Suppliers → Internal Logistics → Operations → Outbound
Logistics → Marketing → Sales → Service → Customers

The problem with using the value chain on services is that it assumes that productive operations are performed on some physical goods. It is physical goods that are supplied, inbound, operated on, sold, and serviced, but services are quite different. For example, what are the "raw materials" used in financial services—money, information, transactions? And who are the suppliers? In some cases even customers act as suppliers.

But the value chain analysis may help us see financial services in a different way, as a business which produces a product, because the purpose of the value chain is to assign a *value* to each step of the production process. Most financial institutions have a hard time assigning the appropriate values to all of the steps necessary to perform a financial service. Because of that, many institutions persist in performing parts of the services value chain which have little value and in doing so, these institutions emphasize parts of the business which customers do not regard as valuable. It remains for someone like Professor Fahey, or perhaps Professor Porter, to derive a value chain specifically designed for financial services.

The Competitor's Mindset

In this part of the analysis, Professor Fahey concentrates on the *assumptions* that underlie the competitor's strategy. Although they are seldom expressed in detail, an institution's assumptions can be gleaned from published comments by its executives, from documents like the annual report, and can be inferred from the institution's actions. Recognize that the competitor's set of assumptions is critical, not only because they allow you to predict the institution's future actions, but because they allow you to recognize when they are more accurate than yours.

Assumptions tend to fall into two classes, external and internal. External assumptions cover such things as the condition and growth expectations for the industry, the role of competitors, the evolution of regulation and laws, the expectations of customers, and general economic conditions. Internal assumptions cover such things as the organization's resources and capabilities, its position in the market, and its adaptability.

Comparing the apparent assumptions of financial competitors with your own can be both startling and disconcerting. Are most of your competitors emphasizing branch operations, while you are emphasizing home banking? Is one of your competitors actively buying loan servicing, while you and many others are selling? Is a competitor building its trading capability in spot currencies, while you are de-emphasizing yours? These differences may have little or no significance on their own, but they may be very revealing regarding the assumptions the two institutions have made.

The Competitor's Organization

This part of the analysis depends on one of the strangest dichotomies in business: Corporations came into being, and continue to be thought of, as a way to allow a large number of people to be more productive than they would be as individuals—but these same corporations spend much of their time trying not to stifle the productivity of the individuals who work there. This is a particular issue for institutions undergoing significant change. Professor Fahey focuses on three aspects of an organization: its structure, its personnel, and its culture.

An examination of a competitor's structure can tell you whether they will be able to respond to change, either economic or competitive, and it can also tell you something about their assumptions. Is the institution organized along market lines, or product lines; are there executive vice presidents of lending and deposits, or retail and middle markets? How are the various geographies where the institution does business handled? Is transaction processing centralized for all business units, or segmented among the business units?

But, much more important than the present structure is the chain of structural changes that the institutions have undergone. These changes tell a very revealing story about the institution's changing perception of its market, its role in that market, and its best chance of success. Watching the evolution of a competitor's structure may be the most revealing insight competitor analysis can offer.

A close second to structure in both relevance and interest would be personnel. Every corporation is a political hotbed, with the fortunes of its senior executives rising and falling constantly. The corporate soap opera is fascinating as entertainment, but it is much more fascinating as analytical raw material. Every person in a corporation brings his or her own style and background to the job, and those individuals who attain executive status often impose their style and background on their subordinates.

For example, the departure of a charismatic investment banker and his replacement by a low-profile commercial banker may signal a change in operating style for a competitor, and it might suggest that personnel and customers are ripe for the picking. Or the elevation of a marketing guru to head of retail services might mean that the institution will soon be knocking on your retail customers' doors.

Finally, an institution's culture, defined by Professor Fahey as "the dominant values, beliefs, norms and behaviors," can explain why a competing institution does things you would never do, and why they wouldn't consider doing something you would jump at. Not all institutions publish their cultures, but you can always divine their cultures from their actions.

Values are a hierarchical arrangement of things the institution wants to do, and that arrangement is not always obvious. One of the most common values has to do with the importance of transactions and relationships. Institutions can regard themselves as transaction-oriented, in which case they will pursue a specific transaction across a wide variety of customers, or relationship-oriented, in which case they will attempt to maximize the kind and number of transactions they do with a specific customer. This is an expremely important value to determine, because it can tell you how to approach that institution's customers. A transaction-oriented institution may not notice if you steal a customer, as long as you do it with a transaction they don't specialize in, but a relationship-oriented bank will notice every time.

Knowing their values will also help you predict how they will react to your actions. If you announce a special CD offering, will the competitor move immediately to match you across all market segments, across only a few important segments, or not at all? Will a competitor match any transaction you propose to one of its key customers, no matter how unprofitable for them, or will they put profits before relationships? Does the competitor regard loan servicing as a desirable business because it keeps them in touch with their customers, or will they sell servicing to generate capital?

Beliefs, on the other hand, are those things a competitor assumes will happen, sometimes without much supporting evidence. Here, too, the competitor reveals its beliefs through its actions, although it might also articulate them publicly. Beliefs and values are closely related, but, while values are general, beliefs refer to specific patterns of behavior, either theirs, yours, customers', or regulators'.

Beliefs are particularly important if competitors have either more resources or fewer resources than you. Competitors who believe that customers value image above price may be sitting ducks for an aggressive pricing strategy that gives you an entree to their customer set. Those who believe that regulators will not grant you the right to enter new markets may be caught flatfooted if the regulators do. Beliefs are one of the most important areas in which you must compare yourself with your competitors (note the plural). If you see a belief widely held by your competitors, but not by you, it could point out a major flaw in your strategy, or a tremendous opportunity.

Norms of behavior are those things a competitor does as a matter of course, most likely as a result of values and beliefs. For example, one of the decision-making processes a competitor follows might give it an advantage in pricing risk transactions, and might point to an outdated or inappropriate value or belief in your own organization. The way competitors approach a new market or product might give you an advantage if you can influence their norms of behavior early in the process, before they have much experience to go on. The point is, there is always a great deal of information to go on, if we take the effort to find it.

The Third Factor: The Marketplace

The marketplace is where the customer and the products come together, and where the customer chooses between you and your competitors. There has been a great deal of study about marketing and marketplaces, in much greater detail than I can cover here, so I will limit myself to some basic observations.

Product Life Cycles

Marketing experts know that every product has a life cycle. The cycle begins with a slow takeoff as the product is introduced. Here the institution is called a "pioneer," breaking new ground, perfecting systems, educating customers and making significant investments of resources. There is a saying in marketing the "many pioneers get shot by the Indians," but pioneers often reap the biggest rewards.

Once a product catches on, it enters a growth, possibly explosive growth, period. More and more customers recognize its value, but more competitors do as well. In this part of the life cycle, competitors do not concentrate on efficiencies as much as on sales efforts and growth, customers decide more on product quality than on price, and the rate of innovation in the market is high. Market leaders can generate large profits, but they must invest much of those profits in product support and research.

At some point, the product enters a stable, slow-growth phase known as maturity. Here almost everyone who will use the product knows about it, so price begins to emerge as the competitive weapon. Volumes are still high and may be growing, but profit margins are narrower, which means that efficiency becomes much more important. Customers are more knowledgeable about the product, requiring less education, and they become tougher bargainers as well.

Finally, the product enters a decline, as it becomes run-of-the-mill, or obsolete. Sales volumes often decline, price competition becomes fierce, competitors drop out of the market, and profit margins narrow further. Research and market support both dwindle to almost nothing as everyone attempts to wring the last dollar out of the product.

Each of these parts of the product life cycle requires a different marketing approach. If a competitor believes that a particular product is in the growth phase, he may ignore the entry of another competitor into the market, preferring to concentrate on capturing his share of the growth pie. That same competitor in what he regards as a mature market will react instantly to any new competitor, because he knows the importance of maintaining market share.

Market Segmentation

Just as products change over time, so do markets. The most important way in which markets change is by segmentation. Market segments are groups of customers with similar enough wants and needs that they can all be satisfied by a single version of a product. Financial institutions who understand the principle of market segmentation, and take advantage of it, can capture large chunks of a market, even though they do not have the first, most popular, or most advanced version of a product.

Early in the life of a product, there may only be one segment in the market, so each competitor might have one version of the product. As the product matures, and more customers begin to use it, their needs and wants begin to diverge, creating distinct market segments. Smart institutions will be alert to the segmentation of relatively new markets, because those who respond quickly to the new demands may capture a significant market share without a large research and development investment. As products age, the market segments even more and the segmentation process often leads to entirely new products, just as the old ones are entering the decline.

The segmentation of markets can be seen in financial services in such diverse product areas as deposit accounts, interest-rate swaps, and credit cards. In all those cases and many others, financial institutions have generated large revenues and profits by introducing variations on successful, but generic, products.

The Product Portfolio

The final concept we need to understand is the product portfolio. Products and markets are always in the process of growing, changing, and segmenting. Market participants are always fighting for market share and most marketing experts agree that the best profit performance comes from a collection of products that are in strong competitive positions in their markets. Thus the marketing fraternity has developed the concept of the *product portfolio*, or that collection of products that any one company is offering in any one product class.

There has been a large amount of writing, both academic and popular, on the subject of product portfolios, so I am not going to cover it all here. There is, however, a relatively simple way to look at a financial institution's product portfolio, using a matrix originally developed by the Boston Consulting Group (Figure 2.2). This analytical framework, called the BCG Four-Box, looks at products from two viewpoints: the growth being experienced in the market, and the competitive position of the product.

Figure 2.2
Boston Consulting Group Analysis

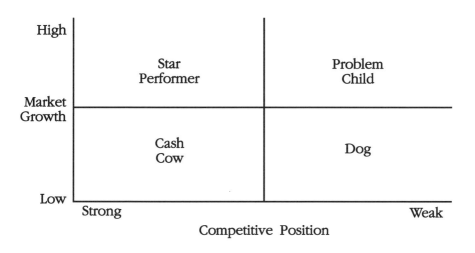

This framework had been around for at least ten years, and the four boxes have been given descriptive names.

Star Performer This is the institution's dream, a strong product in a high-growth market. These products generate a lot of profit, but often require a lot of investment in order to maintain the strong market position and fight off competitors. Star performers are very rewarding, but they demand a lot of attention.

Problem Child This product serves a high-growth market, but has a weak position. In order to become a star it will require an investment, perhaps a major one, and a big push into the market. Problem children have lots of potential, but they can break your heart before they become stars.

Cash Cow This is a strong product in a mature, slow-growth market. Most competitors see the growth potential in this market as diminished; if they are in a weak position they may not choose to compete strongly and leave the field to the entrenched forces. But other strong competitors in this market will fight fiercely to protect their positions and their cash flow, forcing you to keep up the pressure. Cash cows can feed a lot of stars and problem children, but you still have to keep the wolves away.

Dog This product has no realistic hope of generating a good return. It is in a weak position in a market that isn't growing, and probably doesn't justify the large expenditures necessary to make it competitive. Unless you really have to have this product, and be in this market, the best course might be to reallocate resources into more promising areas. In this analysis, most dogs are put to sleep.

Marketing experts have gone beyond the BCG Four-Box to matrices having both nine and 24 boxes, in an attempt to be more specific about the product life cycle and the competitive position. However, some important concepts of managing a product portfolio can be gleaned from the BCG Four-Box. One is that you need products in more than one of the boxes to keep your portfolio healthy. Betting the ranch on one product in any but the most embryonic market is suicidal. Another concept is that the natural movement of products is from the upper left to the lower right. Good products in growing markets always have a way of becoming dogs if left alone too long.

The Competitive Ladder

When I examined these three aspects of building a winning strategy, internal, competitor, and market, I saw that financial institutions naturally divide themselves into four groups, which I have arranged on what I call the "Competitive Ladder of Financial Services" (Figure 2.3).

The four categories are:

Winners, who will dominate their markets and make all the other players march to their drummer,

Competitors, who will be successful and make money, but who won't dominate their markets,

Also-Rans, who will hang on by their fingertips and may not succeed in the long run, and

Victims, who are just waiting to be taken over.

These four categories describe the general mindset of the institution, but I have differentiated them on three fronts, which correspond to the three aspects of the winning strategy: the attitude toward their business, toward their competitors, and toward their marketplace. We can begin with the top of the ladder and work down.

Figure 2.3
The Competitive Ladder of Financial Services

Winners	Innovators Predators Marketeers
Competitors	Implementers Growers Sales Organizations
Also-Rans	Followers Protectors Vendors
Victims	Reactors Targets Order Takers

Winners

Winners are those institutions determined to be the best and to dominate their market. They are product innovators who strive to have their products in the market first, who want to dictate the pace of the action, and who want to be seen at the front of the pack. This doesn't mean that they have to be the first in the world with these products, just the first in their market. However, being an innovator is expensive and potentially dangerous, but these institutions know it is where they want to be.

With regard to competition, they are predators, constantly looking for what their competitors have that is good, and for opportunities to acquire customers, markets, and franchises. They regard signs of weakness on the part of a competitor as an opportunity, and are always looking for new markets and businesses. Not only do they want to grow, they want to expand.

Finally, not content to be sellers of services, these institutions utilize the discipline of marketing, beginning the product development process with market input, and incorporating market input in all aspects of the sales cycle. They are always aware of what part of the life cycle each product is in, and they keep their product portfolio finely tuned to generate the best cash flow and return on equity.

Competitors

Competitors are one level less driven than winners, but they display many of the characteristics of successful companies. Although they do not feel the need to be innovators, they are usually the second or third institutions into the market with a product. Often, they are adept at carving out a significant market share by capitalizing on the imperfections of the innovators' products. They have far fewer costly failures, but they operate at the winners' pace, and are willing to let the innovators call the tune of product introductions.

Competitors want to grow their businesses, and are often successful at doing so, but they aren't necessarily predatory about it. In many cases, they are willing to stay within their current markets, either geographically or functionally, and are content to make the most of familiar territory.

Although they will take an opportunity to expand if presented, they are not watchful for every slight weakness in their competitors, and they may take strength on the part of a competitor as a reason to back off instead of a reason to attack.

These institutions tend to have a strong sales mentality, in which they aggressively promote whatever offerings they currently have. Although they work hard to increase sales volumes, they may not modify products to match market segmentation until the innovators do it first. Since they are not as adept as winners in incorporating market input in the development process, their ability to adapt to changing markets depends to some extent on the ability of their product developers to predict customer preferences.

Also-Rans

Also-rans begin to display some of the characteristics of unsuccessful businesses, and may be more likely to fail than survive. They do not introduce new products until their customers actively lobby for them, or begin defecting to a competitor, and their new products are seldom more than copies of those introduced by innovators and implementers. They are forced to compete on price more than any other basis, so their new products seldom generate large cash flow or returns on equity.

Without an aggressive approach to their business, also-rans think more about protecting their turf than about growing. They are constantly trying to keep their customers, protect their market position, and fend off aggressive predators. With low ROEs, and constraints on capital, also-rans often sell off successful parts of their businesses, fueling the growth of their stronger competitors.

Also-rans are not aggressive sales organizations, falling more into the mold of vendors. They offer their products, but they don't seek out new customers as a matter of course. They may advertise, for example, but the ads are often unfocused, and follow-up is usually haphazard. They sometimes look as if they are selling in spite of themselves.

Victims

Victims are at the bottom of the competitive ladder, and are sitting ducks for those at the top. Their continued existence is usually a matter of waiting for the axe to fall. When others introduce new products, the victims often hold back and attempt to retain customers through price cutting or appeals to loyalty. If they do introduce new products, it is often after they have matured, and long after there is any hope of capturing market share. Sometimes they spend heavily to promote these new offerings, resulting in large losses followed by product withdrawals.

Such product performances leave them unable to defend their market position, and they often lose market share to those at the top of the ladder. After they have lost or sold the successful parts of their businesses, they may continue running up losses in the remaining parts, until they are taken over or forced to merge by the regulators.

Their approach to their marketplace is that they have services available, but customers usually have to ask. This puts them in the position of order-takers, the last institutions to enter a market and the first to exit. Since they have relatively little dialogue with customers, they never seem to know what the market wants, and they act, often rightly, as if their situations were hopeless.

Climbing the Ladder

There is good news and bad news about the competitive ladder. The bad news is that the forces of gravity are at work here, just as they are on a real ladder. If an institution does nothing, if it depends on chance or the regulators to make things happen, the institution will slide slowly down the ladder. We can all think of financial institutions that were winners at one time, aggressive and successful, and are now slipping from competitors to also-rans. In many cases, they are only dimly aware of what is happening, and not at all aware of what to do about it.

The good news is that an institution can climb the ladder, can go from being an also-ran to a competitor, and on to being a winner. And the requirements for doing that are similar to the winning requirements for a sports team. We could stop with those—*good people who keep improving, intensity of effort, and attention to detail*—but that is much too simplistic. We will need to develop a much more detailed and relevant winning strategy. And the first step is building a good business foundation.

3 | Establishing a Good Business Foundation

Management consultants are the subject of as many jokes as there are managers who think they don't need consultants, but the consulting profession continues to do very nicely. Over and over I have sat down with senior executives in the finance industry, and over and over I have heard a phrase something like, "Of course, we don't really need a consultant, but we have this little problem. . . . "

The "little problem" might be costs that are out of control, or internal friction between departments, or a recent loss of market share, or a persistent problem of bad assets. It is always presented as isolated, temporary, externally caused, and on the way to being fixed. Except that it always turns out to be pervasive, permanent, internal, and stubbornly hard to eradicate.

The management consultant is trained to respond, "Perhaps we should take several steps backward, and look at the root causes of this problem. After all, you wouldn't take an aspirin for appendicitis, would you? Well, you have appendicitis of the bottom line."

In all the consulting training manuals, this conversation is supposed to lead to an extensive review of the institution's business strategy, perhaps followed by the strategy's revision or complete replacement. No wonder the consultant starts to grin and the executive starts to groan when the conversation reaches this point.

To make matters worse, most finance industry executives don't feel that they have the time or money to engage in a massive long-range strategy project. In the first place, they are rightly concerned about the next quarter's results. In the second, they have seen their industry change so much over the last five years that they have already thrown out a couple of expensive strategy documents. Another round of deep thinking and staring into space has no appeal for them.

And yet, the consultants have a point, even if their timing is a little off. History has shown that businesses who operate without a plan have only a random chance of long-term success. Furthermore, the plan cannot be set in concrete, or it may do more harm than good. Every industry has examples of companies who achieved considerable success, and then assumed that the world would stay the same forever. Sometimes they wake up to changing conditions in time, and sometimes they don't. But the first step in having a plan is understanding the business of financial services.

The Business of Financial Services

The first step is to look, in more detail, at the business of financial services, and what it comprises. At its most basic we can define financial services *as performing as a business, not as an adjunct to another business, and any of the following: executing or processing financial transactions, participating in financial transactions as principal, or rendering advice on financial transactions.* That not only defines the business, but breaks it into some natural components, organized along the lines of profitability dynamics. But what does it mean to be in each of these businesses, and how do they relate to each other?

Executing and processing financial transactions looks like two, quite unrelated, businesses, but it is, in fact, two sides of the same business. Execution/processing is defined as *acting as agent for other parties to a financial transaction.* Here are some of the businesses that make up this component:

Check processing
Acting as an automated clearing house
Electronic funds transfer
Asset servicing
Letter of credit collections
Capital markets brokerage
Capital markets processing
Custody and safekeeping

Although these lines of business have the common denominator of being agency services, they range all over the lot in terms of perceived profitability, as well as in terms of their perceived keys to success. Most of the processing businesses are thought of by financial institutions as cost centers or necessary evils, while the execution businesses are thought of as profit centers, if not the gold mines they once were. But there are some common denominators we can apply to them all.

In all these cases, *economies of scale are at work*. These businesses depend for profitability on large volumes, because they are not required to be human functions to any great degree. Stock and commodity brokers will argue that point at length, but the shrinking market share of physical exchanges in all instruments is an indication that the brokerage function is losing its manual nature. Economies of scale mean that large, efficient service providers will have a tremendous competitive advantage, and that barriers to entry will become significant when those providers achieve those efficiencies.

Also, in these businesses, *having a franchise is highly desirable,* if not essential. That franchise can be a membership, as in an exchange or a clearing house, or access to a closed system, such as a central bank wire system or money transfer system. The problem with the franchise aspect of the business is that the members are likely to regard the franchise as a crutch instead of an opportunity. It is human nature to think that, if I buy a membership to an exchange or a clearing house, I can collect a "toll" from those who want access. But customers, although they will pay for value, eventually find a way around paying tolls.

The important thing about the execution/processing business is that, if an institution does it well, it provides competitive advantage in the other two businesses. Institutions which regard exchange or clearing house membership as simply an opportunity to exact a toll will find their customers will take that business, as well as other business, away. On the other hand, institutions which excel at such things as asset servicing and money transfer will find that those efficiencies allow them to compete in such areas as securitization and cash management, if they are clever enough to take advantage of the relationship. Although the execution/processing businesses are highly competitive and not very glamorous, they often hold the key to the customers' other needs.

Participating as principal is the most visible of the components, as well as the riskiest. It is where we see most financial institutions most often, whether it is at an automated teller machine (ATM) or in the newspaper. Here are some of the businesses in this component:

Deposit taking
Borrowing
Lending
Leasing
Trading
Performance guarantees
Investing
Issuance of insurance
Issuance of derivative instuments

The primary common denominator of these businesses is that they involve the institution's balance sheet, implicitly if not explicitly. In certain cases, the involvement is obvious, as in the deposit/loan area of banking. In others, like the performance guarantees contained in letters of credit or interest-rate swaps, the involvement is contingent, or outside the accountant's limited vision. But in every case the institution's balance sheet, and thus its capital, comes into play.

Capital comes into play because all of these businesses involve large doses of risk. All financial services involve some risk, of course, but this is the only one where risk is a large part of the product itself. In fact, in these businesses, accepting risk is the service the institution is providing. The problem, of course, is that a measurement of the risk is not normally included in the measurements of financial performance.

Thus lenders can show high net interest income during periods of economic growth by increasing loan volume or by increasing loan risk. Only when the economy turns down do we know whether it was the volume or the risk that they were living on. Trading firms traditionally have volatile and unpredictable earnings patterns, largely because of the age-old trading adage, "There is a world of difference between brains and a bull market."

Risk is seductive because it is the easiest way to grow principal businesses. In that way, it is like the franchise component of the agency businesses. It is much harder to build principal businesses without increasing risk, but it can be accomplished in a couple of ways. One is by *innovation,* particularly in markets which are segmenting. We see this all the time in the new trading products being introduced by exchanges and trading houses, as well as in new deposit and loan products. The other is by *combination,* where principal services are offered in conjunction with other services, or principal services themselves are combined so as to reduce the risk to the institution. In both these approaches *marketing* is the real key to success. In fact, the essence of all principal businesses is enhancing the customer relationship.

Beyond risk management, there is one other profitability dynamic in the principal businesses—*differential pricing.* In order to maximize the profitability of principal businesses, banks must alter their pricing to take account of the risk involved. Banks do this in some ways; for example, varying the interest rate on loans based on term to maturity. In some other ways, though, they do not. For example, at the 1994 American Banker's Association annual convention in New York, Chairman Alan Greenspan chastised the banking industry for not varying loan interest rates by credit risk. He rightly pointed out that homogeneous pricing of loans had prompted banking's best customers to shift to other sources of funds, leaving banks with the worst credits. Differential pricing may be counter to the culture of many bankers, but it certainly is right for the times.

Rendering advice on financial transactions is the Hollywood of financial services. It is where people see the larger-than-life players, as well as the larger-than-life pay packages. It is the home of the Michael Milkens, the Bruce Wassersteins, and the Peter Lynches. It is the Camelot of financial services, where everyone wants to end up. Here are some of the businesses it encompasses:

Mergers and acquisitions
Securities underwriting
Corporate finance
Financial engineering
Personal financial planning
Investment advisory
Investment management

Although these are the glamour areas of financial services, they are startlingly hard to succeed at. One reason is that *the only product you have to sell is your brains.* Customers aren't paying you to perform a processing service, and they aren't paying you to accept risk; they are paying you for what you know. But, smart as you might be, you have to keep your ego out of the equation, because customers are really paying you for what you know that makes *them* money, not you.

These businesses are also enormously competitive. Any endeavor which holds the opportunity for huge rewards will attract smart, aggressive, highly motivated people. The larger the stakes, the smarter, more aggressive, and more motivated they will be. In addition, the operating environment where these people excel is unstructured and creative, not the structured, efficient environment which exists in many financial institutions. Thus, successful advisory departments often sow the seeds of dissent within an organization because they make people in other groups feel like underpaid functionaries.

Actually, a successful financial institution must have some of all three components. The execution/processing part can feed the principal part, the principal part can generate business for the advisory part, and the profitability of the institution can increase manyfold. The problem is to bring out the best in each kind of business, and that requires a good business foundation.

The Business Foundation

A good business foundation is made up of some basic tenets, which one might think of as granite blocks on which to rest the business. Those tenets, because they will be few and relatively permanent, must be well conceived and tested. If they are, and if they last through time, they will keep the business strong no matter what the economic or industry conditions.

For the foundation to work for financial institutions, it must apply to all of its businesses. It must also involve, and motivate, all the institution's employees. It must stand the test of time, not having to be rebuilt every time conditions change. And, it must enable the institution to prosper in any kind of market, from highly successful to depressed. So what are the blocks that make up this foundation?

The Building Blocks

The institution's mission is to maximize its return on equity (ROE). Like all the building blocks, this one seems simple and obvious, but it most assuredly is neither. It involves a great deal of thought and commitment, and it will affect the institution and its employees in many ways.

Most businesses have the goal, either stated or implied, of making money, and financial institutions are no exception. But making money is a vague, and perhaps misleading, concept. As long as an institution shows a profit, no matter how small, it satisfies that criterion, but just making money won't guarantee success or survival. There are lots of examples, in all kinds of businesses, of companies that were profitable right up to the point when they ceased to exist.

A variation on the profit theme is the objective of maximizing profits. This objective is significantly more useful than just making money, since it raises the performance bar. Institutions with an objective of maximizing profits will make some good decisions, but they may also make some bad ones, because a pure profit objective says nothing about *limitations* or *efficiency.*

Maximizing ROE gets right to the crux of what an institution is in business for. It recognizes that all businesses, and finance in particular, operate under restrictions, and the limitation of equity is the most important. Having the objective of maximizing ROE keeps everyone's eye on the need to work the limited capital as hard as possible.

And everyone has to keep their eye on the ball. Not just the CEO, not just the heads of the lines of business, not just the people who see themselves as profit producers, but everyone in the organization. This means that support functions must see a connection between their jobs and ROE. It means that the processing businesses must have a measurable impact on ROE. And it means that individuals, and business units, must be given incentive to work together to maximize ROE. In an organization of any size, gaining such a broad acceptance of a single objective is extraordinarily difficult. It has been attempted many times, utilizing corporate mottos, executive speeches, internal publications, and departmental meetings, to name just a few methods. Sometimes all those things work, and sometimes they don't, but there are two measures which will usually make a significant difference.

The first is *the incentive compensation system.* Simply put, compensation systems which reward individuals and departments for their individual and departmental success may increase ROE, but only accidentally. This concept of accountability, which is as widespread in financial services as it is generally, almost always has the effect of pitting department against department in such areas as allocation of capital, access to customers, corporate focus, and career path. Many of the ills of corporate America, such as excessive corporate politics, lack of market focus, and inability to respond to competition, can be traced, at least in part, to the prevalence of accountability, and the compartmentalization it fosters.

An alternative incentive compensation method is based entirely, or largely, on ROE. That can be done in two ways, one easier, and one more effective. The easier way is simply to relate the ROE incentive compensation to the organization's ROE as a whole. It is easy to set up such a system, but employees may lose their own focus, since their ability to affect ROE might be unclear or very small. The more difficult, but more effective, method is cross-compensation. Here, departments have a bonus pool to be awarded only to employees *outside* their department who made a significant contribution to maximizing their ROE. Where it has been used, cross-compensation has fostered much higher team spirit, and the increased cooperation has made the organization more responsive.

The other measure is *corporate advancement.* Within any corporation there is a political process by which people advance their careers. The larger the corporation, the more political the process becomes. Employees, as well as competitors, are aware of the politics, and they pay particular attention to who advances and why. Institutions where corporate advancement is a function of the person's contribution to ROE, and where that fact is publicly acknowledged, stand a much better chance of maximizing ROE, and of improving the quality of their service.

The most important product the institution has is quality. Of all the arenas in which an institution can compete, the most fruitful one is quality. Unlike price competition, quality does not cut into profit margins. Unlike advertising, the effect of quality lingers. And unlike special promotions, quality breeds customer loyalty. Now that we have been more explicit about the three components of financial services, we can be more specific about what constitutes quality in each of those components.

In Chapter 2, I mentioned a book by Valerie Zeithaml, A. A. Parasuraman, and Leonard Berry, called *Delivering Quality Service.* In that book are the results of a study the authors did on the relative importance of various aspects of quality in service. Included in the list of aspects were:

Reliability, or consistency of performance and dependability

Responsiveness, or the willingness or readiness to provide service

Competence, or possession of the required skills and knowledge

Access, or approachability and ease of contact

Courtesy, or politeness, consideration, respect, and friendliness

Communication, or keeping customers informed and listening to them

Credibility, or trustworthiness, believability and honesty

Security, or freedom from danger, risk, or doubt

Understanding, or knowing the customer

Tangibles, or the physical accessories and evidence of service

In the vast majority, if not all, of the studies the authors conducted, the most important aspect of quality service was *reliability.* The other aspects were either held to be less important by customers, or were assumed to be present, and thus not open to discussion. But we need to be more specific about quality service as it pertains to the finance industry.

In the execution/processing arena, the first thing we think of when we talk of quality is reliability, in this case accuracy. Processing and execution errors are more than an annoyance, they expose the customer to financial risk. Misposted credit card charges, securities delivered out of the wrong custody account, or letter of credit (L/C) payments against the wrong goods do more than make customers angry, they make him doubt the quality of the rest of the institution's services.

Among the other aspects of quality service, two which have particular importance in this area are access and security. More and more customers are demanding access to their information and/or markets, not on a batch basis, but in real time. And, with transaction information worth millions of dollars, assurance that the information is safe, both from loss and from prying eyes, has great value.

In the principal area, the perception of quality by customers is much less clear. Since the customer is buying part of the institution's balance sheet, the price at which the space is sold has an overwhelming position in the customer's mind. But, since it is easy for the institution and the customer to slip into adversarial roles during negotiations, those aspects of service quality that work to reduce the adversarial relationship have great weight.

Thus, other very important aspects here are responsiveness, communication, and credibility. Showing an understanding of the customer's real needs, being willing to take the time to make sure a customer understands a transaction, and being honest about the institution's capabilities and priorities all make customers feel that they and the institution see eye to eye.

When an institution is rendering advice, much of the service quality is perceived in the quality of the advice. Thus, competence and understanding head the list. Knowing which stock is a good buy is important, but knowing which is a good buy for a particular investor is more important. Knowing how interest-rate swaps function is valuable, but knowing how a particular customer can benefit from them is even more valuable.

One part of rendering advice that gets less attention than it deserves is credibility. By definition, advice givers should know more than their customers, so there is always the unasked question whether the customer is getting *all* the advice, or just some of it. In the same vein, access can be important, since no one wants to sit on hold, or wait for a callback, during an emergency.

In the end, however, service quality is still a new subject, and institutions will have to blaze their own trail much of the time. There won't be operations manuals to read, or procedures to follow, or checklists to refer to. Like someone once said about good art, you may not be able to describe service quality, but you will certainly know it when you see it. And you will have to depend on the quality of your people, which brings us to the next building block.

Your institution is only as good as your employees and the effort they put forth. Managers in all aspects of finance are fond of saying, "It's a people business," but they sometimes act as if that were not their real feeling. Work areas are referred to by such demeaning names as "the cage" or the "back office." Incentive programs are often restricted to executives. And career advancement is often a matter of the "old boy" network.

Winning institutions and their managers must recognize that their employees are the most important hidden asset they have, and they must know that every single asset has to work very hard for the institution to win. But working hard and making a contribution are a result of much more than exhortations, or even bonuses. There are three key rules to making the most of your employees.

1. *Hire good people.* Employee quality starts here; there is no substitute for finding and hiring the best people you can. That means hiring good people throughout the organization, for every job, in every location. And yet, when you look around some institutions, you wonder who was in charge of hiring, and what they were trying to accomplish.

In order to hire good people, you have to know what qualities you are looking for. Here are a few that will help you find the right people, no matter what job you are filling:

❑   *They must be intellectually curious.* That may sound like an odd first quality, but intellectually curious people will not do things the old way just because everyone else does. Intellectually curious people will challenge old ideas, offer new ones, and keep everyone thinking. Without this quality, the employee will never improve, and the institution won't either.

❑   *They must be competitive.* This might also appear to be an odd quality, but finance is becoming a very competitive business, and people who easily accept losing won't help you win. People who don't regard a competing institution as a threat to themselves won't find weaknesses in their approach to improve on and won't find weaknesses in their competitors' to exploit.

❑   *They must be comfortable on a team.* This is the complement to the competitive quality. However, team players aren't those who go along with the will of the majority, or accept the orthodox view. Team players help others to improve, cover for their teammates, and give up the opportunity for personal glory in the interests of winning. Team players aren't blindly loyal to the coach, but they are fiercely loyal to their teammates.

Of course, finding good people is half the effort—hiring them is the other half. Book after book has been written about the interviewing/hiring process, dealing with all the hidden signals and manipulations practiced by both sides. It is important to remember that people work for more than money, although compensation is very important. The people I have just described will respond well to a certain kind of approach, and will want to work for a certain kind of institution.

❑ *They will want a challenge.* If you give the impression that you are looking for a spot-filler, or someone who quietly does what he or she is told to, you won't attract winners. If you indicate that the road to responsibility is long and bumpy, you won't attract winners. If you appear autocratic, or your institution appears very hierarchical, they will look elsewhere.

❑ *They want to work for winners.* Many people, particularly when they are young, choose among employers, either consciously or subconsciously, largely because of the image the company presents. If your institution fosters a winning attitude, if your employees think of themselves as winners, if you place winning high on your list of priorities, you will attract winners.

❑ *They will want an incentive compensation system.* Winners want a chance to prove themselves and a chance to be rewarded. That applies to *all* employees. If your institution has a bonus program for tellers or secretaries based on the performance of their unit or the institution as a whole, you are on the right track. There is nothing like an incentive system to keep people focused, and that brings us to the next point.

2. *Help your employees improve.* Over the long haul, it is not enough to find and hire good people—they must want to, and have the environment to, improve. Such an environment does a hundred times more to improve morale and productivity than do no-layoff policies. There are some key points on employee improvement:

❑ *It applies to everyone.* Most employee improvement programs apply to those people management has identified as "promotable," but the real benefit comes when every employee, no matter what his or her job or background, knows that the company wants him or her to improve. A tremendous amount of service quality and productivity comes from the efforts of people who have low-level jobs. Quantum improvement in quality and productivity comes from small investments in those low-level people. That is why . . .

❑ *It should lead to a better job.* The effort an employee makes to go to night school or take a correspondence course should result in his or her having a higher value to the institution. And that should be reflected in an employee's responsibilities and compensation. Of course, there are countless ways of improving one's self that don't make you more valuable to an employer, and they may not make you more promotable, but job-related improvement programs will cease rather quickly if they don't result in a better job for the participant.

❑ *It must be the basis of self-selection.* Not everyone in an organization will make the extra effort that self-improvement requires. Not everyone will go to night school after a long day of work. Not everyone will read up on new regulations and accounting treatments in order to find ways to use them or deal with them. Only those employees who really want to improve themselves will do that.

So, the institution must take notice and encourage such actions. Tuition assistance programs are one way to do that. Recognition of employee accomplishments in corporate publications is another. Personal notes from top executives recognizing the accomplishments of employees at all levels can do wonders for keeping spirits and effort high when an employee might not have much else to show for it. It is amazing how hard people will work when they think they are appreciated.

3. *A business that isn't growing has probably already begun the process of shrinking.* The world of economics and business is a world in constant change. Even when things appear stable, there are changes occurring under the surface. Someone is planning to introduce a product, or take one off the market. Someone is working on getting into a new business, or deciding to get out of one. Someone is adding to his or her work force, while someone else is laying people off.

This all means that a business must be growing all the time. It must have new products in the pipeline, it must be looking for new customers, and it must be watchful for new businesses to get into. If it isn't growing, it is already losing ground. Organizations that are shedding businesses, without getting into new ones, are in a shrink mode. Institutions that are getting out of markets are leaving vacuums for winning institutions to fill.

But growing a business is hard work. It requires investment in research and development, as well as marketing and sales. Growing institutions need capital, both human and financial. And growth puts a strain on the institution's organizational and technological infrastructure.

What I am really saying is that *an institution may not be able to grow all its businesses, in all its markets, at the same time.* It must husband its resources, applying them to those businesses it has a chance to dominate. It must know its customer base well, not only providing the services those customers need today, but looking ahead to the services they will need tomorrow. It must combine products and businesses, so that customers are presented with easy buying decisions.

Most of all, it must have a plan. Businesses don't prosper and grow without knowing where they are going and how they will get there. But there are plans and there are plans. Good plans combine both internal and external information, take stock of both the institution's and its competitors' strengths and weaknesses, and provide for both a primary strategy and a contingency. Here are some basic questions a plan must answer:

- ❑ *What customers do we want to serve?* Markets segment themselves in a variety of ways, and the institution must know which market segment it is after. Retail or wholesale, or both? What geography? What income level?

- ❑ *What products do we want to sell?* Within the three basic product groups in financial services is a myriad of offerings. Which ones will the institution offer? Which ones have the largest potential market? Which ones will be the most profitable? Which ones have the best growth path? Which products feed customers to which other products?

- ❑ *How should we be organized?* The way an institution is organized often has a large effect on how it approaches its customers. Should we be geographically organized, or by some other segmentation? Should product departments be grouped together, or included as part of marketing departments? Should all principal businesses be together, or should they be aligned with processing and/or advisory businesses?

- ❑ *How should our employees be compensated?* Since employee compensation has a huge effect on employee effort, this question affects every aspect of the institution. Should everyone have an incentive plan, or just those people who are in "production" departments? Should compensation be compartmentalized, or should it be centralized? Should "sales" people have an open-ended compensation plan, or should they be compensated like everyone else?

These aren't all the questions a business plan should answer, but they are typical of the list. Writing a business plan is an art, not a science, because each institution is different, with different values, histories, and market conditions. And business plans aren't cast in concrete, either. As soon as a plan is completed, it should be assumed to be a little obsolete. No institution is more vulnerable than one which had a very good business plan several years ago, but has made no changes since then.

II | The Winning Strategies

In any endeavor, winning begins with getting the fundamentals right. Good sports teams practice the fundamentals until they are second nature. Good armies drill on the fundamentals until every soldier can execute them in the heat of battle. And good businesses keep the fundamentals uppermost in the minds of all their employees.

But the fundamentals themselves won't win for you. Sports teams need a winning game plan, armies need a winning battle plan, and companies need winning strategies. In financial services, winning institutions will have to focus on six specific objectives—the six winning strategies. They are:

Maximizing noninterest income

Enhancing asset quality

Optimizing capital

Marketing financial services

Managing financial risk

Controlling expenses

At first glance you may say, "Of course, we know that. We know those things have to be done. What's so new about these strategies?" But knowing about these strategies and incorporating them into the everyday life of the institution are very different things. There is a tremendous amount of detail behind each of those headings, detail that spells the difference between wanting to incorporate the strategy and carrying it through.

And that's not all. Achieving one or two of these strategies isn't nearly enough; you have to incorporate them all. In fact, these strategies aren't discrete jobs, they are part of the fabric of the business. They have a part to play in every decision, every customer contact, and in every employee's job. They are the six commandments of financial services, which come together to make a powerful, predatory, winning institution.

4 | Maximizing Noninterest Income

There is no strategy which has been at the forefront of financial services for longer than the strategy of maximizing noninterest income (NII). I can remember at least 15 years ago, the most forward-thinking bank managers were stressing those businesses which generated revenue without entailing the balance sheet. For at least that long the annual reports of all kinds of financial institutions have prominently featured NII. And for at least that long the stock prices of financial institutions have been, at least partly, a function of NII.

And yet, NII has been, for at least 15 years, stubbornly hard to come by. Rare indeed is the bank whose noninterest revenue represents more than 15 percent of total revenue. And even worse, in most institutions, most noninterest revenue is made up of loan origination and deposit account fees, which are themselves derived from selling space on the balance sheet. True, there has been some progress on this front in the United States in the last few years, but only among the larger banks. As generators of real NII, most banks, and particularly the smaller ones, have to be regarded as minor successes at best. But why?

The Nature of Noninterest Income

At the very core of this issue is the definition of noninterest income. For our purposes we will define it as *derived from the execution/processing business, the advisory business, and that part of the principal business which does not entail buying space on the balance sheet.* That complicated definition is necessary because some forms of NII, like loan origination fees, are actually interest charges or payments. The Financial Accounting Standards Board recognized this in their Statement of Financial Accounting Standards #91 (SFAS 91), dealing with the treatment of origination fees.

SFAS 91 says, in simple terms, that origination fees in excess of the actual cost of originating a loan are interchangeable with the interest on the loan, and must be amortized over the loan's life. This treatment was in response to some financial institutions' practices of granting loans at below-market rates and then collecting large origination fees, thus "front-loading" the income stream. Although SFAS 91 is interesting in the abstract, it points up the more difficult issue of separating the NII derived from selling the balance sheet from the income derived from selling something else.

The Sources of Noninterest Income

When we look at it, we can see that all revenue comes from selling something. In finance, it comes from selling the institution's services, its balance sheet, or its brains. Taken generally, and without too much examination, those categories correspond to the three parts of financial services. However, just as the three separate parts of the business interact, the three sources of NII interact. Let's look, then, at the specific sources of NII.

Execution/processing sources:

Check processing fees (including returned items)
Automated Clearing House (ACH) and Electronic Funds
    Transfer (EFT) fees
Letter of Credit (L/C) collection fees
Credit card origination fees
Merchant debit processing fees
Brokerage commissions of all kinds
Trade processing fees
Custody and safekeeping fees
Asset servicing income

Principal transactions sources:

Trading profits
Monthly deposit account fees
Securitization profits
Origination and underwriting profits on assets sold
Profits (not premiums) on risk products

Advisory sources:

Merger and acquisition fees
Investment management and advisory fees
Corporate and municipal finance fees
Personal financial planning fees
Mutual fund sales commissions
Insurance sales comissions

This list of sources is by no means complete, but it is indicative of the whole, and, more importantly, of the categorization of NII. That is because, although financial institutions seldom group their businesses this way, the keys to maximizing NII are different in each of these three categories.

Maximizing Execution/Processing Income

All of the businesses in this category are heavily dependent on *volume* and *efficiency* for profits. Although stockbrokers regard brokerage as distinctly different from transaction processing, the fact is it is moving rapidly toward the "commodity" side of the pendulum where its profit dynamics will be much like those of processing. Already, based on the actions of many retail securities firms, the profitability of securities brokerage is becoming heavily dependent on the total volume of brokerage the institution processes.

At the same time, being in these businesses is often a function of a *membership* or *franchise*. Access to or ownership of an execution or settlement medium has become, and will become more of, a key to success. The problem is that such an advantage can be very temporary. For example, as access to exchange marketplaces opens up, the business of pure brokerage will shrink to almost nothing. In such a market, with efficiency the watchword, a seamless connection between the trade center and the settlement center may be the crucial ingredient that separates the successful markets, and their participants, from the also-rans.

The same set of issues confronts banks in the payments processing business. In a Banker's Roundtable report published in 1994, and prepared by the banking consultants Furash & Co., the authors sound the warning that banks have been restricting their payment processing efforts to the most efficient and least profitable parts of the business, and leaving the more profitable ancillary businesses to non-bank competitors. As payment processing shifts from check processing and merchant debit processing to EDI and value-added networks, banks will have to make the effort to expand their processing businesses or risk becoming irrelevant.

In addition, as both the execution and processing businesses become more efficient and more electronic, they will depend less and less on human beings. In the processing arena this is already occurring, as processing entities extend the entry point (and information delivery point) closer and closer to the end customer. And the people responsible for extending the entry point aren't always the banks. Microsoft Corporation recently offered $1.5 billion for Intuit Corporation (the manufacturer of the Quicken program) because the chairman, Bill Gates, saw the potential of Quicken's ability to extend the household bill-paying function to the home computer. Eventually, all sorts of processing entities will be electronically connected, so the passage of money, ownership, financial claims, and financial information will involve almost no human intervention. If banks do not take the lead in transforming these payment systems, they may involve almost no bank intervention.

By the same token, the execution business is becoming much less of a human process. There are exchange floors all over the world where those are not very welcome words, but they are true nonetheless. In every venue where physical exchanges operate, there are pressures to move to electronic trade match. One by one, the exchanges are giving in to the pressures by instituting electronic trade match after regular trading hours, by allowing orders to arrive on the floor electronically, or by replacing a trading floor with a computer. In doing that, they are following the lead of the biggest exchange success story of the last 20 years, the National Association of Securities Dealers Automated Quotation system (NASDAQ), which has overtaken the New York Stock Exchange (NYSE) in trading volume by executing all trades on a computer.

These businesses will continue to concentrate, because a minimum critical mass will be necessary in order to be profitable. Over the last several years concentration has accelerated in several of these businesses, like check processing, custody and safekeeping, merchant debit processing, and mortgage servicing, as the efficiencies of critical mass become apparent to all the participants. However, since these businesses also give their providers access to, and control of, huge amounts of financial information, institutions will abandon them at their peril.

A classic example of the risks associated with giving up the processing business involves the sale of mortgage servicing. Many institutions have done that to generate regulatory capital, but they have sold their information, as well as their customers, at the same time. Smart institutions who know how to use mortgage servicing can acquire not only an income stream, but also the information necessary to securitize those loans, and, in the process, acquire new customers for their other financial services.

Maximizing Principal Noninterest Income

If the formula for maximizing execution/processing income is relatively straightforward, the formula for maximizing principal noninterest income is anything but.

While execution and processing are pure services, principal transactions involve an institution's *balance sheet* and *risk*. In fact, one could say that principal businesses are not really services at all.

Certainly, many financial institutions approach these businesses as something other than services. As a result, there is a tendency for the customer and institution to take adversarial views and assume adversarial roles in the negotiations that accompany many of these transactions. Sometimes financial institutions come to assume or believe that customers are not even essential to the process. The best example of that kind of thinking is what happens in trading.

Trading Profitability

Not only is trading enormous in its totality, it has become central to the profitability of all financial institutions, because the world's capital markets are the balancing mechanism for the world's financial systems. Thus, even as the capital markets apply pressure to the profits of financial institutions, they offer new ways for those same institutions to make money.

But trading profitability may be the most arcane subject in all of financial services. There are any number of banks and dealers who can attest to the difficulty of building a winning trading organization. Some traders are paranoid and difficult to work with, and seem to resist management. Then, just when these traders do get it right, and the desk seems to be hitting on all cylinders, the markets turn on a dime and bury everyone in losses. The volatility of trading profits is a good reason why the stocks of trading firms have low price/earnings ratios.

One reason for the volatility is that trading is essentially a *zero-sum game.* Whatever money one trading organization makes must come at the expense of another. Of course, market participants come to the market for different reasons, with different measures of success, but the zero-sum nature of the markets puts everyone a little at odds. And the decline of pure brokerage, which used to add some service component, has made the adversarial nature of markets even more apparent.

At the same time, the markets themselves are changing rapidly, which makes trading profits even more elusive. The whole history of markets has been one of a march toward efficiency, which means better service for participants, but lower profits for dealers and brokers. Naturally, brokers resist the march, and certain exchanges have withstood the trend, but even the New York Stock Exchange has suffered a significant loss in market share because it has not embraced change and efficiency. Thus, dealers and exchanges who depend on market inefficiencies for profits will face a long, hard, losing struggle.

But the same forces which restrict the profitability of some entities, change and efficiency, represent an opportunity for others. That is because the changes in the market are customer driven, and those trading firms and exchanges that respond to the demands of the customer will open new avenues of opportunity. NASDAQ is one example of such an exchange.

This necessarily means *getting closer to the customer.* It means finding out earlier and more accurately what the customer wants and needs. It means developing and delivering more quickly what the customer wants and needs. And it means maintaining contact with more customers, and more kinds of customers, all over the world. The changes currently affecting the U.S. markets aren't coming solely from the United States, so participants who look solely to the U.S. customer will be late in responding to those changes.

It also means *keeping an educated eye on a wider range of instruments.* More and more, the price of anything that trades in any market is a function of other instruments in other markets. Stock prices are affected by currency rates, currency prices are affected by interest rates, and interest rates are affected by financial-futures prices. Furthermore, the patterns of interdependence are constantly shifting, so one of the keys is an ability to scan markets in real time, looking for emerging relationships and patterns which lead to trading opportunities.

Another key is *maintaining an electronic connection to an array of customers.* That electronic connection allows a two-way sharing of information, making both customer and dealer more efficient. It allows easier access to markets for the customer, and a better view of the customer's current and future intentions for the dealer. It is one of the few instances of increased efficiency which benefits both dealer and customer, and it serves to defuse some of the adversarial nature of the relationship.

Finally, the trading firm will make more money by *working together more.* Most trading organizations regard their trading units as independent profit centers, but customers are more often doing business across instruments. For example, dealers who can combine currencies and securities trading can bring new efficiencies to international investment managers, who must oversee portfolios of holdings in a myriad of countries and currencies.

Other Principal Businesses

The same drive to efficiency, and the same opportunities, exist in some other principal areas. Risk products, for example. These are the quasi-off-the-balance-sheet products institutions and their corporate customers use to manage their financial risk. They go by such names as swaps, caps and floors, forward-rate agreements, swap options, and the like. They are bilateral agreements in which a financial institution agrees to absorb or lay off a financial risk.

These products can be likened to trading, except that the instruments are not standardized and positions are carried by the financial institution for a long time. Thus, while trading positions can be priced reasonably easily and come and go quickly, risk-instrument positions can be very hard to price and can stay with the institution for years. But even more important, because they aren't carried on the institution's balance sheet, the fact that their value can shift violently may not be apparent until their damage (or benefit) has been felt. Over the past year or so, several banks and their customers have suffered large losses in derivative instruments. I will cover this in more detail in Chapter 8, Managing Financial Risk.

Risk products have grown substantially over the past 10 years, until the volume of contracts in force stood at over $2 trillion. In spite of that huge volume, the markets for these instruments remain neither liquid nor regulated. On the one hand, that represents an increased profit opportunity for financial institutions, because illiquid and unregulated markets are by definition inefficient. On the other hand, it represents increased risk, since large mistakes can be hard for management to detect and get out of.

Many of the same keys to profitability that apply to trading apply to risk products. Getting close to the customer, keeping an educated eye on a wide range of markets, connecting electronically, and working together are all applicable here. One additional key has to do with developing and structuring new products. Because of the illiquidity of the markets, an ability to predict the performance of new instruments under a variety of market conditions becomes crucial. Thus, the programs which are used to construct and price risk products must have the ability to create a pro forma of the instruments' prices under a wide range of market and economic conditions. And it is very beneficial if the process is reversible, so the institution can derive the conditions which would lead to adverse price performance. Finally, because so much of the pricing of these instruments is mathematical, it is essential that banks not rely on the same people who run the models and trade the instruments to mark the positions to market.

Another adjunct to trading is the field of securitization, where assets are modified in form to make them more tradable in the financial markets. Since the advent of the Government National Mortgage Association (GNMA) pass-through in the late 1960s, the volume and variety of securitization has picked up speed. By far the largest amount of securitization has been done in residential mortgages, but the practice has spread to auto loans, credit-card balances, and home-equity loans. With the imposition of the risk-based capital guidelines, the ability of institutions to securitize corporate debt will become more important. One effect of securitization which many banks seem not to be aware of is its acceleration of the trend toward disintermediation, particularly in the thrift industry.

Like the development of risk products, the securitization of assets will be driven by customer demands, but the customers in this instance will be securities customers, not lending customers. And that is not the only difference. In fact, the secret to success in securitization is to do the job itself backwards.

On paper, the process of securitization begins with asset origination. Then the assets to be securitized are selected from all those oroginated, and the security is structured. Then the security is underwritten, which means it is created, and finally sold to the investors. However, professionals in the securitization business know that the securities are actually sold first. That is, the appetite of the market for a specific security is determined, measured, and priced. Then the structure of the security is derived, and the sale to the customer is committed for some time in the future. Then the assets are either selected from an existing portfolio, or originated. Doing the job backwards might look illogical, but it gives you the best chance of having a successful sale, without having unsold product in your inventory. Following the chronological path will ensure that your chances of success will be random at best.

Finally, the principal business generates fees which come from the maintenance and assumption of certain kinds of accounts. Foremost among these is deposit account fees, which are the fees banks charge for deposit accounts, as well as the management fees charged to money-market mutual funds. These fees are generally a fixed amount per month for deposit accounts, but a percent of assets under management for money-market funds. That difference, while subtle, is extremely important. Given that structure, and depending on the relative fees and net-interest margin, it may make sense for the bank to encourage customers to move excess balances from a deposit account to a money-market fund, even though it might not make economic sense for the banks branch staff to do so.

The final principal source of NII that we need to note is credit-card fees, in particular, the annual fees for maintaining an account and the issuing bank's portion of transactions fees. These fees, taken together, have generated very significant profits for some banks, but the margins on both of those businesses have begun to decline. Within the last four years, marketing schemes, mostly involving extended warranties or product insurance, have swept the market, which indicate that the margins earned for processing and accepting credit-card debits are narrowing. In addition, interest rates on card balances have begun to come down, and American Express has introduced a card which gives the customer a grace period on all purchases, even if there is an outstanding balance. These facts point to a dramatic slowing of growth in the credit-card field, and the increasing importance of efficiencies of scale in this area, making the small credit-card issuer a vulnerable species.

Maximizing Advisory Income

The advisory businesses, as I have said, are the glamorous part of financial services. They attract many of the top finance graduates of each year's MBA class, the highest-paid employees and the most public scrutiny. But they are extraordinarily competitive, and institutional newcomers have found their success elusive at best. In the case of commercial banks, those advisory businesses where they traditionally maintained strong positions, like investment management and cash management, have become significantly more competitive in the last ten years, and banks have been losing market share in those specific areas, where the profit margins have been high.

Remember, in the advisory businesses, customers are paying you for what you know—that can help them. Given that fact, the advisory businesses can be divided into two general areas: *transactions-driven* and *volume-driven*. Transactions-driven businesses generate revenue when transactions are done. Mergers and acquisitions is an example of a transactions-driven business, as is personal financial planning and most of corporate finance. Volume-driven businesses generate revenue based on a designated volume of assets under management for the fiduciary businesses. The related business of corporate trust generates fees based on the size of corporate issues under trusteeship.

These two categories may look very similar, but they actually are not. Not only are the keys to doing a good job different, so are the keys to maximizing the income. Transactions-oriented businesses require a high degree of creativity and an aggressive sales technique, while the volume-oriented businesses require a high degree of trust on the part of the customer and steady, long-term performance. Many bankers do not understand the differences between these businesses and the different kinds of people they attract.

Of course, there are some similarities. In both cases, success is a matter of being sharper than the competition and knocking on a lot of doors. Success tends to breed success, so that once customers begin coming in the door, they tend to come in droves. And in both cases, once customers start leaving, for whatever reason, the trend can be extremely difficult to reverse.

But for these businesses, the connection between performance and profitability is very different. On the transactions-oriented side, performance is generally measured by the success rate of transactions: the number and size of mergers accomplished, the number and size of corporate issues underwritten. These transactions have a direct relationship to profitability.

On the volume-oriented side, the quality of the performance has a more tenuous relationship to profitability. In the fiduciary businesses, the amount of assets under management can be a function of the performance of the portfolio managers, but it can be just as much a function of an elusive chemistry between the managers and the customer, based on an espoused investment philosophy, or simply on the quality of the record keeping and quarterly reporting.

The impact of all these cross-currents is that the advisory sector has become heavily individualized. It depends on the efforts of individuals more than most other financial services. As a result, individuals are more richly compensated here than in the other services. But it also requires more individual approaches to customers. Even if the institution employs a largely mass-produced approach to these products, each customer wants to feel as if his solution is his alone. Banks have been struggling to deal with this highly individualized market and personnel environment by doing such things as spinning off their advisory departments, so as to give the personnel an equity interest in the business.

Unfortunately, those attempts have had spotty success, largely because the advisory businesses are as subject to economies of scale as any other. Thus, *the real key to profitability is the development of efficient, replicatable services that look to the customer as if they were devised just for him or her.* For example, portfolio management is a matter of fitting market opportunities to a wide variety of portfolios, which have a wide variety of restrictions and objectives. The more successful a fiduciary business is, and the more customers it attracts, the harder it is to provide its essential service differentiator.

In the future, success in money management will probably require sophisticated computers, scanning the market for opportunities, matching those opportunities to the appropriate portfolios, and delivering the results as if they were individually arrived at. That structure will be hard to sell to current fiduciary employees, who place a high value on their individual expertise, unless their equity interest prompts them to look for more efficient ways to deliver their services.

Making the Most of the Business

When we look at the whole picture, given the methods of success in each of these categories, the real benefits come from combining and expanding the individual categories. In fact, the benefits come from building businesses on top of other businesses, and from developing new products and services. However, both these efforts require a disciplined approach.

The Noninterest Income Matrix

Cross-fertilizing one business from another, and one customer from another, requires some discipline like the Noninterest Income Matrix in Figure 4.1. Like most bilateral matrices, it plots a set of alternatives against two sets of parameters. In this case, the alternatives are sources of NII. The horizontal axis divides the sources of income by the requirements of the business. The vertical axis divides the same sources by the markets served. We need to recognize that, in a business as complicated as finance, there is always some overlap. Some businesses could be considered to serve either capital markets or the wholesale market, for example. In

Figure 4.1
Noninterest Income Matrix

	Execution/ Processing	Principal	Advisory
Capital Markets	Trade Processing Brokerage Custody/ Safekeeping	Trading Securitization	Investment Management Mergers and Acquisitions
Retail	Check Clearing Mutual Fund Sales EFT	Deposit Account Fees Credit Card Trans Fees	Personal Financial Planning Personal Trust Insurance
Wholesale	ACH EFT L/C	 Risk Products	Corporate Finance Cash Management

other words, the matrix isn't perfect, but it can help us see things more clearly and build a business plan.

The first thing we can do with the matrix is to determine if there are any obvious holes in it. Are there businesses which are a natural for the bank to be in, given its current product/market mix? Are there any services which are conspicuous by their absence? Why are we not providing those services, or serving those markets? The answers to these questions might appear to make sense on the surface, or within the bank's current culture, but they may be pointing to needed changes in thinking instead of logical reasons to stay where we are.

The next thing we can do is highlight those services the institution is good at, and being good could be measured in terms of profitability, market position, or customer satisfaction. Are they concentrated within one vertical column? That probably means that the institution is heavily concentrated in one product area or line of business. Although that can be attractive, from the point of view that emphasizes focus, it can also be bad news. The largest flow of NII will probably come from combining all three business categories, not depending exclusively on one.

All the highlights in one row says that the institution is heavily dependent on one market. For institutions with limited resources, this is an attractive choice, but it too carries some risks. In particular, it requires that the institution keep a close eye on the preferences of that customer set and market, because missing a change there can mean curtains.

Finding highlights scattered throughout the matrix is both a benefit and a warning. The benefit is based on having a diverse portfolio of product offerings, targeted for markets which are in different stages of the product life cycle. It is a marketing axiom that the most successful companies have a diverse portfolio of products, so that those products in mature markets, known as cash cows, can subsidize products that are earlier in the life cycle. The warning is that, unless there are highlights everywhere, the institution may be wasting opportunities to build success upon success.

Migrating around the Matrix

That brings us to the best use of the product matrix, as a guide to building a winning portfolio of noninterest businesses. There are natural affinities between products, and those affinities offer easy paths for migration into new businesses. One migration path is horizontal, where you offer more, and different kinds of, products to your current customers. For example, in capital markets it might make sense to focus trading efforts on those customers for whom you already provide custody or safekeeping services. Or, in the wholesale arena, you might target your current trade finance customers for risk products or cash management. The benefit here is that you already serve this corporate customer, often the same contact person as the customer, and your delivery processes might be very similar.

Another migratory approach might be vertical, where you offer services in one category to a different market. For example, in the advisory category, doing well at cash management services for corporations might translate to offering those same services to state and local governments, since their cash management expertise might be lower than that of corporations. In the execution/processing category, being efficient at EFT for corporations might translate into a nice EFT business for individuals, or perhaps trade processing for securities firms.

The most difficult migratory path is diagonal, where the institution moves into a new product area as well as a new market at the same time. That migration often requires large investments in both product development and marketing, with uncertain results. This is one of those situations where buying into a market by acquiring a company with both the product and market expertise is often the best policy.

Developing New Products

By far the most rewarding strategy, although it is the most difficult, is developing products entirely new to the banking industry—those not offered by your competitors yet, although they may be offered by some other industry. This is not just diagonal migration, it is, in a sense, migrating out of the matrix altogether. Although many institutions can see the benefits of striking out into other products and markets, they have very little confidence in their ability to make it work, so they don't attempt it often, and they bring it off even less often.

Market-Driven Product Planning

There is, however, a process for developing new products, called market-driven product planning, and it is depicted in Figure 4.2. It is called *market-driven* product planning because the process incorporates information about the conditions in the marketplace, as well as the conditions within the institution, to derive products that utilize the institution's strengths and play to the best audience.

In looking at Figure 4.2, we can divide the market-driven product planning process into four distinct phases, the first two of which we will cover here. Phase 1 involves the generation of a product strategy. Phase 2 involves the generation of an implementation plan. Phase 3 involves the introduction of the product. Phase 4 involves the evaluation of the product's success and any resulting adjustments to its makeup or marketing.

Phase 1—The Product Strategy

The product strategy is a result of combining two bodies of knowledge: knowledge about what is going on outside the institution, called market conditions, and about what is going on inside the institution, called situation analysis.

The Market Conditions section contains information on three subjects: customers, markets, and competitors.

Customers: The first step in this process is establishing a profile of the institution's current customers. The profile will answer the following types of questions:

Figure 4.2
Market-Driven Product Planning

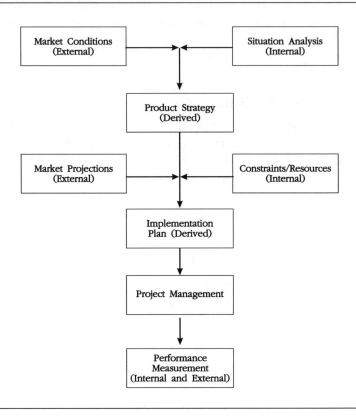

- ❑ What products or services will the customer buy, or what products or services are they currently buying from others?

- ❑ What attributes of those products or services are most important to the customers?

- ❑ How do customers make buying decisions for those products or services?

- ❑ Are customers likely to link the purchase of new products or services with current products or services?

- ❑ How many current or potential customers are there for each new product or service?

Much of the information necessary to answer these questions is available to the institution, through its current processing of customer business, but much of it will require market research, probably conducted by a market-research firm.

Once a profile of the institution's current customers has been prepared, the institution needs to expand that profile to potential buyers who are not currently customers. In addition to the above questions, there is an additional category covering possible impediments to winning over the customers of other institutions to these new products.

Market: The same market-research firm used above could probably provide the answers to the following kinds of questions about the market for new products or services:

❑   How large is the current market for these products or services?

❑   Has the market segmented, and how are the segments differentiated?

❑   What has been the growth rate in the market over the last three years, and is it accelerating or decelerating?

❑   What are the competitive positions of the current providers of the products or services?

❑   What barriers to entry exist in the market, and what barriers can be erected?

This information, when placed alongside the customer information, gives the institution a feeling for whether the market is a desirable one, as well as whether it can be entered effectively.

Competitors: The remaining set of questions refer to the institution's competitors in the new product or service:

❑   What capabilities or resources do competitors have or have access to that could affect their ability to compete?

❑   What mindset, values, or beliefs do competitors have that could affect their ability to compete?

❑   What relationships, alliances, or organizational differences do competitors have that could affect their ability to compete?

❑   Based on the above, and on observations of their actions, what are the competitors current strategies?

❑   Based on the institution's entering the market with a product or service, what is the range of expected reactions by competitors?

Situation Analysis: At the same time that the institution is assessing the array of market information, it needs to assess its internal situation. This assessment, while useful in and of itself, is really meant to be compared to the information just covered regarding competitors.

Resources: This part of the process covers the things the institution can *bring to bear* in an effort to make the product a success. It is distinguished from the things the institution can *do*, which are discussed in the next section. Here are some kinds of resources:

❑ Financial—for example, regulatory capital, cash flow, and stock price

❑ Regulatory—for example, approvals, franchises, access to insurance, and business restrictions

❑ Information—for example, transaction records, internal and external databases, and the ability to manipulate any of these

❑ Human—for example, key executives, people with key contacts, and those with special expertise

Capabilities: These are the things an institution can do to make a product a success. They are organizational capabilities, as opposed to individual ones, which are covered above.

❑ Processing—for example, payments processing, ownership records processing, and account record keeping

❑ Marketing—for example, accessing a large current customer set, fostering a wide acceptance of similar products, and projecting a well-recognized corporate image

❑ Delivery—for example, a large branch/ATM network, a wide network of electronic access, and membership in a clearinghouse or exchange

Culture: These are the organizational behavior patterns that can affect the institution's ability to introduce a successful product.

❑ Values—These are the priorities an institution uses to regulate its behavior, like profits, market share, customer satisfaction, risk assumption, and quality of product.

❑ Beliefs—These are the assumptions that underly the institution's behavior, about things like customer loyalty, regulatory patterns, competitor's behavior, and economic conditions.

❑ Structure—This is the way the institution is organized, both visibly (the organization chart) and invisibly (the underground), and the way it deals with problems. It determines such things as the institution's ability to react to change and to take advantage of opportunities.

Product Strategy: Bringing together the above information and analyses, the institution can develop the product strategy. It is very important that all the departments and people involved in launching the product be in agreement on this strategy, because it carries the seeds of either success or failure.

The product strategy will cover the following subjects:

❏ Product Description(s)—Obviously, this part describes the product, but is also describes the variations of the product necessary for different market segments. Included in the description would be such things as the customer benefits, the legal arrangements necessary, and the relationship between the institution's products and the competitor's.

❏ Target Segments—This is a description of the customer segments the product(s) are targeted at. The relationship between the segment needs and wants and the product features should be explained, and a comparison should be made between the product's fit and its competitor's fit.

❏ Pricing—The pricing section covers not only the cost justification for the pricing, but the marketing impact of the price, as well as alternative pricing strategies for different markets and/or different economic conditions.

❏ Delivery—This section covers both the method by which the product is produced (which can be somewhat amorphous in the case of services) and the method(s) by which it is brought to the customer. The same product can be delivered to different market segments by totally different means. For example, mutual funds can be delivered to busy executives through self-service devices, with one cost structure, and to "widows and orphans" through a financial planning service, with a significantly higher cost structure. Most banks who offer mutual funds do not utilize such disparate delivery channels and cost structures.

❏ Marketing—This section covers the way in which the product is introduced to the market (as opposed to how it is delivered), how customers are made aware of it, and how they are given incentives to buy it. Included are such things as the product image, introductory programs, and customer satisfaction surveys.

Phase 2—The Implementation Plan

Once the product strategy is agreed upon, there is one more job to be done before the product is developed: *the implementation plan.* This is the road map the institution will follow in bringing the product to market at the lowest possible cost and with the largest possible impact. The implementation plan starts from the product strategy, and adds two more analyses: market projections and constraints/resources.

Market Projections: Because the implementation of any project introduction takes some time, it is important to make some projections about the market, so the product will be right, for the right market segment, introduced the right way, when it is ready. The following subjects need to be addressed.

Product Life Cycles: As the institution moves from strategy to implementation, a clear understanding of the life cycle(s) of the products becomes paramount. This is particularly important because many products that are new to banks have been available to their customers for some time. Although life insurance may be a growth product to a bank, it is probably in the mature stage of its life cycle overall. Life-cycle analysis will answer the following kinds of questions:

- ❑ At what point in the product life cycle (emergence, growth, maturity, decline) is the product in general? How does that compare to the products position within the banking industry?

- ❑ How rapidly will the product move along the life-cycle curve?

- ❑ How much segmentation has already occurred in the market, and how rapidly will it continue? Are any of the market segments particularly accessible to the bank?

- ❑ How possible is it that products in or approaching the mature/decline stage can be relaunched?

Competitors' Strategies: Also as the institution moves from strategy to implementation, a set of projections about competitors' possible strategies and reactions to the institution's actions have to be folded in. These kinds of questions have to be addressed:

- ❑ Based on past performance, what are our competitors' most likely future strategies?

- ❑ What possible future strategy would be the most damaging to us?

- ❑ What strategy would be the most helpful to us?

- ❑ Is there anything we can incorporate into the implementation plan that could influence our competitors' choices of strategies?

Economic Variables: However good the product strategy is, it can all come to naught if economic conditions shift. Thus, this analysis needs to address the following kinds of questions:

- ❑ What are the most likely economic changes during the implementation period, and what impact could they have on the implementation?

❑ What economic changes could cause the most damage to the product introduction?

❑ What adjustments to the product's design or introduction would be necessary to counteract negative economic developments?

❑ How will the institution be able to determine what economic changes are occurring before it is too late to react?

Other Variables: In addition to economic changes, other kinds of changes during implementation can represent either threats or opportunities:

❑ Regulatory—What regulatory changes for the institution, its competitors, or its customers could impact the implementation plan?

❑ Accounting—What accounting changes for the institution, its competitors, or its customers could impact the implementation plan?

❑ Taxation—What tax changes for the institution, its competitors, or its customers could impact the implementation plan?

❑ Demographic—What demographic changes could impact the implementation plan?

Constraints/Resources: As a complement to the market projections, the institution needs to assess its ability to implement the strategy. That requires an objective assessment of the institution's constraints and resources. The assessment is done in four parts:

Financial/Capital: This is a measure of the financial resources that can be brought to bear on the implementation. It addresses such issues as budget allocations, the implementation's impact on the institution's capital base, and its impact on the institution's return on equity over the next several years. Included here is an assessment of the alternative methods of financing the implementation.

Personnel/Competencies: This is an assessment of the human resources that are necessary to implement the product, and an assessment of the human resources the institution can marshal. It addresses the alternative uses of those human resources, and alternative sources besides those internal to the institution.

Size/Geography: This is an assessment of the institution's ability to introduce the product on a scale and in the locations necessary to make it a success. It addresses such alternatives as staged introductions, joint implementation, and product resizing.

Regulatory/Alliance: This is an assessment of the institution's regulatory environment as it pertains to its ability to complete the implementation. It addresses such things as regulatory limitations on lines of business or geography, as well as alternative corporate structures or alliances to deal with regulatory limitations.

Implementation Plan: Given the results of these analyses, the institution can formulate an implementation plan, which is the last step before the implementation project begins. The implementation plan has four main parts:

Action Plans: These are all the specific steps necessary to implement the product. They include, among others, such things as alliances, systems development, advertising and public relations, and regulatory approvals. Because the institution has already completed the product design during the strategy phase, these steps are specifically designed to get the product into the market as quickly and as profitably as possible.

Resource Allocations: These are the hard decisions about where the resources to complete the job will come from, how they will be paid for, and how their efficient use will be encouraged.

Schedule: This is the expected chain of events, and the expected completion points along that chain. If the work has been done properly before this point, the institution will have a fairly firm idea of the completion points and will have the ability to tailor the process to account for uncertainties in certain steps.

Performance Measurement: This is the set of criteria by which the implementation team will be judged. Although it incorporates accountability, it needs to encourage the flexibility, on the part of the both the implementation team and management, that is necessary both to take advantage of opportunities and to avoid disasters.

Having done all this work, the institution can start the implementation process, comfortable in the knowledge that it has a winning product and a winning implementation, and that it will be maximizing its noninterest income.

5 | Enhancing Asset Quality

In business, as in other aspects of life, things tend to move in cycles. For a time, one aspect of a business is center stage, and then another aspect gains the footlights. Business strategies burst on the scene, capture everyone's attention, and then become passé, seldom to be mentioned again. Yesterday's excesses become today's reactions, and perhaps tomorrow's forgotten issue. Sometimes it makes you wonder if we will ever learn.

In financial services, the hottest topic until the last few years was enhancing asset quality. Every financial institution has had its brush with credit problems, and some have foundered on them. Entire sections of the country have endured large-scale economic downturns, waves of loan defaults, and the resulting spate of banking collapses.

But things always seem to come around. In the late 1970s and early 1980s, Texas and the rest of the Southwest were boom country, where raw land turned to money right before your eyes. By the mid-1980s, this same section of the country was an economic dust bowl, its banks were knee-deep in defaulted loans, and the FDIC was knee-deep in failed southwestern banks. By the early 1990s, the Southwest was coming back, and the banks that had purchased Texas franchises from the FDIC were using the profits from these purchases to subsidize their more recent credit losses at home, in the Northeast, the Southeast, and California. By the mid-1990s, credit problems in general had receded from banking center stage, with the exception of some lingering commercial real estate problems. In fact, the significant improvement in bank profitability in 1993 and 1994 were almost entirely due to reduced loan loss provisions. But in 1994 there were already storm clouds on the horizon. At the 1994 ABA convention, Federal Reserve Chairman Alan Greenspan felt obligated to warn bankers that the Fed was already seeing signs of credit excesses, and he urged bankers to begin differential loan pricing based on credit.

The Texas lending cycle of overenthusiasm, overlending, contractions, defaults, and bank failures is not a purely regional phenomenon. Lending institutions have demonstrated the ability to make the same kinds of mistakes on a national basis, if not an international one. The corporate leverage binge of the 1980s, where raiders with access to over-willing lenders bid up the stock prices of public companies, still hangs over the financial arena. Whether the raiders were American businessmen, or foreigners like Robert Campeau or Alan Bond, their singleminded pursuit of corporations at ever more stratospheric stock prices has left many lenders queasy over their assets, if not downright sick.

But it is important to realize that it is the lenders themselves who make these cycles of excess possible. In fact, it is lenders who drive the cycles. It was the lenders who chased after real estate developers in the 1980s and showered them with land-acquisition and construction loans. It was the lenders who courted the corporate raiders, vying to structure the most attractive bridge or mezzanine financings. And it was the lenders who seduced the American consumer with credit cards and home equity loans, which are the next credit catastrophe, waiting in the wings.

The Dichotomy of Financial Assets

Hindsight, of course, is 20/20, but it doesn't take a business genius to see that all these credit cycles were very predictable. The history of finance, going back two hundred years, is a parade of boom and bust. Economic growth always seems to lead to economic frenzy, followed by a financial collapse somewhere in the economy, followed by a financial panic, ending in a severe economic contraction. When the financial excesses have been wrung out, *which means when the volume of financial assets again approaches the volume of real assets,* an economic recovery can begin.

Astute economists have known for years that the financial sector has played a major role in economic cycles, but not much has been written about why. We can best understand the role of financial institutions in this cycle if we understand the *dichotomy of financial assets.*

Somewhere in Economics 101 we learned about the ability of the banking system to expand the money supply by accepting deposits and relending them. In the economics texts, the only limit to the expansion of the money supply was the reserve ratio imposed by the central bank. The time-honored formula said that the multiplier by which an increase in the reserves could increase the money supply was the inverse of the reserve ratio. Thus a 20 percent reserve ratio generated a 5 multiplier, for example.

That simplistic approach to financial assets misses the important fact that at any point in time there are only so many quality financial assets to be created. When financial institutions in the aggregate attempt to increase their holdings of financial assets, they degrade the quality of financial assets in general. *The best way to ensure that the quality of an institution's assets continues to stay high is to curb the urge to create them.*

Unfortunately, the clear thinking necessary to resist the lending frenzy that often comes at the end of an economic expansion is made more difficult by the high interest rates and large commitment fees offered by the borrowers. To make things worse, the value of the collateral for many loans made at the end of a cycle is universally viewed as both high and ensured.

Thinking about Financial Assets

In order for the winning institution to avoid the dichotomy of financial assets, where the desire to create more income leads to the desire to create more assets, the institution needs to reshape its thinking. Here are some starting points.

1. *There is no such thing as a "secured" loan because collateral is the most overrated factor in the lending game.* Loans are paid back out of cash flow, and, if the cash flow isn't sufficient to cover the debt service, the collateral most likely won't be sufficient to cover the principal. More bad loans have been made on the market value of collateral than on any other basis.

2. *The worst place in the world to discuss repayment of a troubled loan is in a bankruptcy court.* Negotiations about troubled assets are most effective when they are directly between the borrower and the lender. The more parties involved in the conversation, the harder it is to bring it to a successful conclusion. A bankruptcy referee is charged with weighing the interests of a variety of claimants, and the larger the number of claimants, the more convoluted the conversation in a bankruptcy court.

3. *The optimal structure for an asset is the one that optimizes the combined positions of both the borrower and lender.* The American business system has long been built on the adversarial model, where participants in financial transactions are assumed to have opposite interests. That is why we have more complicated contracts and more lawyers than countries like Japan, which don't utilize the adversarial model. However, the best result one can expect from a lending transaction occurs when both borrower and lender prosper as a result, and this is often a result of proper structuring. Structuring financial assets is an exercise in balancing the interests of both parties.

4.   *Underwriting loans is important, but not as important as monitoring them.* In my presentations to commercial bankers, I often ask how many people ever made a bad loan, and many of them raise their hands. When I tell them I mean a loan which was in trouble at the time it was made, very few people ever raise their hands. Almost every loan is good when it is made; the bad ones go bad later. Spending more money to improve loan underwriting will probably have much less value than spending it to improve loan monitoring.

The Role of the Balance Sheet

The items just covered are important reference points, but they really serve to lead us to the basis of asset quality: the role of the institution's balance sheet. Traditionally, bankers have regarded their business as one of taking deposits and making loans. In fact, Congress and the regulators define banking as the business "of taking insured deposits and making commercial loans." Since U.S. banking law defines banking as being composed of both those functions, some corporations have formed "nonbank banks," which perform only one of those functions.

That widely accepted definition of banking has in the past led everyone, bankers and nonbankers alike, to regard deposit-taking and lending as the primary businesses in banking. It naturally follows that the same people regard the primary source of banking income as the spread between the cost of deposits and the yield on assets, known as *net interest income.* The next step of reasoning says that the larger the bank's balance sheet, the larger its ability to generate income.

We now know, of course, that this line of reasoning ignores the impact on asset quality of rapidly increasing the bank's balance sheet. As competition increases, and net interest margins decline, as they have recently, the easiest way to increase the size of the balance sheet and the net interest margin is by creating assets of ever lower quality. These assets, because they carry higher relative interest rates, and high commitment fees, appear to generate large amounts of income. Only later, when the principal of the asset is deemed uncollectible, does the real impact of the asset on net income become clear.

There are two rules about balance-sheet lending that address this dichotomy, and they go hand in hand. The first is: *The balance sheet isn't there to be tied up, it's there to be turned over.* Every asset should be created not to be held, but to be sold. This is true first because the size of the balance sheet is the limiting factor on the amount of business an institution can do. Leaving assets on the balance sheet arbitrarily reduces the institution's ability to do more business. It is also true because the market is an excellent determiner of the right relationship between an asset's quality and its interest rate. If assets are created to be sold first and to be held second, then assets that are poorly priced or of too low a quality will not be created in the first place.

The second rule is: *The balance sheet isn't there to generate income, it is there to generate business.* When interest spreads are narrow, as they are today, an institution that manages its balance sheet superbly can make just enough money to become a good target for an acquirer. In order to make enough money to be an acquirer itself, it must generate significant noninterest income. One of the best ways to build sources of noninterest income is through the balance sheet. By making space on the balance sheet available to the right kind of customer, an astute institution can open up opportunities to generate noninterest income from the same customer.

Taken together, these two rules set the foundation for enhancing asset quality. By changing the emphasis from holding assets to creating marketable assets, the institution brings the market's discipline to bear on its underwriting decisions. By changing the balance-sheet emphasis from income generation to business generation, the institution replaces the need to create high yielding assets with a need to create good customer relationships.

Turning the Underwriting Process Around

But there is a much bigger issue banks must deal with in enhancing asset quality, and it is best illustrated by the situation Citicorp Mortgage Corp (CMC) found itself in a few years ago. Under pressure from senior management to increase servicing volume and origination fees, CMC embarked on an aggressive marketing program, which included an underwriting process which dropped requirements for documentation of such things as income levels and employment history.

The program was successful, in the sense that CMCs origination and servicing volumes took off, but it was a major disaster in terms of the quality of loans originated. As the economy turned down, many of CMCs loans went into default, and its lax underwriting practices made it quite difficult for CMC to keep track of its problem loan portfolio. Things got bad enough that Citicorp itself had to inject about $200 million of capital into CMC, and it lost its franchise to sell and service loans for the Federal National Mortgage Association (FNMA).

At that point, there were some changes in CMCs management, and the lax underwriting standards were tightened up. This brought down the incidence of defaulted loans, and restored their FNMA seller-servicer status, but it was at the expense of a drop in originations and subsequent servicing volume. Even streamlining the underwriting process did not really have the effect of increasing accepted loan volume. It appeared that CMC was caught in the classic dichotomy of credit quality—the only way to keep the asset quality up is to say no more often, and the streamlining of the underwriting process just allowed them to say no more often faster.

The real problem is that bankers, like insurers, tend to regard underwriting as an essentially reactive event. Customers come in to apply for a loan, and underwriters say either no or yes. If they say no too often, loan volume and revenue suffer. If they say yes too often, asset quality suffers, and they have to take some write-downs. As far as they are concerned, they have to walk the middle line. After all, there are only so many good loans to be had.

But their more creative competitors, including the nonbank lenders, have learned to use the loan underwriting process as a proactive, instead of reactive, tool. Instead of waiting for customers to come in at random, assuring themselves of an average sampling of borrowers, these lenders are doing their loan underwriting before customers apply, based on financial information available to them from a variety of sources. By preunderwriting potential loans, these lenders can select the best quality borrowers, according to their criteria, and actively market their loan products to these customers. Because these are what the lenders regard as the cream of the borrowing crop, the lenders can offer very attractive rates, thus accomplishing the differential pricing Fed Chairman Greenspan advocated in 1994. By turning the underwriting process around, these winning financial institutions have escaped the dichotomy of asset quality, and have assured themselves of being winners.

Dealing with Current Assets

However, that approach to underwriting still leaves unaddressed the institution's need to enhance the quality of the assets it currently has on its books. Market disciplines are fine, until the market goes overboard for a certain kind of asset, and noninterest income is fine, but it won't save an asset that has already gone bad. Thus, the institution must implement a three-step process designed to enhance its asset quality.

❑ It must underwrite the assets well—ensuring that it solicits from and lends to only credit-worthy borrowers.

❑ It must structure the assets well—ensuring that both it and the customer have the best business result.

❑ It must monitor the assets well—ensuring that it keeps its finger on the financial pulse of the customer.

Underwriting the Asset

Obviously, enhancing asset quality begins before the asset comes into existence, with underwriting. Almost any financial institution will tell you that they already have adequate processes in place to underwrite assets. However, that doesn't explain the cycle we have repeatedly seen of overlending, and the resulting defaulted assets. One only has to look at the collection of wildly optimistic loans on commercial real estate, or some of the corporate acquisition loans that were obviously headed for trouble from the start, to conclude that good underwriting, if not a lost art, is far from a common one.

The underwriting process is one of gathering and analyzing information, and the first kind is borrower information. Most financial institutions collect a significant amount of information about potential borrowers and about the collateral which may be offered. There are some basic pieces of information, recognized by everyone, and some that may be less apparent, either in availability or impact. Borrower information requirements differ, depending on whether the borrower is a household or a business. Here are some categories of borrower information:

Household Borrower Information

> Credit history
> Employment history
> Balance sheet
> Past and projected cash flow
> Collateral description

Business Borrower Information

> Credit history
> Business history
> Balance sheet
> Past and projected income statements and cash flow
> Supplier experiences
> Business case for loan
> Collateral description

Of all the kinds of information required to underwrite an asset, the borrower information is the most common, and most institutions believe that they do this part of the job adequately. That isn't necessarily true for the second category, market information. This is information about the borrower's marketplace, and the borrower's position in it. Obtaining borrower's market information evidences a recognition by the lender that the borrower's ability to repay may be affected by things outside his or her own control.

Market information falls into two categories: the nature of the market for what the borrower produces, and the borrower's competitive position in the market. On reading those descriptions, it would be easy to assume that we are only referring here to the corporate or business borrower, but that is not the case. The household is also a producer of something—the marketable skills of the working members of the household. There is clearly a market for those skills, robust or otherwise, and the borrower clearly has a competitive position in that market.

Although it is more difficult to determine a household's market position than a business's, it can be done, and the effort to do it will highlight any glaring potential problems, like having skills of use in declining industries, or being positioned at the bottom of the skills ladder.

It is in the corporate arena, however, that market information has the most impact. Corporate borrowers all operate in markets, whether the borrower is a real estate developer, manufacturing concern, services provider, or in any other line of endeavor. Given that universal fact, the financial institution must answer the following kinds of questions about a potential borrower:

❑ What is the borrower's product mix, and what is the profitability of each product?

❑ At what stage in the life cycle is each of the borrower's products?

❑ Who are the major competitors for each of the borrower's products?

❑ What is the competitive position of each of the borrower's products?

❑ In light of all the above, what are the best strategies for the borrower to pursue, and how likely is he or she to pursue them?

The potential borrower should have answers to the above questions. If not, that fact itself should raise some red flags in the mind of the lender. Given that the answers are available, the lender should prepare a matrix like the one in Figure 5.1, which should point out any potential problems looming for the borrower.

Figure 5.1

Product	Profitability ROE	Life Cycle	Competitor	Competitor Strategy
Shock absorbers	15%	Mature	Ace Shocks & Struts	Outsource manufacturing and cut prices
Hydraulic Rams	21%	Growth	Amalgamated Construction Gear	Build new plant and acquire dealer network

It may appear that this kind of analysis is excessive and too expensive to be justified. While it may be too much effort to make for small loans, it can be systematized and automated to a large extent, and it is essential to prevent the large losses that come from lending to poorly positioned borrowers in mature or declining markets. In addition, it will often point out potential customers who may not currently be doing business with the financial institution, and who are much better credit risks and much more profitable customers.

The combination of borrower information and market information is two-thirds of what is needed; the remaining piece is economic information. This refers to the status and recent history of the economy, as it applies to the borrower. It is a recognition of the fact that a borrower's ability to manage its business or personal affairs and its position in a market are both affected by changing economic conditions. Changes in things like the price of raw materials, levels of economic activity in a particular region, tax laws, and regulation can greatly enhance or reduce a borrower's ability to pay. Changes in shopping patterns made city department stores poor credit risks, just as their owners were leveraging them to the hilt. Airline deregulation and an economic slump has forced many of them into bankruptcy, just after some raiders went heavily into debt to acquire them. And a saturation of the airwaves with video entertainment, as well as a public rebellion against cable rates may make loans to the cable and local broadcasting market a poor bet in the future. Of course, economic good news can make what looks like a marginal asset a very good one.

Analyzing the Information

Collecting all this information has value in and of itself, but the real benefits come from analyzing it. There are analyses and then there are analyses, but the best kind for underwriting assets is a *stress analysis*. A stress analysis determines the causal factors of a borrower's ability to carry the debt service, and attempts to determine the impact on that ability of a variety of changes in its own situation, the market, and the economy.

The basis of a stress analysis is a mathematical model which places the borrower's cash flow as the dependent variable, and has as independent variables such things as expenses, market structure, competitor strategies, and economic conditions. Most people think of a stress analysis as being run "forward," that is from the independent variables to the cash flow, and that process can give meaningful results. However, the best use of a stress analysis is probably to run it "backwards," from the worst case cash flow to the conditions that would prompt it. In most mathematical models, there are multiple combinations of independent variables that could produce the worst case scenario, but the institution will fairly quickly be able to spot the most likely combination, and should be able to evaluate the probabilities of that combination of events occurring.

Structuring/Restructuring the Asset

Asset underwriting is a tried and true part of the process of enhancing asset quality, so much so that it gets almost all the attention. The problem is its effect on asset quality is limited. This is because things change over time, including the financial condition of the borrower (which we will cover in the next section), and because a very significant aspect of asset quality is the asset's structure.

Asset structuring is based on the fact that financial assets are essentially claims on cash flows. What generates the cash flows, who else has a claim on them, which and how many corporate structures they must pass through, and what obligations the borrower has to fulfill are just some of the questions that are addressed by the asset's structure. As with most other aspects of enhancing asset value, some parts of structuring are well understood by most financial institutions, and some are not.

Structuring concerns can be divided into four broad classes:

- ❏ The form of the asset contract
- ❏ The financer's position on the borrower's balance sheet
- ❏ The financer's position in the borrower's cash flow
- ❏ The financer's position vis-à-vis other financers

The Asset Contract

This aspect is what most people think of when structuring is brought up. In its simplest form, it covers the interest rate, maturity schedule, collateral, and any covenants the borrower agrees to. For a simple consumer loan, the contract can be created using a boiler-plate approach and can be one or two pages long. For a highly technical transaction, it can run literally hundreds of pages, most of them filled with covenants.

However, as complicated as the contract might become, it describes a fairly simple relationship. One entity lends another money, and the borrower agrees to repay, with interest, over a specified period of time. To ensure payment, the borrower may pledge collateral to the lender. That transaction, replete with any number of conditions, is both ancient and venerable. It has, however, some major flaws. One is well known, that the lender bears all the negative risk and has almost none of the profit potential. The second, less obvious, is that the bankruptcy courts have evolved a process which weakens, and can invalidate, the terms of the contract.

The bankruptcy laws, which were originally designed as a way for borrowers to work their way out of problems and for lenders to realize as much of their principal and interest as possible, have become an arena for invalidating and renegotiating the original contract. Except that a bankruptcy court is the last place the lender wants that to occur, because the lender is negotiating with a judge, instead of a borrower, and because the entire process involves all the other creditors. Thus, the financial institution must put in place a contract which gives it the best possible bargaining position in case the borrower has problems, and must be willing to renegotiate directly if it appears that bankruptcy is a real possibility.

One aspect of Chapter 11 bankruptcies is that the referee almost always moves immediately to secure those things that are necessary to the production of the product, and arranges the funds to pay for them, even while denying the creditors access to their funds. This accepted method of administrating a reorganization argues forcefully for the substitution of an ownership and lessor position over that of a lender.

The Balance-Sheet Position

Ever since double entry bookkeeping was perfected, lenders have realized that there is a great deal of import associated with where on the borrower's balance sheet their debt appeared. One only has to look at the balance sheet of a finance company, an electric utility, or a bank, to see clearly the concept of layering debt.

Layering has become quite an art by now. A highly leveraged company will have first mortgage debt, second mortgage debt, senior unsecured, subordinated unsecured, income debentures, preferred stock, and perhaps preference stock, before one gets down to the common stock. In addition, there may be off-balance-sheet debt, like leases or obligations to perform on such things as interest rate or currency swaps, which might not show up in an orthodox credit analysis, but could have a huge impact on credit quality, and in a bankruptcy proceeding. To make matters more complicated, some layers are convertible into other layers, either at the option of the lender, or upon the technical default of one of the covenants.

Each of these layers carries what the market feels is an appropriate interest rate for its position, but each lender must determine if his or her balance-sheet position is being properly compensated, both initially and during the life of the asset. If it appears that the borrower's position has deteriorated, the lender needs to negotiate a remedy before the situation moves out of his or her control and into the court's.

Cash-Flow Position

Balance-sheet position has traditionally been the measure of safety and protection for the lender, but a more useful measure might be cash-flow position. Where balance-sheet position refers to the lender's claim on principal, cash-flow position refers to the lenders claim on the debt service.

In addition, cash-flow position reflects the fact that there really is no such thing as a real-estate loan or a working-capital loan or an acquisition loan. All loans are paid back out of cash flow, and, if the cash flow is insufficient to cover the debt service, the collateral will most likely be insufficient to cover the loan amount. Thus, the astute financial institution will pay at least as much attention to its position regarding the borrower's cash flow as it will to its position on the balance sheet.

The reason financial institutions do less about cash-flow position than they do about balance-sheet position is that cash-flow position is harder to determine, since it requires the institution to get fairly deeply into the borrower's business. However, following the path a borrower's cash flow takes is not only a good credit practice, it exposes the institution to some opportunities to do business with the borrower, and perhaps improve its cash flow position at the same time.

One critical question regarding cash-flow position relates to the choice between lending to a holding company or one of its operating subsidiaries. Many lenders opt for loans to holding companies, reasoning that such a loan gives them a claim on a wider variety of assets. A better practice might be to apportion the loan among the operating subsidiaries, getting the same diversification of collateral but affording a much better position with regard to the cash flow.

Competitive Relationship

The final issue under structuring assets results from the fact that, when the borrower's cash flow is insufficient to service the debt, the lenders are in competition to access that cash flow. As a borrower's financial condition begins to deteriorate, institutions who entered into the transaction as peers quickly become competitors, and the institution which is alert and creative can substantially better its position.

One key to making the most of its competitive position is the institution's ability to come up with an alternative structure that the borrower will regard as beneficial and the other lenders will not regard as prejudicial. In addition, recent bankruptcy rulings have invalidated renegotiations accomplished prior to a bankruptcy which the court felt had the effect of forcing the borrower into the bankruptcy, under a doctrine called "equitable subordination." This is the most ticklish part of being a lender, and is a point in the administration of an asset where all the effort the institution made to understand the borrower's business, as well as its market position, can pay tremendous dividends.

Another key to optimizing your competitive position, as well as most of the other structuring issues, is keeping an eye on the borrower's fortunes. That is the arena of monitoring.

Monitoring the Asset

If you want a good dose of the negatives, attend a meeting of lenders to a company which has filed bankruptcy. There is nothing like a big loan gone bad to ruin a banker's disposition. What astonishes me about such meetings is the universal belief that this disaster could have been prevented if the bankers had just done a better job of loan underwriting. The conversational common denominator is, "Man, we never should have made this loan."

Rubbish! The plain fact is that some precentage of loans will always get into trouble for reasons that were completely unpredictable at the time the loan was made. For most financial institutions, it is axiomatic that large additional amounts of money spent to improve asset underwriting will bring only small marginal benefits. The same amount of money spent to improve asset monitoring will generate proportionately much larger benefits.

The problem is that it's not very exciting work. The glamour is in originating new assets, not keeping an eye on old ones. Most institutions have a pretty effective way of measuring the profitability of asset origination, and have an incentive program for the people who do that work. I have found that, in the vast majority of cases, the same institutions have little or no understanding of how effective their asset-monitoring program is, how much it contributes to profits, or how to compensate the people who do it. No wonder it is an ignored art—and a very fertile field to be plowed.

Developing a Good Monitoring Program

So, the first step in developing a good monitoring program is to determine its value to the institution. That means finding a way to measure and put a value on the losses prevented, never an easy task. Two possible comparative methods relate the institution's credit losses to those of competing institutions, and to losses incurred before the monitoring program was instituted, but both have flaws. In the first case, there is no recognition of the impact of good underwriting, and the second has no recognition of the impact of changing economic conditions. However, a comparison of the institutions losses to its competitors both before and after the institution of the program could give the institution a useful measure of the benefits of monitoring.

That still leaves the fact that asset monitoring is regarded as the dirty work of financial services. The "workout department" is seldom the part of the institution with a waiting list of applicants; it is seldom on the fast track to the CEO's office. Talking to borrowers about all the money they are going to make after you give them the loan (and thinking about all the money the institution will make as well) is much more satisfying than arguing about when the institution is going to get paid back.

Because monitoring occupies a less attractive position, management must make a long-term commitment to upgrading its function. Compensation programs must be structured so as to make it a financially rewarding career. Employees who do an excellent job in this area must be singled out for recognition throughout the institution, not just in their own department. Running the monitoring function must be a stop on the "rotation" of promising executives.

All of those things add up to making the monitoring function a positive one, which is perceived by everyone as adding to the institution's bottom line, but it will take a concerted change in the way it is done to make it really effective for most institutions. Monitoring is really the same thing as underwriting—it is *collecting and analyzing the right information, and then making the right choices as a result.*

Collecting the Information

Collecting the information necessary for asset underwriting is relatively easy, because the borrower wants the loan, so he or she will provide the information requested. Once the loan has been disbursed, however, the borrower's motives with regard to information turn 180 degrees. Before, the more information the institution got, the better off the borrower was. Now, the more information the institution gets, the more vulnerable the borrower feels, because it is more likely that the bank will see problems at the same time as, or perhaps sooner than, the borrower.

And that's the key to the monitoring business. When a borrower starts to have trouble, no matter how important the borrower or how long-standing a customer, he or she will shield negative information from the institution. Borrowers all think their problems are just temporary, easily within their ability to correct, and that bringing them up will only alarm the institution unduly. As things get worse, the borrower comes to regard the institution as a taskmaster at best, and a potential enemy at worst. Just when open communication with the borrower becomes crucial, the borrower loses all interest in communicating.

There are three things an institution can do to improve the information flow under these conditions. It can utilize the same market and economic information it used during the underwriting function. It can collect the information as part of another function. And it can make it worthwhile for the borrower to volunteer the information.

Market and Economic Information: If the institution utilized market and economic information in underwriting the asset, and if it did a stress analysis, then it follows that gathering and analyzing the same information after the loan has been disbursed will have at least as much value as it did before. Is the borrower's market share rising or falling? Is he meeting the volume projections he used in applying for the loan? Are his competitors reacting as expected to his marketing strategies? Is the market as a whole growing as projected? Is it segmenting as expected? Are the products exhibiting the life cycles that the institution projected? If an institution pays attention to these factors, it is unlikely to be surprised by an adverse trend in the customer's cash flow.

Painless Collection of Information: Requesting quarterly financial statements from borrowers, which is as much as most institutions do, is woefully inadequate as a collection process. What is much more effective is gathering information about what passes through the borrower's checking accounts. Are receipts rising? Are employee expenses rising faster than receipts? However, there is another, more effective, method of information collection. By processing a borrower's cash flow, an institution can get a much earlier warning of trouble.

Many small- to medium-sized businesses spend a reasonable amount of money, either internally or externally, on such functions as accounts receivable, accounts payable, and payroll. These functions are just the kind of processing businesses that a bank can perform well, particularly on a large scale. By taking over those functions for a borrower, not only can the institution save the customer some money and generate additional noninterest income for itself, it can also obtain priceless information on the financial fortunes of the borrower, and long before it would be able to otherwise.

Making it Worthwhile for the Borrower: Whatever the institution does to mask the collection process, it will encounter resistance if the borrower sees no real benefit to giving up the information. But all borrowers have one universal motive, to succeed in business. If the institution develops and offers a financial consulting service for small and medium businesses, the borrower's motives will likely shift from one of sheltering the information to one of volunteering it. Naturally, there might be some skepticism on the borrower's part about the benefits to him of her, but, if the service is well constructed and presented, one dominant fact will surface: both the borrower and the institution have a powerful incentive for the borrower to be successful.

This kind of planned approach to loan monitoring will have several benefits. It will make the flow of information easier, of better quality, and more timely. It will change the institution's relationship with the borrower and the way the borrower views it. It will keep assets that were well underwritten and well structured in good condition. It will generate additional noninterest income. In short, it will move the institution a lot closer to the winner's circle.

6 | Optimizing Capital

The financial services industry is something of a chameleon, appearing to be a different business, with different problems, depending on who is looking at it. For commercial bankers, it is a business of taking deposits and making loans, and the biggest problems are costs and asset quality. For investment bankers, it is a business of doing deals, and the biggest problem is over-regulation. For the customer, it is a service business, and the biggest problem is the quality of the product. But for the regulators, it is a business of taking risks with the public insurance funds, and the biggest problem is insufficient capital.

The fact that capital is important to the regulators makes it important to bankers, but it is important to bankers for another reason. Banking is a unique business in the world, because what the rest of us think of as an asset, namely money, banks think of as a liability. In fact, the real money in banking is capital. Furthermore, because of the way regulation is done in this country, and because of the regulators' risk-based capital guidelines which took full effect in 1992, *the primary constraint to an institution's being a predator, a survivor, and a winner, is capital.*

If capital is that important, it would be nice if everyone could agree on what it comprises, what makes it rise or fall, and where it comes from. No such luck! In fact, there are three distinct forms of capital, each with its own sources, measurements, and rules.

The Three Forms of Capital

The advent of double-entry bookkeeping, and its evolution into accounting, established the first form of capital—*accounting capital* or *book value.* Accountants define book capital as the difference between the carrying value of assets and the carrying value of liabilities, which is a simple concept but a much more complicated reality. Because book value is so dependent on the carrying value of assets and liabilities, accountants have developed a whole range of treatments for transactions that impact those carrying values. We will look at some of those treatments later in this chapter.

Double-entry bookkeeping came about because of the advent of common stock ownership, which leads to the second form of capital—*stockholder capital* or *market value* (sometimes called market capitalization or "market cap"). In its simplest form, market value is the number of shares of common stock outstanding (which is often less than the number of shares issued) multiplied by the last sale price of the stock. In theory, that amount should approximate the present value of the expected future earnings of the company. Obviously, the market value of an institution can vary from its book value. When market value exceeds book value, the difference is said to be the *stock premium.* When market value falls short of book value, the difference is called the *stock discount.*

Stock premiums and discounts have a great deal of importance in the arcane world of corporate finance. When a company's stock is selling at a discount, the management and directors are often reluctant to sell more stock to the public, even if the institution needs more capital, because the sale itself would reduce the book value of the stock currently outstanding, a process called dilution.

When a company's stock is at a premium, any company which acquires it by buying all its stock creates an intangible asset called *excess of purchase price over book value,* or *goodwill.* Goodwill has a negative connotation in corporate finance because the acquiring corporation must amortize it or reduce it to zero by subtracting a percentage of it from net income every year. In addition, that amortization is not recognized as a tax deduction by the IRS.

In banking, goodwill has an even worse implication because banks must subtract it, in its entirety, from the third form of capital—*regulatory capital.* While book value and market value have fairly objective definitions, regulatory capital is whatever the regulators say it is. Since the regulators' prime concern is the cushion between the banks' total assets and their exposure as deposit insurers, their definition of capital might not have much resemblance to either book value or market cap.

The Interplay of the Three Forms of Capital

We can see how these three forms of capital connect if we look at one of the most common, if not most popular, financial transactions among banks in the late 1980s and early 1990s—the establishment of a bad debt reserve against a class of assets.

The impact of a bad debt reserve on book value is relatively straightforward: it reduces the book value by transferring funds from retained earnings into the reserve, since accountants do not count bad debt reserves as part of capital. The effect on market value, on the other hand, is not at all straightforward because market value is determined by the investing public, not the accountants. In many cases, the market will have already made the adjustment in the value of the assets reflected by the reserve, so market value may not go down. In fact, it might go up, for the following reason.

When a financial institution sets aside a bad debt reserve, the IRS does not recognize that as a tax deduction; they only recognize the actual write-down of the loan. Thus, an institution which has set aside a bad debt reserve has a hidden tax benefit. If the loan does in fact prove to be uncollectible, the institution will have an income tax deduction, but no accounting loss, so the deduction can shield other income. If the asset proves to be collectible, the institution reverses the reserve, showing a tax-free profit, since the IRS doesn't recognize the profit, not having recognized the loss.

The effect of a bad debt reserve on regulatory capital is a function of how closely tied the reserve is to specific assets, and what the regulators' treatment of the assets has been. If the regulators have already required the institution to restate the value of the assets (for regulatory purposes, but not necessarily for accounting purposes), the establishment of a reserve will have little or no effect on regulatory capital. If the regulators have not already revalued the assets, the establishment of a reserve might cause them to do so, and that would reduce regulatory capital. If it does not cause them to restate the value, the reserve won't affect regulatory capital.

The Role of the Three Forms of Capital

All of this is interesting, but the real questions are: What roles do these three forms of capital play? Which one is more important, and why?

In and of itself, book value has the least important role. Book value seems to be important only to accountants; stockholders look at market cap, and the regulators use their own measure. But book value has a huge derivative role to play because most changes to book value are made through the income account. With the exception of the sale or retirement of equity securities, or transferring funds between equity accounts (as in declaring stock dividends), all changes to book value must involve increasing or decreasing net income. For example, the establishment of a bad debt reserve like we just discussed can have a devastating effect on income, turning a pretty good quarter into a disaster.

The role of market value is much more important than the role of book value. First, it is a reflection of the investing public's interest in, and confidence in, management's ability to run the institution. We know that market capitalization is made up of stock price multiplied by the number of shares outstanding, now we need to look at the components of stock price.

Like market capitalization, stock price is made up of two components: *return on equity (ROE)* and *price/earnings ratio (P/E)*. Management can have a direct impact on ROE, but it can only have an indirect impact on P/E. Much of this book is about how a bank can increase its ROE, but it is also about how it can increase its P/E. P/E is really a measure of how sanguine the stock market is about the future prospects on any company, and, by that measure, the stock market in 1994 was not very sanguine about the prospects for banks, particularly large ones.

In October of 1994, I looked at the P/Es of banks in the United States and determined that the lowest ones, below nine, belonged exclusively to the largest banks. NationsBank, Chase, Chemical, Bankers Trust, and BancOne, among others were below the magic nine level, while Citicorp and BankAmerica were just above nine. All those banks above 15 were smaller institutions, or were in the process of being acquired. Thus one must ask the question, "If large size means lower P/E, why are some banks so determined to grow through acquisition?" The answer was articulated by the president of NationsBank in the *American Banker* when he pointed out that the president of a very large bank makes more money than the president of a small one.

Thus the management of any company will be attuned to the company's stock price and market cap, but there is an even more compelling reason for financial institutions to pay attention to market cap: it is their ticket to independence.

The consolidation of the finance industry will not be accomplished by one institution's paying cash for another institution's stock—there is too much leverage already in the finance industry. Virtually all the mergers that are affected in this industry will be stock-for-stock transactions, not only for the reason just stated, but because such transactions have the possibility of being accounted for as poolings-of-interest instead of purchases, allowing the resulting institution to avoid booking goodwill on the balance sheet. Thus a high P/E and a large market capitalization will give a strong institution a commanding platform from which to bid for other institutions.

Anyone who is familiar with the ins and outs of mergers will notice a disparity in the merger scenario in banking. Under normal conditions, the company with a higher P/E has an advantage in a stock takeover, because it can offer a lesser amount of stock and actually increase its earnings per share by doing the transaction. Let's see how that works.

Lets imagine that there are two banks, each with one million shares outstanding. Each bank earns $1.00 per share. Bank A's P/E is nine, so its stock price is $9, and its market capitalization is $9 million. Bank B's P/E is 15, so its stock price is $15, and its market capitalization is $15 million. Now lets suppose that Bank B offers $10 in stock value (.67 shares of its stock) for each share of Bank A's stock. The impact of the transaction is shown in Table 6.1.

Table 6.1

	Bank Merger Illustration		
	Bank A	Bank B	Merged Bank
Shares Outstanding	1,000,000	1,000,000	1,670,000
Earnings	$1,000,000	$1,000,000	$2,000,000
Stock Price	$9.00	$15.00	$15.00
Earnings per Share	$1.00	$1.00	$1.20
P/E Ratio	9	15	12.525
Market Capitalization	$9,000,000	$15,000,000	$25,050,000
Offering (in shares)		0.67	

The illustration shows that, as long as the merger doesn't depress Bank B's stock too much, it can increase the market capitalization of the merged bank over the sum of the unmerged banks, simply by offering a higher P/E stock for a lower one. But, more often than not, it is the lower P/E stock of the larger banks which is being offered for the higher P/E stocks of the smaller banks. This transaction results in a significant dilution of the larger banks earnings, and goes a long way toward explaining why the P/Es of the larger banks continue depressed, and why the market value of very large banks in the United States isn't any higher than it is.

Based on that analysis, we can conclude that the best way to get a large market cap is to grow your business and profits, which will increase both ROE and P/E. But that effort brings you squarely into contact with the regulators and regulatory capital. For this reason, regulatory capital is without a doubt the most important form of capital in the day-to-day running of a financial institution. And, to make matters more complicated, the regulators have just completed imposing a new and strikingly different measurement of regulatory capital, both actual and required, called the *risk-based capital guidelines.*

The risk-based capital guidelines, a product of the so-called Basel Agreement, completely changed the way financial institutions calculate the amount of regulatory capital they have and, more important, the amount of regulatory capital they are required to have. Before the Basel Agreement, banks in most countries were required to maintain capital as a percentage to their deposits, the regulators feeling that their exposure was to the depositors. The Basel Agreement, signed in 1988 and fully implemented in 1992, changed the capital requirements to a precentage of the banks assets. Instead of being a function of how much you *owed,* regulatory capital became a function of how much you *owned.*

Why would the regulators go from a quintessentially logical basis for capital—deposits—to the much less intuitive basis—assets? Because they discovered that depositors never line up outside the bank looking for their money unless the bank has an asset problem first. Banks think they are in the business of taking the depositors' cash and turning it into paper, and it is the quality of the paper that always turns out to be the problem. In other words, banks don't really fail because their depositors come home to roost, but because their assets have flown the coop.

In establishing the risk-based capital guidelines, the regulators recognized only one form of risk, credit risk. They were cognizant of the fact that assets come in a range of creditworthiness, so they constructed the guidelines accordingly. To begin with, the Basel Agreement, as interpreted by the Fed, requires a bank to have capital equal to 8 percent of assets, beginning in 1992. That capital must be half in tier 1, which is made up almost entirely of stockholders' equity, and half may be in tier 2, which can be in other kinds of stock (like preferred) and long-term debt.

Then the regulators said that, in calculating the required capital, the amount carried in each asset class would be multiplied by a percentage, specified by the guidelines, and then by the 8 percent. Here are the classes, the percentages, and the required capital per $100 of asset:

All corporate obligations and all consumer obligations except certain first mortgage debt	100% or $8.00

Consumer first mortgage debt with a loan-to-value ratio of 80 percent or less	50% or $4.00
Government agency debt (including mortgage-backed securities) and most senior bank debt	20% or $1.60
U.S. government debt longer than 90 days to maturity	10% or $0.80
U.S. government debt shorter than 90 days to maturity	10% or $0.80
U.S. government debt shorter than 90 days to maturity, OECD government debt, and cash equivalents	0%

The Impact of the Basel Agreement

The first impact of the Basel Agreement is that it makes regulatory capital the limiting factor on the size of a bank's balance sheet. No matter how well an institution runs its branch network, no matter how large its net interest margin, no matter how many institutions or branches become available for purchase, an institution that is low on capital cannot grow its balance sheet. In fact, the specter of the capital guidelines has already prompted many banks, both large and small, in the United States and other countries, to shed assets and shrink their balance sheets. It also had a major impact on Japanese banks, which have traditionally been run on narrow capital bases. The risk-based capital guidelines, along with credit and profit pressures in Japan, prompted these banks to severely curtail their lending activities in the United States, a factor which contributed to the economic downturn in the United States in the late 80s and early 90s.

The second impact of the agreement is that it makes asset selection a more complicated, and more important, function. Because capital is the limiting factor on the amount of assets you can hold, it places a tremendous burden on the institution to choose wisely, particularly because different classes of assets have different capital requirements.

Optimizing Regulatory Capital: Asset Selection

The best way to think about the issue of maximizing regulatory capital is to imagine that the institution starts every day with a finite amount of capital, and that it must use that capital to maximize ROE. That raises two questions. The first question relates to which asset the institution should select, and we can see how it works in this simple example:

The assumptions:

Base capital requirement	8%
Corporate debt capital ratio	100%
First mortgage capital ratio	50%
Agency capital ratio	20%
AAA corporate interest rate	10%
First mortgage interest rate	9%
Agency interest rate	8.5%
Cost of funds	7%
Available free capital	$8.00

The question is: starting with $8.00 of free capital, should the institution invest in corporate debt, mortgage debt, or agency debt, so as to maximize ROE? Here is how the math works:

AAA Corporate Debt

($8.00 capital/8% ratio)	Amount	Rate	Income/(Expense)
Asset	$100	10%	$ 10.00
Liability	92	7%	(6.44)
Net	$ 8	3%	$ 3.56
ROA 3.56% ROE 44.5%			

First Mortgage Debt

($8.00 capital/4% ratio)			
Asset	$200	9%	$ 18.00
Liability	192	7%	(13.44)
Net	$ 8	2%	$ 4.56
ROA 2.28% ROE 57%			

Agency Debt

($8.00 capital/1.6% ratio)			
Asset	$500	8.5%	$ 42.50
Liability	492	7 %	(34.44)
Net	$ 8	1.5%	$ 8.06
ROA 1.61% ROE 100.75%			

This problem is simple enough with three assets, all approximately equal in interest rate risk. Now imagine, not three choices, but three hundred, all with different degrees of credit and interest rate risk. Also, imagine a set of constraints concerning the concentration of assets, along such lines as industry, geography, collateral, and asset form. Finally, imagine that there are noninterest income implications for some of these assets—such as the fact that certain borrowers would be more likely to choose the institution as a money manager for their pension fund if there were a lending relationship. All in all, that makes for a gargantuan optimization problem. Fortunately, there are computers and optimization models available for such purposes, because an analysis like that must be run monthly, if not more often.

Optimizing Regulatory Capital: Asset Turnover

Managing the balance sheet superbly is a necessary, but not sufficient, condition for optimizing capital. In fact, managing the balance sheet superbly will make an institution profitable enough to become a good target, but not a good predator. If the balance sheet is not there to be tied up, but turned over, then assets aren't there to be tied up, but to be turned over.

Up to now, turning assets over mostly meant selling off participations, or selling assets servicing released (i.e., letting the buyer service the asset). Selling participations can serve a useful purpose, but it virtually requires that the buyer be a bank. The real pools of investable funds, the pension plans and the life insurance companies, have not been ready buyers of participations.

Much the same reasoning applies to selling assets servicing released. Since servicing assets requires a presence in the local market, as well as the ability to perform the servicing function, servicing released selling virtually requires that the buyer be a bank.

But there is a much more important reason not to sell assets servicing released, one related to marketing. Servicing is a method of keeping contact with the customer, as well as a method of maintaining pools of information on individual customers and the market. The institution must understand that servicing-released asset sales, as well as the sale of the servicing itself, are in fact the sale of an institution's customers.

All these facts argue persuasively for the securitization of assets as a method of turning them over. Securitization allows the institution to retain servicing, with its customer contact as well as its wealth of customer information. Securitized assets are much more suitable for sale to traditional securities purchasers, like pension plans and mutual funds. And securitization, when accomplished through the federal agencies, greatly reduces the capital required by the asset, even if the institution decides to keep it.

In Chapter 4, I discussed the process of securitization and how it is accomplished by a process which runs backward—from sales to origination. That process ensures that assets are originated to respond to the demands of the market, not to respond to the institution's need for interest or noninterest income. Assets which are properly originated and securitized are available to be turned over at a moment's notice, whenever the optimization analysis points in their direction.

Although securitization of assets was a popular strategy in the overheated 1980s, when assets were being created all over the place and banks were capital-constrained, it is a much less popular strategy in the 1990s, when assets are harder to come by, and banks are much better capitalized. Nowadays, bankers ask, "Why would I want to securitize my assets? I can't find enough of them as it is." But that reasoning misses the point. Securitization is a good discipline, even when the institution has no intention of selling the assets, partly because it enforces market pricing on the institution, and partly because securitized assets are easier to use for financing purposes than unsecuritized ones, and you never know when interest rates will run up. Banks which securitize assets as a regular business practice will be much better prepared for the future than those that don't.

Maximizing Regulatory Capital

Since regulatory capital is the primary constraint on the volume of business an institution can do, its maximization expands the institution's horizons in both the volume and kinds of business it can do. Since market capitalization depends on stock price, which depends on the price/earnings ratio, which depends on the level of earnings, an institution's regulatory capital will be a key to its ability to stay independent.

Maximizing regulatory capital involves some obvious steps, and some that are not so obvious. It begins with understanding the definition of regulatory capital: the difference between what the regulators regard as the value of the institution's assets and what they regard as the value of its liabilities. Notice that we refer to "what the regulators regard as the value." That may be very different from what the bank's auditors regard as the value, and will probably be quite different from what the stockholders see.

Since the regulators' view of liabilities is fairly circumscribed, the essence of maximizing regulatory capital is to maximize the regulators' valuation of assets. There are several methods for doing that:

Monetize all fixed assets whose market value exceeds book value. Fixed assets are carried at cost, less depreciation. In some cases, especially office buildings which have been occupied by the institution for some time, the value of those assets may be quite a bit higher than book value. By selling such assets and arranging for occupancy rental, the institution can generate substantial regulatory capital.

A special case of monetization involves the popular transaction known as *outsourcing,* where institutions arrange for outside organizations to provide services they had been providing for themselves. Such arrangements can achieve significant cost savings, since the service provider is presumably expert in its specialty, and since outsourcing servicers can often achieve significant economies of scale. A popular outsourcing arena has been the institution's data center, where the bulk of the data processing is done.

While that transaction has been thought of as a cost-reduction measure, it can also generate regulatory capital if the market value of the data center exceeds its carrying cost. The market value of a data center is only partly a function of the value of the computers and other equipment in it, and the real estate. It can also be a function of the volume of business done there. The institution could think of the outsourcing process as putting a value on its entire data processing function, much as an outside processor would, and selling the business for that amount. In that way, the institution can monetize a much larger source of capital than it could by just valuing the fixed assets.

Create or convert assets into a form that minimizes their capital requirement. The risk-based capital guidelines separate assets into very specific categories, with very different capital requirements. Changing the nature of an asset slightly, or creating it a little differently, can have a substantial impact on the required regulatory capital.

For example, most consumer debt carries the maximum capital requirement: 8 percent. That means the bank must put aside $80 of capital for every $1,000 of credit-card debt it puts on. By encouraging customers to pay off their credit-card balances with home-equity loans, the bank can cut the capital charge in half, and free up $40 of capital. In addition, depending on the customer's tax status, the bank could help turn interest charges from nondeductible to deductible. Bankers have been reticent to do this up to now, largely because of the interest differential between mortgage and credit-card debt, but that differential has been dropping as the competition in the credit-card business heats up, and credit-card rates are now quite close to second-mortgage rates. If bankers treat a home-equity loan as a second mortgage, even if they own the first mortgage, they will have the best of both worlds.

Another structuring opportunity is the creation of mortgage assets as agency mortgage-backed securities. Although mortgages carry a 50 percent capital ratio, or $40 per $1,000, agency mortgage-backs carry a capital ratio of less than half that: 20 percent, or $16 per $1,000. Not only are mortgage securities less capital-intensive than the underlying mortgages, they are more liquid and cost less to finance (in the repurchase market), and the agencies will likely absorb a good portion of the credit risk—no small matter in a period when mortgage defaults are rising.

Take a very careful look at off-balance-sheet commitments. One aspect of the risk-based guidelines is that they impose a capital requirement on off-balance-sheet commitments, like letters of credit and many of the risk products like interest-rate swaps. Because these businesses were a ready source of noninterest income, many banks have built up large portfolios of commitments. With these positions now requiring significant capital backup, the institution needs to examine these positions to determine their real profitability. Because risk is such an important characteristic of these commitments, I will cover this subject in more detail in Chapter 8, Managing Financial Risk.

If the institution decides to try to reduce its exposure in off-balance sheet commitments, it must be careful how it does that. These commitments are not liquid securities, they are bilateral agreements. Thus, the institution can't just sell the position, and entering into an offsetting agreement with another party may not reduce the capital requirement; it might double it! In many cases the only ways out are to get another institution to replace you in the contract with the current contra-party, with the consequent profit or loss, or get the contra-party to annul the transaction. That last possibility might arise more often than you think, if the contra-party is an active user of derivatives. The institution might discover that it has offsetting positions with the same party, and could cut down on check exchanges for both sides by eliminating the offsetting positions, freeing up some capital in the process.

Maximizing Accounting Capital

Although accounting and regulatory capital appear similar, they are in fact distinctly different; and the methods of maximizing them, although similar, are also different. The primary difference between the capital types is in who determines them. The regulators have as their primary mission to protect the deposit insurance funds, so they look at capital as a cushion between the insurance funds and disaster. The auditors, who determine accounting capital, perceive that their mission is to report the financial condition of the institution to its stockholders.

As I mentioned earlier in this chapter, the main impact of accounting capital is that most of the changes to it have to be run through the income statement, and that process is anything but simple. Over many years, as corporate structures and financial transactions have become more complex, accounting rules have become more complex in order to deal with them. As a result, today's accounting rules can generate some counter-intuitive, if not surprising, results. Maximizing accounting capital is largely a matter of utilizing these complex accounting rules.

The first rule covers the carrying value of assets and liabilities. Based on the original accounting practices for manufacturing companies, assets are divided into current assets, which are planned to be turned into cash over one business cycle, and fixed assets, which are planned to be used up over their economic life. This treatment works well for distinguishing between inventory and accounts receivable on the one hand, and plant and equipment on the other, because all the assets—even the financial ones—are assumed to be related to manufacturing.

The manufacturing treatment works less well when almost all the institution's assets are financial. In particular, the assumption that current assets will turn into cash within one business cycle doesn't work when you are a lender, and the assumption that you will consume fixed assets during the manufacturing process doesn't work if you aren't manufacturing anything.

The accounting profession has dealt with this until now by treating the lending of money, which is the exchange of cash for a promise to pay, as an exchange of equal value, having no impact itself on the income statement. Until recently, the receipt of fees from the borrower upon initiation of the transaction was regarded as revenue, but FASB has decreed that such fees must now be amortized over the life of the asset.

Once the asset is on the books, the receipt of debt service is treated as revenue to the extent that it is a receipt of interest, and the reversal of the lending process to the extent that it is a repayment. At no time does the value of the financial asset change, *unless its repayment is deemed to be in doubt.*

That event creates the charges to income that result from reserves being established against doubtful assets. Based on this treatment, it would appear that a class of assets suddenly went bad, which of course isn't the case. The deterioration very likely began some time before, and only became apparent, or measurable, recently. In a way, the large charges taken by financial institutions in establishing bad debt reserves are really a restatement of prior years' earnings to reflect the deterioration of asset quality.

In the early 1990s FASB published for comment a proposed accounting change which would require all public companies to value financial assets and liabilities at market for reporting purposes, and to run the valuation changes through the income statement. There has been a storm of controversy about this proposed ruling, and FASB and the banking regulators have indicated that they will substantially weaken it. However, the sentiment to adopt such a ruling remains strong in both the accounting and regulatory communities, so we should expect it to reappear if the banking business has any more problems with unexpected market risks.

The marking to market of both sides of the balance sheet will, if adopted, give interest-rate risk management (often called asset liability management) a direct impact on the income statement. Until the introduction of this ruling, the immediate impact of interest-rate risk management was restricted to its impact on this year's net interest margin. Funding a five-year asset with overnight money might incorporate enormous risks, but they would be seen in the income statement year by year. Under the now amended ruling, the full impact of a mismatch could be seen each year. In a year when rates rose, the present value of the mismatch would be deducted from income, and in a year when rates fell, it would be added.

Maximizing Stockholder Capital

Of the three kinds of capital, stockholder's is the most important in the consolidation arena. Financial institutions are not generally in a position to make large acquisitions for cash, both because of their already high leverage and the negative regulatory impact of goodwill. As a result, stock-for-stock combinations are the best form of merger, as well as acquisition of business units or branches.

But the real lesson we can learn from recent history is that stockholder valuation will be inversely related to the institution's dependence on principal transactions. This fact has begun to become apparent in the lending arena, but it applies to the trading arena as well. All balance-sheet businesses involve risk, and risk is seductive. When institutions depend on risk businesses to generate income and stockholder value, the natural tendency is to accept higher amounts of risk to generate higher amounts of income. But the low price/earnings ratios of both lenders and trading organizations bear out the fact that stockholders are risk-averse.

There are three things financial institutions can sell: their services, their balance sheets, and their brains. Selling services generates volume, customers, and information. Selling the balance sheet generates risk. It is selling your brains that generates the real income, and putting all three together generates the highest stockholder value.

7 | Marketing Financial Services

There is a very good case to be made that the American paradigm is a salesman. Shortly after the first settlers moved up the Hudson or through the Cumberland Gap, they were pursued by the itinerant peddler, with his wagon full of necessities and luxuries. Most of our economic history was written by visionaries who knew what the public needed and could sell it to them. From Frank Woolworth to Marshall Field, from Henry Ford to Edward Land, from Professor Harold Hill to Willie Loman, many of our central figures, in life and in fiction, have been people who practiced the fine art of salesmanship.

Except in financial services. People do not think of John Pierpont Morgan as a salesman. For most of their history, banks and bank branches didn't look like stores; they looked like vaults. In the press, and in literature, bankers aren't pictured as salesmen, beating the drum to make quota; they are pictured as stern guardians of the nation's finances, if not its scruples. The image most of us have of a banker isn't of a smile and a handshake, but of a starched collar and a frown.

Even the image projected by securities, the most sales-oriented part of the finance industry, is decidedly restrained. Stockbrokers have been careful to downplay the sales aspect of their jobs, for fear of scaring away potential customers. Mutual funds, even when they advertise, stress words like "safety" and "fidelity." Even the market regulators play their part in delivering the anti-sales message. Only the life insurance agent stands apart as an out-and-out drummer.

When you think about it, it is not too surprising that marketing was never an important part of banking, and of minor importance in the financial markets. In banking, the common perception was that banks were where you took your money for safekeeping, and borrowed it back with interest. Everyone had to have a bank account, except those few relics of the Great Depression who didn't trust banks and kept their cash in a coffee can. And, when you applied for a loan, the bank was doing you a favor to lend it; they didn't have to sell you on the idea.

In the financial markets, the exchanges and their members had a monopoly, very much like the local power company. For almost two hundred years, if you wanted to buy or sell the stock of a major industrial or utility company, the New York Stock Exchange was the only game in town—or in the country. Until the 1970s, stock commissions were fixed, so the member firms didn't even have to compete on price. When you made enough money to have a nest egg, and when it outgrew a savings account, you had to get yourself a stockbroker. It was that simple.

Well, those truly were the "good old days." Things aren't that simple any more. With deregulation, competition, and razor-thin profit margins, *salesmanship* has become the watchword of financial services. Not only have banks become sales organizations, bankers have become salespeople, and financial transactions have become sales. And banks have begun advertising on television during the last five years (just when astute observers have begun to question the economics of television advertising).

All of which might suggest that the finance industry has really entered the marketing age. But sales and marketing are very different things. How different? *Sales is getting the customer to buy the product. Marketing is getting the product the customer will buy.* Most of sales happens after the product is developed; most of marketing happens before. It is a subtle difference, and many businesspeople in many industries still don't understand the distinction. In many companies, both in and out of finance, marketing departments are given such tasks as advertising and sales promotion, while some other department designs and develops new products.

Marketing in General

Traditional marketing has evolved over many years to meet the needs of the industrial sector, but it has only recently begun to adapt to the special needs of the services sector. In order to apply marketing to financial services, we must understand its more basic form as it applies to manufactured goods.

The most basic expression of being market driven instead of product driven is the concept of *making saleable products, instead of selling the products you make.* A simple concept to grasp, but one which incorporates a wealth of detail and thinking. If the market is a participant in the design and development process, instead of the recipient of the finished product, then we have to know a great deal about it before we start designing the products. Countless books have been written on marketing and market analysis, in much more detail than I can hope to accomplish, but I will lay out here some simple starting points in marketing, for both goods and services.

1. *Markets are made up of more than customers; they are made up of the institution, its customers, and its competitors.* Many people think that marketing is about determining what the customer wants, and delivering it. But it is easy to go out of business delivering what the customer wants. A market is a mosaic of products, customers, competing institutions, and economic forces, which constantly determine the profitability of an institution. Marketing is the science and the art of crafting a success from that mosaic.

    In such an arena, marketing is about determining which customers to serve, which products to deliver, how to deal with competitors, and how to allocate scarce resources. All of business is about making choices—between products and production methods, between geographical areas, between distribution channels, and between research projects. Marketing is the incorporation of market information into those choices.

2. *Markets are always changing, almost always to the detriment of the producer.* The essence of competition is that it fosters change. Products improve, new producers enter the market, prices drop, profit margins shrink, and customers get more sophisticated in their tastes. I wish I had a dollar for every time I have heard an executive say, "This business has gotten so hard. What ever happened to the good old days?" Competition happened to the good old days.

    The point is, change and competition aren't passing oddities—they are the facts of life. An institution whose management thinks the market will stand still while it wrings a little more money from its product line, or while it develops a new product, will find itself getting to the train station just in time to wave goodbye to the express. As tough as we think today's markets are, they are tomorrow's good old days.

3. *Understanding market segmentation is as important as understanding the market itself.* Over time, markets segment, as customers' wants and needs become more specialized. This is as true for financial services as it is for automobiles or computers. Institutions that ignore or misunderstand market segmentation stand to lose market share, even though they may have had the first product into the market, and may have the best one in the market at the moment.

    In order to understand the impact of market segmentation, look at credit cards. Initially, there was one charge card, the American Express card. Then the bank credit cards arrived. Then there were charge cards, credit cards, and extended-payment cards. Then there were cards with frequent flyer mileage arrangements, with sports team affiliations, charity affiliations, and with extended insurance protection. Now there are cards which earn you discounts on automobiles or long distance telephone calls.

But it is important for bankers to understand what it is that causes market segmentation. It is *not* customers which cause the market to segment, it is your competitors. In an effort to differentiate their products, your competitors will create new versions which appeal to ever narrower segments of the market. If they are successful, they will attract some of your customers and eat into your market share.

The question is, are you going to leave it to your competitors to segment the market, or will you do it? Remember, the winners are the innovators, even if it means cannibalizing their own products. Of all the marketing lessons bankers could learn, the most valuable, and the most difficult, is that *it is always better to compete with yourself, and obsolete your own products, than to let your competitors do it for, and to, you.*

4. *Every product has a product life cycle with approximately the same shape* (Figure 7.1). Whether it lasts a few weeks or many years, every product goes through the same S-shaped life cycle. The cycle is divided into four distinct phases:

Figure 7.1
Product Life Cycle

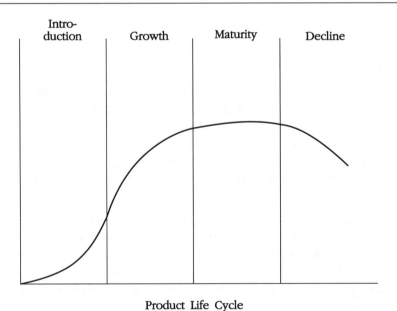

Intro-
duction   Growth   Maturity   Decline

Product Life Cycle

Phase 1 is *introduction* or *infancy*. This is when a product takes a lot of research and development (R & D), and generates very little in the way of profit or cash flow. Customers are generally uninformed about the product, so the market is unsegmented, and profit margins are high, although volumes are low. A lot of products never make it out of this phase.

Phase 2 is *growth*. In this phase the product's popularity takes off. Volumes increase, so manufacturing costs drop, but more competitors enter the market, so unit profit margins might actually shrink, although aggregate profits grow. As customers become more knowledgeable, the market begins to segment, and satisfying these segments requires significant additional R & D expenditures. Thus, although the product is profitable, it may not have a large positive cash flow.

Phase 3 is *maturity*. Here the growth rate slows markedly as the market is saturated. Volumes are high, so unit costs are low, but competition is intense, so profit margins continue to shrink, and the market is highly segmented. Certain producers have dominant positions in certain segments, which they will defend against all comers. With growth slowing, large R & D projects for this product are viewed as unwarranted, so marketing emphasis is placed on sales promotion and cost reduction. This is the first stage where replacement products begin to appear, as some producers look for differentiators.

Phase 4 is *decline*. Here the volume actually decreases, as replacement products begin their growth phases. Producers begin to exit the market, as profit margins shrink to almost nothing. Low-cost producers hang on, wresting the last profits from a highly segmented, price-conscious, competitive marketplace. In a shrinking market, all R & D for this product ceases, as well as most promotion, as producers go into a defensive posture. At this point there are usually strong replacement products, and their growth has probably contributed to the decline.

5. *In the mind of the customer, if not the producer, products are linked.* Customers' choices about products, in all kinds of markets, are often linked to their choices about other products. This is certainly true in financial services. Examples of linked products would be home mortgages and homeowners insurance for individuals, letter of credit collections and foreign exchange for corporations, and securities trading and custody for capital markets customers. Institutions that have a good relationship with customers in one product area often have an advantage in offering that customer set newer or related products, but only if they use it.

This becomes increasingly true as markets for financial services segment. Institutions that have successfully introduced a new financial service have a golden opportunity to build relationships with the customers of that service. As those customers become more knowledgeable, and the market begins to segment, competitors will offer these new customers variations of the product. If the institution does not follow the market segmentation by offering these customers additional services, it stands to lose contact with the customers it fought so hard to win.

6.   *The most important ingredient in good marketing is good information.* Since marketing is making the most of a market, success in that effort is based, in large part, on what you know about the market. It is based on what you know about current customers, and what you know about potential ones. It is based on what you know about current competitors, and what you know about potential ones. And it is based on what you know about economic conditions, as well as some predictions about the economic future.

This information comes from a wide variety of sources. Some comes from the institution's own business, except that many institutions don't know how much they know. For example, what is the average amount of money that passes through a retail account in your institution? Why would you want to know that? Because it is vital input in market segmentation. Or which of your retail customers work for your corporate customers? Why would you want to know that? Because it might tip you off to a new service offering, like payroll processing. Or which ATMs, yours or a competitor's, do your customers use most? And why would you want to know that? Because it might indicate where you need additional branch coverage. The answers to these questions are often available from records of the business that the institution currently processes, if only the institution knew how to look for it.

Other information is available from regulatory, governmental, and published sources. Competitors' strategies, both current and future, are often discernable from regulatory and audit reports. Demographic changes, as well as economic ones, are available from a variety of sources, and both Congress and the regulators telegraph the changes they are contemplating long before they are put into effect. The point is, the institution has to compile this information and, much more important, make sense of it. Raw information, by itself, is good only for postmortems, determining where a strategy went awry. It is turning information into intelligence that will make the institution a winner in the market.

Marketing Financial Services

Although there is a wealth of knowledge, both academic and empirical, about marketing in general, there is much less knowledge that is specifically adapted to the marketing of financial services. One reason is that services marketing is itself a new discipline. Marketers are used to dealing with things that you can pick up, look at, and put in a shopping bag. Most graduate marketing courses, and most of the case studies they use, are devoted to marketing in the manufacturing arena, where there are some common marketing denominators.

For example, it is easy to understand what "research and development" means to a manufacturing company. R & D generally impacts one of two things, functionality or manufacturing cost. It is easy to picture research labs, where scientists concoct new formulas for stainless steel or floor wax, or software development labs. But it is not nearly so intuitive to imagine a "lab" where a new kind of checking account is invented, or where a new securitized asset is developed. However, that is just what must happen, so where in your bank is the new products lab? If you can't point to one, you might need to rethink your product development strategy.

On the other hand, it is not to hard to imagine the kind of cost reduction research in financial services that is a matter of course in manufacturing. In financial services, the initial reaction to an increase in volume, as occurs during the growth phase of the product life cycle, is not to become more efficient, but to increase the number of people in the department. However, recently some banks have undertaken cost reduction research during good times, although not many banks are doing that. I will cover this subject in more detail in Chapter 9, Controlling Costs. So research and development is still a largely unexplored facet of marketing in financial services. And yet, R & D is at least as important to financial services as it is to manufacturing.

Another manufacturing concept that has not translated well into financial services is the concept of marketing contribution, or the contribution to profitability that can be attributed to marketing. In many companies, this attribution is accomplished by having the production departments "sell" the product to the marketing department at manufacturing cost plus an appropriate profit margin for production. Then it is up to the marketing department to maximize the market acceptance of the product, and thus the marketing contribution.

Such a concept has some meaning in some parts of financial services, particularly the execution/processing part, and perhaps the advisory part. But it has much less validity on the principal side of the business. Even though many banks have "loan production offices," principal transactions do not have very many of the "production/sales" characteristics common to goods. Principal transactions aren't "produced" like other things are, and they aren't "bought" in the same way either.

In fact, the idea of having salespeople in the principal businesses leaves many astute observers uneasy. This is because the institution doesn't realize a profit when it *institutes* (or opens) a principal transaction, but when it *unwinds* (or closes) it.

This is true in both lending and trading, and yet the sales force in both cases is usually compensated for opening (and only sometimes for closing) transactions. More and more, however, financial institutions are getting away from sales incentive programs which are driven by opening transactions. Nonetheless, bankers should look carefully at the applicability of the marketing contribution concept for their business.

Finally, the nature of financial products dictates that barriers to entry in many markets and products are low, and product life cycles are correspondingly short. Lots of loan officers, traders, and portfolio managers have been heard to say that the window of opportunity is so short that it almost doesn't make sense to introduce new products. All your competitors have to do is clone your product and they are in business.

It is very true that it is easier to clone an asset-backed security than a VCR, or to knock off an interest rate swap than a car, but there are several ways bankers can deal with the easy-entry/short-life-cycle phenomenon.

1. *Incorporate barriers to entry into your new products.* By tying new products to successful older products, you make it harder for competitors to simply clone your offering; they have to clone the older product as well. An example would be automobile insurance where the premium is included in the monthly car loan payment. Or, by utilizing customer information that you and only you have, you prevent your competition from generating an exact match for your product. Using mortgage servicing information to target market home-equity loans is an example. And by delivering your product through a unique pipeline, you make your product itself unique. Several banks, incuding Citicorp, allow their customers to purchase stocks through their ATMs.

2. *Market the product aggressively as soon as it is available.* In products with short life cycles, the first few days or weeks may be the only period during which the market is essentially unsegmented, and when competitors can be caught off guard. Customers won during those early days may be hard for competitors to win back, particularly if they are well served by the product. A cautious introduction of a short-life-cycle product almost ensures that your competitors will jump on the bandwagon with you.

3. *Be ready for market segmentation.* Many short-life-cycle products are targeted for relatively sophisticated customers, who learn about the product very quickly. As a consequence, the "honeymoon" period for these products is very short, and segmentation begins almost immediately. The institution that doesn't listen closely to its customers, and that doesn't aggressively adapt its products to changing customer needs, will likely find itself trying to sell vanilla ice cream while its competitors have become Baskin-Robbins. This is

a prime example of the benefits of cannibalizing your own produc
cially successful ones.

Specific Marketing Strategies

Given the body of knowledge that currently exists about marketing, and given the
differences between manufacturing and finance, there are four specific marketing
strategies that can make a large difference in an institution's fortunes over the next
several years.

Target Marketing

One of the most familiar concepts in marketing generally, and yet one of the least
realized, is target marketing. In its most basic form it is simply the development of
different products for different market segments and the delivery of the product
and sales message through different channels. Whether it is Procter & Gamble
with laundry detergents, or General Motors with automobiles, there is a long and
honorable heritage in target marketing.

Target Marketing in General

Before we apply it to financial services, we should understand target marketing in
general. It begins with product design, in particular, with designing products in
response to the documented wants and needs of the customer segment you have
chosen to serve. In addition to being designed to respond to customer parameters,
the product is designed to take advantage of the institution's strengths and its
competitors' weaknesses. So, the perfect product design fills a niche defined by
customers' wants, wants the competition hasn't adequately filled, and which the
institution has a relatively unique capability to fill. Financial products are among
the best adapted to this aspect of target marketing.

However, product design is just the beginning of target marketing. The delivery of the sales message, and the delivery of the product itself, must also be
targeted. Targeted sales-message delivery is old hat to advertisers. They know that
you advertise Chevrolets on NASCAR broadcasts and Cadillacs on golf broadcasts.
Procter & Gamble spends a bunch of money advertising detergents in the *Ladies
Home Journal,* but none in *The New Yorker.* And you seldom see women's clothing
ads in the sports section of the newspaper.

Targeted sales-message delivery has taken on a new urgency in the last few
years, as manufacturers and advertisers have adopted a skeptical view of the real
value of mass advertising. The sale of network television time has plateaued, general readership magazines have fallen on hard times, and both cable television and

special interest magazines have filled in the gap. Advertisers are finding that they get better responses from advertising messages that reach fewer, but more likely, customers. Banks are also finding targeted message delivery to be valuable. Advertising for 50-plus financial products appear, in publications aimed at the retired, while private banking ads appear in upscale periodicals.

All of this targeting depends heavily on market research. Traditionally, market research has meant a range of interviewing processes, done in varying degrees of breadth and depth, to try to determine the real wants and needs of the customer segments. Although a lot of work has been done on enhancing the quality of market research, most experts in the field still regard it as equal parts art and science, and most advertisers take the output with a healthy dose of salt.

Recently a new school of market research has begun to emerge, one which advocates garnering the information through a direct connection with the customer or potential customer. This approach is so new that it is being played down as untested by the marketing establishment, but it is worth examining by any financial institution that takes target marketing seriously.

In a book, titled *The Great Marketing Turnaround*, Stan Rapp and Tom Collins explain many of the concepts and practices of the new target marketing. Much of what they suggest involves the use of publications, like newsletters, by which vendors communicate directly with customers, or the formation of customer interaction groups, like computer user groups, where customers can interact directly with the vendor. Very few banks have attempted to establish such direct connections, which could go a long way toward explaining the low image banks have in the minds of their customers. While there are still only rudimentary examples of direct interaction in the banking industry, that is largely because the concept of a direct connection between the customer and the vendor is so new that it is still being refined.

Target Marketing in Financial Services

Clearly, the most unobtrusive way to conduct market research is without asking the customer any questions at all. Market researchers know that customers will sometimes tell you one thing and then do another, so the traditional market research has a relatively high error potential. But customers' actions seldom lie, so financial institutions have a distinct advantage in the market research field, in fact in the entire arena of target marketing.

To the extent that financial institutions process and execute their customers' transactions, they possess extraordinary information concerning their customers' wants and needs. That information is almost always discarded, sometimes after the transaction is processed, and sometimes with the processing itself, as when processing is sold or outsourced. If you doubt the value of the information an institution obtains through processing, consider this: I have often offered to process a financial institution's transactions free, with the proviso that the information generated from the processing is mine, to use or sell to anyone I wish. I have never been taken up on that offer.

So the first step in target marketing is using the information generated in processing transactions. That information, when properly organized, can tell you what products a customer, or set of customers needs. But you have to ask the right questions.

For example, what is the average amount of money that passes through a retail checking account (cash flow) in your institution during a year? What is the cutoff cash-flow point for the top ten percent of your retail customers? Are those customers potential targets for a financial management program, perhaps including a personal computer, software, and a modem connection to their account?

Or, which of your middle-market corporate customers spend more than 50 percent of their cash flow on payroll? Is their payroll expense rising faster than their revenue? Are they good targets for financial management counselling, which might also serve to enhance the institution's asset value? Should your institution be doing their payroll?

Or, which corporate customer has a largely variable interest expense, and does it track market rates? Is such a customer a likely target for the institution's interest-rate hedging programs? Based on the information the institution has, what kind of interest-rate hedges are appropriate?

Or, where do your customers tend to use ATMs when they aren't using yours? Are there patterns of location and timing that indicate that some of your retail customers who use your ATMs during business hours (indicating that you have branches where they work) use someone else's at night (indicating that they have branches where the customer lives or shops)? Is the opposite true, indicating that you have the customers covered at home but not at work?

Getting the right information and analyzing it is the first step in target marketing. Developing the right product is the second step. In Chapter 4, Maximizing Noninterest Income, I covered the process called market-driven product planning—the same process to be used here. You can read that chapter for the detailed explanation, but I will summarize it here.

Market-driven product planning utilizes input from two sources: external conditions and the internal situation. Under external conditions, the process assimilates information on customers, markets, and competitors. Under customers come such items as their wants and needs, the process by which they make buying decisions, and the total number of potential customers. Under markets come such items as market segmentation, product life cycles, and barriers to entry. Under competitors come such items as their resources and capabilities, their mindset and culture, and their alliances.

The counterpoint to market analysis is the internal-situation analysis, which covers things pertaining to the institution itself. It would include the institution's resources, such as financial, regulatory, informational, and human. It would cover the institution's capabilities, including processing, marketing, and delivery. Finally, it would cover the institution's culture, including values, beliefs, and structure.

That work will result in the institution's having the best possible products for the target-market segment, delivered in the optimal way. The remaining task is to deliver the best marketing message through the best medium. That medium may not be the typical advertising media—the press, radio, or television.

In fact, advertising might be directly to the customer, using the methods the institution currently uses to communicate. Monthly statements are usually read by customers in substantial detail, and may be the best place to alert the customer that he or she is ideally qualified to take advantage of a new product. Most banks include stuffers in their statements, but most of those are undifferentiated in nature. The winning banks are using their customer information files (CIFs) to create customized stuffers for their statements. ATMs also represent an opportunity to deliver a personalized message concerning new products, at a time when you know you have the customer's undivided attention. This is another area where most banks have missed the boat in target marketing. Each customer carries a unique ATM card, so the bank could use that information to display a personalized greeting, but very few do. And, where home banking has caught on, the customer's personal computer can be turned into an advertising medium. All it takes is imagination.

Conduit Marketing

Conduit marketing is simply marketing someone else's products. Although that might sound like a new concept to some financial institutions, it is an established practice in most other businesses. Sears Roebuck makes almost none of what it sells, for example, even though it puts its label on much of the merchandise. And the Big Three car companies all sell vehicles made by other manufacturers.

Conduit marketing also applies to most services. Doctors send samples to laboratories for analysis, construction companies subcontract much of their work to others, and auto mechanics send specialized parts to specialists for repair. It even occurs in finance more often than you might think. Brokerage firms sell mutual funds managed by others. Insurance companies lay off their risk with reinsurers. But, in spite of its frequency in most other businesses, conduit marketing is still rare among banks.

The first aspect of conduit marketing we need to look at relates to the three parts of financial services as I defined them earlier: processing/execution, principal, and advisory.

Processing/Execution

We have already seen that processing businesses depend for their profitability on volume and efficiency. If that is true, smaller institutions will be at a disadvantage in delivering these services, and may well contract for them to be performed by others. In some cases this is called outsourcing, but in others it is referred to as a service bureau. Generally, *outsourcing* refers to a function performed specifically for one client, on dedicated equipment, while *service bureau* refers to processing performed for a collection of clients, all on one set of equipment.

As cost pressures escalate on financial institutions, the question of whether to outsource the processing/execution business becomes very important. The institution must weigh the advantages of reduced cost against the disadvantages of losing control of its information. If outsourcing reduces costs by reducing the availability or quality of the information, it may very well be false economy.

However, there is a completely different way to look at outsourcing, and that is to become the outsourcer instead of the outsourcing customer. Banks which are just a little too small by themselves to justify processing their own transactions could reach the plateau of efficiency by processing those transactions for others. This is particularly applicable where the other banks are not geographic competitors of yours, so that they would have little or no fear of entrusting you with their transaction records. This approach could easily lead to alliances of medium-sized banks across the United States, who have gotten together to attain the efficiencies of large processing bases without being worried about getting involved with local competitors.

Taking this role will require the bank to take a particularly active stance with regard to its technology. Undertaking to perform processing for a range of customers implies that the bank will keep up with the latest technology, and make it available to its customers. The service bureau and outsourcing fields are already crowded, and the competition is intense, so any bank that wants to enter the field will have to make a commitment to be technologically topnotch. Of course, there are benefits to making that commitment, one of which is that the bank will be much better able to use its information to achieve competitive advantage.

One area of processing where conduit marketing is particularly dangerous is the field of *payment processing*. Because banks sit at the center of the world of payments, they have become the payment processor of choice, both internationally and domestically. In fact, banks have come to regard payment processing as their private fiefdom, but that is no longer true, particularly in the value-added part of payment processing, where much of the profit margin now resides.

A 1994 study comissioned by the Banker's Roundtable, conducted by Furash & Co., and titled, "The Future of Payment Systems," pointed out that banks have generally restricted themselves to the most basic, undifferentiated, and low-profit parts of the payment processing business, leaving the more differentiated parts, with high information content and profit margins, to the nonbanks. The study warns that banks are in danger of becoming permanently irrelevant in the payment processing field, and that only if they treat payment processing as a profit center will they be able to protect their position. Astute bankers view the attempt to purchase Intuit Corp. for $1.5 billion by Microsoft as a first foray by Bill Gates into the business of retail payment processing.

Principal Transactions

The issue of conduit marketing is much less obvious in relation to principal businesses. Whether the business comes in the form of deposits, loans, or trading positions, it is antithetical to most bank managements to market someone else's principal products. But we already know that a heavy reliance on balance-sheet businesses limits the profitability of the institution. Thus, balance-sheet businesses actually represent a golden opportunity for conduit marketing.

The first example of this that comes to mind is securitization. When a financial institution originates assets to satisfy the demands of the securitization market, it is conduit marketing someone else's balance sheet. The bank normally collects origination fees and passes some of them through to the asset buyer, but, because it is selling the asset and not keeping it on the balance sheet, it can recognize as immediate income those origination fees not passed on.

In addition, the bank can market balance-sheet offerings of other kinds. On the asset side, it can offer loan or lease programs from other institutions, or other kinds of companies. For example, where banks do not need tax shelter, they can offer tax-related leases from other lessors to their customers. On the liability side, the institution can offer a variety of deposit or quasi-deposit products, such as mutual funds, in order to keep customers from leaving the institution when it doesn't want to be ultracompetitive on rate. If customers know that the institution will endeavor to find them the best rate on their deposit, even if it means placing it elsewhere, they will have much less reason to shop around, which translates into a lot of saved time for them. Very few banks avail themselves of the conduit-marketing opportunities that exist in the principal businesses, but they should take note of the fact that the nonbank competitors who have been stealing their best customers for years, the brokerage and mutual fund industries, are much more willing to utilize conduit marketing than the banks are. Do you think there is a connection?

Advisory Businesses

These businesses are the glamour side of financial services, and the source of the most lucrative fees; therefore many institutions are trying to get into them, not trying to market someone else's offerings. But there are so many kinds of advisory businesses that only the very largest institutions could possibly provide their customers with all the services they could want. That leaves the smaller institutions, which may have a strong presence in their market but limited resources with which to provide an almost unlimited array of advice.

Fortunately, there are top-notch advisory organizations throughout the country, in a wide variety of disciplines, who lack the kind of marketing coverage necessary to find all those customers. It is a marriage made in heaven for the local institution to deliver these quality services to its loyal customers. Whether it is corporate finance, personal financial planning, or mergers and acquisitions the ability of the institution to deliver customers, and of the advisor to deliver the service, makes both organizations more profitable and the customer happier. But the banks management must realize that the management of the advisory organizations might not be innovative enough to recognize the value of the alliance, so the bank might have to initiate the conversation, and even suggest the form of the alliance.

This approach may require that both organizations rethink their relationship. Up to now the focus may have been on competition, but that needs to change. As resources become scarcer, and the demands of the market for efficiency and value get tougher, institutions will have to align themselves in ways that were unthinkable just a few years ago. That is true everywhere, not just in financial services, but it will be the key to conduit marketing for banks.

Other Products

Conduit marketing has value in all of the traditional finance products, but its explosive power comes when we turn to other products. Financial institutions have the ability to target market all kinds of financial products because of their wealth of financial information, and because they process the payments for just about everything.

There are only two limitations to the kinds of things a financial institution can market—the limitations of its charter and of its imagination. Generally, banks are limited to businesses "closely related" to banking, but the regulators are more and more disposed to allow banks to expand their reach, as long as the new businesses do not appear to increase risk greatly. A classic example of the regulators' attitude is the Fed's continued expansion of the exemptions to Glass-Steagall through their interpretation of Section 20.

Given that attitude, there are numerous possibilities open to financial institutions in the area of conduit marketing. Let's look at a simple example and compare it to the kind of business a bank currently does.

Typically, a bank currently charges a fee of about two points for committing to make a mortgage loan. (For purposes of this comparison, we are not going to count the interest spread on the loan, since that is the "rent" the bank receives for space on its balance sheet.) In most states which have a state lottery, lottery sales agents receive approximately a 5 percent fee for the sale of tickets. There is no technological reason why state lottery tickets cannot be sold through ATMs. The customers get a more convenient way to buy the lottery ticket that they would buy anyway. The state lottery agency gets its money approximately two days earlier than it would if the ticket were sold through a stationery store. And the bank makes twice the fee it would if it lent money.

Of course, selling lottery tickets is not a business we normally associate with banking, and the regulators, when the idea was voiced to them, expressed concern that the practice made the bank look like it condoned gambling. But they soon saw that the bank was really offering a service that both the public and the state lottery agency desired. When asked whether they wanted banks to generate income through taking mortgage-loan risk or through marketing someone else's products, the choice became clear to them.

But taking advantage of this kind of opportunity will require a distinct change in thinking by your typical bank. It will require looking at their services from the customers point of view instead of their own. It will require probing questions about what services their customers are buying from someone else that they could be buying from the bank. And it requires that the bank challenge the thinking of regulators when that thinking is misguided or outdated. That is the kind of thinking you find in winning financial institutions.

Electronic Delivery

Over the past several decades, America has become a study in *self-service*. Perhaps those of us older than sixty can remember going into a local grocery store with a shopping list, giving it to the proprietor, and having him or her bring the food out to the counter. If you are over fifty, you may remember doing the same thing in the local hardware store. If you are over forty, that image applies to an auto parts store.

Gradually, however, those images are being replaced by images of self-service. Now we push a shopping cart up and down the aisles of a supermarket while we pick up food, and, in some parts of the country, a lot more. The local hardware store has become the self-service "home center." The local auto parts store is becoming the "auto center," with parts and catalogs in the aisles.

In fact, some parts of American shopping, that no one ever thought would become self-service, are. Service stations, where the smiling attendant used to wash your windshield and check the oil, are now self-service stations, where you wash the windshield and check the oil. Fast food restaurants have begun to install keypads on the counters, where customers can enter their orders instead of giving them to the person behind the counter. And certain airline tickets, on frequently flown routes, are dispensed by machines at the airport.

The Cost Advantage

There are two reasons for the growth of self-service. The first, and most obvious, is cost. More and more, we have discovered that people will wait on themselves, and that eliminates a certain "people cost." In addition, in almost every business it is cheaper to deliver and get paid for the product in an automated way. Fifty years ago, Horn and Hardart discovered that when they introduced the Automat. As methods of payment became more electronic, and as technology has gotten better, more and more goods and services have been delivered "people free."

The finance industry has played a major role in that process, by making more and more transactions cashless. At the same time, banks have entered the self-service world through the medium of ATMs. It certainly is true that attitudes toward ATMs have been in the past ambivalent on the part of both banks and customers. But I now see more lines, with more people in them, in front of ATMs than I see in front of tellers.

In fact, the dichotomy of the ATM versus the branch was brought home to me recently when I visited a branch of a well-known, successful bank in Charlotte, North Carolina. It was a flagship branch, about 3,000 square feet, with luxurious appointments and a wealth of service offerings. It was staffed by eight people, four tellers and four professionals, and probably cost in excess of $1 million to build.

I was in the branch for about twenty minutes, talking to people about how they did their jobs. During that time, *one* customer came into the branch. When I stepped outside, into the 90-degree heat, I found a lone ATM in the wall next to the door. There were *four* people lined up in front of that ATM, just a few feet from the air conditioned luxury of the lobby! They might as well have been across town.

In the last several years, bankers and banking consultants have jumped on the self-service bandwagon, almost entirely for reasons of cost. In 1993, the Bank Administration Institute (BAI) and First Manhattan Corporation did a study of retail delivery methods, and concluded that the future for all banks, and for all classes of customers, lay in self-service instead of branches, solely because of cost advantages. As a result of studies like these, bankers have begun downplaying branches in their marketing strategies. That could be a tremendous mistake if it is done for cost reasons alone, a subject I will cover in Chapter 14, Looking beyond Branch Automation. But there is another, much more important reason to utilize self-service—its marketing advantage.

The Marketing Advantage

As much as cost has to do with the growth of self-service, a much bigger factor is marketing. There is no doubt that supermarkets are cheaper to run, per dollar of sales, than a mom-and-pop store. But the real reason for the growth of self-service is that you buy more when you help yourself. Marketers have discovered that in almost every sales function.

People who push their shopping carts up and down the aisles invariably arrive at the checkout counter with more than was on their list. It doesn't matter whether the store sells food, hardware, clothing, or housewares, merchandisers have learned that the best salesperson is "friendly, competent, self-help." *Self-service has turned into self-sales.*

As powerful as self-sales is, it has its weaknesses, and it demands a different kind of approach to the customer. With no salesperson to follow up with the customer, your first shot is your only shot. In self-sales situations, first impressions are crucial, and ease of access can make the difference between seeing the customer stop and buy and seeing him or her pass by. It is no accident that food and soap manufacturers pay so much attention to packaging and shelf position. But how often do bankers think about how appealing their products are to the self-seller?

The fact is that, in financial services, self-sales is in its infancy, if it exists at all. Financial institutions that get their customer in front of an ATM do almost nothing to capitalize on that contact. The messages the customer sees are canned, impersonal and unappealing. Anyone with any expertise in self-sales would cringe at the idea of saying, "Check our auto loan rates" to every customer while his or her transaction is being processed.

Over the next several years, winning banks and other financial institutions will make tremendous strides in self-sales. ATMs will greet customers by name, and will carry personalized messages to customers about financial opportunities. Financial institutions will give both retail and corporate customers direct access to a wide variety of their services. Employees of corporate customers will be able to check such things as the value of their 401(k) plans directly, and retail customers will buy insurance directly, buy airline tickets at bank ATMs, and sell themselves any number of other services. The banks who enable their customers to do this will be the real winners. It's just a question of self-sales.

Cross Marketing

Two of the buzz words of the 1980s in finance were "cross selling"—the selling of one service as a result of the customer buying another. As part of the sales mentality that swept banking during the 80s, tellers were trained to suggest additional services or products to people who appeared at their window, and platform officers were as well. Branch automation, another of the hot ideas then, was designed to turn both the platform officer and the teller into salespeople, by relieving them of their more mundane duties.

Cross selling was supposed to have a significant, if less obvious, impact on corporate banking. The corporate calling officer has been given more and more financial products to sell, from lock boxes to cash management to risk management products to corporate trusteeship to pension investment. With the emergence of the calling officer as the single point of contact for the corporation, cross selling has become his or her primary, and perhaps only, job.

But cross selling has been a significant disappointment for most financial institutions. Too many retail customers never talk to a bank officer, and seldom enough to a teller. Past studies have shown that about 80 percent of a bank's assets are originated outside the branch environment, where the bank's employees never get the chance to cross sell. And even when the opportunity presents itself, when the retail customer appears in the branch, the customer has his or her own agenda, and the bank's employees are ill-prepared or ill-advised to break into it.

On the corporate side, there has been a little more progress, but not much. For decades corporations have been moving financial transactions outside the U.S. banking industry, utilizing the commercial paper market, Wall Street firms, and foreign institutions. Gradually the calling officer has lost contact with many aspects of the corporation's business, and specialization within the corporation has exacerbated the problem, since it requires the officer to talk to several people instead of one or two.

Cross Marketing versus Cross Selling

The basic problem is that most financial institutions have gotten the cart before the horse. In this case the cart is cross selling, in which employees are expected to offer targeted products to specific customers, based on transactions the customer is currently making. But that job requires an encyclopedic knowledge of two things: the customer's financial transactions and the institution's financial products.

The simple fact is that very few employees will know enough about both of those things to cross sell effectively. Everyone recognizes that as certainly true of tellers and clerks, but it is equally true of corporate calling officers and platform officers. Institutions that continue to expect employees to be the originators of cross selling will continue to experience disappointment.

The horse in this analogy is cross marketing, or the use of customer and product information to tailor offerings for customers based on their business patterns. Much of the requisite financial information is already in the institution's possession, because it processes so many financial transactions. Other kinds of financial information are available to the institution from outside sources, or from expanded processing offered as a fee-based service. Already several financial institutions have departments of cross-marketers, scanning customer transactions in search of opportunities for both the customer and the institution. The difference is that they are being proactive, searching out the customer instead of waiting for him or her to come in the door.

However, in order to cross market, the institution must be able to retrieve and view the information in a flexible way, and no one can predict which way the information will have to be viewed. In addition, information about the customers and the products will have to be related, in order to allow the right customers to be targeted for the right products. That process can run in two directions: certain combinations of customer transactions can suggest certain products, or certain combinations of products can suggest certain kinds of target customers.

So there are two components of effective cross marketing: knowledgeable employees and effective information technology. The employees must be knowledgeable about the financial products they are seeking to cross market, and about the customer profile that these products apply to. They must be expert in compliance and suitability, so that they don't recommend the wrong products to the wrong customers. And they must be creative, for it is creativity that makes cross marketing so effective. The information technology must allow these knowledgeable employees to get at and make sense of the information they need to do their jobs. Although most banks have enough information to cross market effectively, they often have a hard time getting at it in any meaningful way, often because their systems were designed to process transactions and account for them, not market them. In addition, many of the banks products use incompatible systems, making it difficult or impossible to combine information of customer positions or the impact of a transaction on the customers financial position. Many bankers recognize that their current technology not only doesn't assist in cross marketing, it actually hampers the effort.

But they must ensure that they have the right technology, and the right employees, because cross marketing is critical to the banks future. Not only does cross marketing have to precede cross selling, it can sometimes replace it. For example, if market research indicates that customers with a certain level of credit-card debt can achieve significant savings in interest and taxes by shifting those balances to home-equity lines, the opportunity can be presented to them as part of their monthly credit-card statement, with the annual savings calculated and shown. It is hard to think of a more effective sales presentation than that.

Putting It All Together

As with most of the other chapters of this book, there are advantages to implementing each of these suggestions alone, but the real benefit comes when they are combined. In other words, cross marketing can identify customers who are prime candidates for certain kinds of products, based on their historical and current transactions. Conduit marketing provides some of those products which the institution doesn't or can't currently provide itself, but which can easily be offered through the institution's marketing network. Target marketing identifies the customer sets which are most likely to respond to particular presentations of these products. And electronic delivery allows the product and the message to get to the right customer, in an attractive way, even though that customer may never come into a branch.

The implication here is that there is a two-way interchange between the institution and its market. As market conditions change, as new products are demanded, as competitors react (or fail to react) to changes, the institution adjusts its product mix, its customer contact, and its pricing so as to maximize its ROE. For marketing professors this is all old hat, but for financial institutions it is one of the most important keys to winning.

8 | Managing Financial Risk

Most of the winning strategies in this book have one thing in common: the results of their successful implementation are visible and measurable. The results of good work in the area of maximizing noninterest income can be seen in specific line items of the income statement. The results of good work in marketing financial services can be seen in the lists of new customers and new products. The results of good work in enhancing asset quality can be seen in reduced bad-debt reserves and lower charge-offs.

There is one winning strategy, however, that is so arcane and so hidden that the outside observer cannot usually tell if it is being done at all, let alone if it is being done well. It is managing financial risk. Professionals in the finance industry know that financial risk has been around for as long as financial transactions have been. It is the hidden factor in every decision a financial executive makes. One aspect of it, credit risk, comprises the lion's share of one complete strategy—enhancing asset quality.

As ubiquitous as financial risk is, though, it is poorly understood and measured. As long as it has been around, its management has evolved relatively little. Most financial institutions acknowledge that risk is an important part of their business, and most have some kind of program to deal with it, but very few feel that they have the situation well under control. In addition, after several years as a prominent subject in the 1980s, global risk management became something of a backwater in the early 1990s. Then, just when everything looked calm on the risk front, after the worst of the credit risk problems had passed, risk reappeared with a vengence in the area of derivative instruments. And there is another risk, suitability risk in the sale of investment products, which is waiting just offstage for its cue. It is these mysterious appearances and disappearances that make financial risk such a perplexing topic.

Understanding Financial Risk

Perhaps the most perplexing aspect of risk is its amorphous nature. Like the shadows at the edge of a campfire's glow, risk seems to change its nature constantly, always staying just out of reach. Only when the institution least expects it does risk appear, in the form of unexpected losses. One year the losses come from bad loans. Another year they come from trading positions in complex derivative instruments. Or perhaps from currency exposures generated in some half-forgotten foreign branch. Or, closer to home, from the dreaded asset-liability mismatch.

Getting one's arms around financial risk seems like trying to capture "The Blob." As soon as you get it under control in one form, it transforms into another. When you have it cornered in one place, it disappears there and reappears in another. As financial risk twists and turns, changing shapes and reappearing, the institution could be forgiven for thinking that it is an animal beyond capturing.

The reason risk is such an elusive quarry is that, at its most basic, *risk is about the unknown*. Financial risk is embodied in unknown financial events, unknown either because they haven't occurred yet or because we can't predict them. The future financial condition of borrowers is an unknown; the future price performance of financial instruments is an unknown; the future path of interest rates is an unknown; and the strategies and future actions of competitors are an unknown.

The business world is full of unknowns, which is what makes it such a challenge. Because the unknowns take so many different forms, risk itself takes a great many forms. In fact, there is some element of risk in every form of business. In particular, there is some form of risk in every kind of financial service. Thus, in understanding risk we need to know three things: what kind of risk it is, what events give rise to it, and how it manifests itself.

But we must recognize that, because risk is about the unknown, it is impossible to measure definitively. All sorts of schemes have been developed to measure and equate different forms of risk, but they are all, by necessity, estimations. In many cases, there isn't even an agreed-upon method of quantifying risk. For example, fixed income traders may try to conceptualize it in "two-year note equivalents," or the risk equivalent to holding a specified position in two-year treasury notes. Clearly, that kind of concept could be applied to currency trading, but it becomes too strained to use when we apply it to other kinds of assets, like loans or leases, or other kinds of businesses, like custodial services.

The problem is that, in order to manage financial risk, an institution must be able to identify and measure it across its entire business, and be able to relate one kind of risk to another. It must also be able to identify the causative factors for each kind of risk, so that it can make some attempt to predict those unpleasant events that make it up. Finally, it must identify the business processes and events which give rise to its risks, so it can manage its business in such a way that risk is minimized.

Kinds of Financial Risk

Let us begin by defining risk as the *possibility that the institution will incur a loss.* Then we can divide risk into classes, based on the kind of event which could cause such a loss. Although it is not often done, it is most appropriate to use the same classification for risk as we have done for the kinds of financial businesses—processing/execution, principal, and advisory.

Processing/Execution Risk

This is not a business which people normally associate with risk, but there is certainly risk involved. As processing/execution volume increases, and as it becomes more automated, the financial impact of errors becomes large enough to merit a lot of attention. This is particularly true as the fees for processing/execution drop, which is what normally happens as markets mature.

In many areas of processing/execution, financial institutions have gone to great lengths to grapple with security risk, or the risk that outside parties will tap into the system processing the transactions. Thus ATM, ACH and EFT networks normally incorporate high levels of access control, identification and authentication keys, and encryption. Because the high volume and automated nature of these businesses give the potential criminal a substantial incentive to break in, institutions who have large processing/execution businesses must spend a lot of time and money keeping ahead of the bad guys.

These same institutions may not have focused the same level of attention on error risk, or the risk that errors in the processing/execution will expose the institution or its customers to loss. In most cases, the bulk of these errors are human in nature. They can range from misposting credit card or mortgage payments, where the level of risk in the individual error is low, but the incidence can be high, to delivering out the wrong securities from a custody account, where the incidence may be low but the individual risk can be high.

A particular class of error risk is the risk of software bugs, which can wreak havoc in automated systems. Two widely different examples come to mind. One was a software bug in Chemical Bank's ATM network, where it double-debited customer accounts for ATM withdrawals for a short period, not only generating financial losses for the bank, but also creating both ill will and damage to its reputation. A different type of software bug affected the National Association of Securities Dealers Automated Quote System (NASDAQ). NASDAQ has been upgrading its electronic market on the fly, and a new version of their communications software failed shortly after being introduced, leaving thousands of brokers and millions of customers without access to the market or market information. Most software bugs occur as new systems, or enhancements to old systems, are being introduced.

Finally, as the finance business becomes a global, 24-hour operation, institutions must come to grips with availability risk, or the risk that a processing/execution service will not be available when the customer requires it. In some businesses, like ATM switching or credit-card verification, the loss of the service for an hour or so might be regarded by the consumer as an inconvenience, although the financial institution whose service was unavailable will regard it as a bona fide disaster. In other cases, like the EFT and transactions routing systems that serve the nation's financial markets, a failure during an active and volatile market period can threaten the viabilities of the markets themselves.

The common denominators in dealing with processing/execution risk are *safety, reliability,* and *backup.* In many cases, the points of highest risk are when one processing system connects to another, where information moves from one system to another. It is here that errors most often occur, and it is here that intruders are most likely to gain access. As a result, institutions are forging more secure connections between their own systems and the other systems they have to connect with, and they are beginning to move the points at which information enters processing systems into the customer's location.

For example, for years custodian banks took delivery and receipt instructions from institutional investors by telephone, telex, or fax. Then their clerks would enter those instructions into the processing system. Now custodians for large institutional investors have begun installing terminals in the offices of those institutional investors, allowing them to enter delivery and receipt instructions themselves, not only reducing costs but also eliminating a significant processing risk.

In the same vein, corporate banking departments have begun installing personal computers and terminals in the offices of their corporate customers, allowing the customer direct access to its accounts. This way the corporate treasurer can keep a close eye on balances and check on the status of financial transactions, while the bank eliminates the expense of having bank officers execute these transactions. Another, perhaps more powerful, incentive for the bank to inaugurate such a service is the substantial reduction in error risk that comes from having the customer enter his or her own instructions.

All this automation of the information flow actually increases the availability risk, partly because it increases everyone's dependence on systems, and partly because, when other risks are eliminated or reduced, availability risk becomes the primary concern. Fortunately, high availability is a well documented and highly developed subject in both computers and telecommunications. That is not to say, of course, that breakdowns will not occur, but the use of redundant processors and communications lines and the prevalence of backup facilities means that those who have an availability problem in this day and age simply chose not to prepare for them.

Principal Risk

It is the principal part of the finance business where risk is most prevalent, and where the attention of risk managers is most often focused. It is certainly true that engaging in principal transactions is essentially engaging in risk businesses, and that is true whether the transaction is a lending one or a trading one. But less well understood are what kinds of risk the institution encounters in principal businesses.

Identification: The problem is that the first step in dealing with risk—identifying it—is anything but a science. For example, risk managers tend to differentiate between credit risk and trading risk, as if they were somehow mutually exclusive. But every trading transaction encompasses some credit risk. What we need is a rigorous method of categorization. We can categorize principal risk in three ways: by its cause, by its effect, and by the transaction which generates it. Categorizing by transaction tells us when to expect a risk; categorizing by effect tells us what to expect; and categorizing by cause tells us what to do about it.

Risk categorization by transaction would lead to the following kinds of headings:

Lending risk
Trading risk
Underwriting risk
Asset/liability risk

Risk categorization by cause would lead to the following kinds of headings:

Interest-rate risk
Credit risk
Market risk
Performance risk

Risk categorization by effect would lead to the following kinds of headings:

Capital risk
Income risk

Opportunity risk
Legal liability risk

Each risk inherent in principal transactions has three descriptive components, one for each category. For example, the possibility that currency prices could move against a position the institution holds would be a trading risk, caused by market movement, resulting in a capital loss. Holding a fixed-rate loan in a rising rate environment would be a lending risk caused by interest-rate movement, resulting in an income penalty. By keeping in mind the three categorizations, you can determine whether someone is describing the transaction where risk occurs, its cause, or its effect. One of the important things you will be able to tell about risk from these two examples is that the causes are often correlated. In this case market movement of fixed-income instruments and interest-rate movements are positively correlated, so these two risks themselves will have a positive correlation.

Measurement: Although identification is the first step, by itself it has almost no value in management until the risk is measured. But you will note that I said earlier in this chapter that risk is impossible to measure accurately, since it encompasses the unknown. Most measurement schemes attempt to quantify risk in terms of potential loss based on some specified change in a variable. This measurement system is most advanced in, and best exemplified by, fixed-income trading, where trading positions are equated by measuring their price movements as a result of a change in interest rates. In many firms, this is expressed in equivalent positions in a "common denominator" security, often the treasury two-year note.

That measurement system is useful as far as it goes, but it doesn't really go very far. Many firms use it for constructing hedges in trading accounts, but it misses such fundamental factors as shifts in the yield curve, and it doesn't work at all in measuring such trading instruments as currencies. The more we attempt to apply an exact measurement process like that one across a variety of risks, the more frustrated we become, again because risk is about those things that defy measurement.

In fact, the measurement process for risk must attack the problem from the opposite end. Instead of trying to eliminate the unknowns, the measurement process should be designed to reduce the unknowns to a minimum. Instead of attempting to predict financial results, the system should be designed to issue warnings when the expected results are not occurring. Instead of attempting to measure risk, the system should monitor events, match their results against expectations, and highlight results that go against those expectations.

This concept has a special impact in the rapidly changing world of financial markets. If risk is about the unknown, then the longer a financial transaction has been around, and the more we know about it, the less risky it becomes. Unfortunately, these are the familiar transactions that many risk managers and risk management systems concentrate on. Rather, they should be concentrating on the new, untested transactions that history has shown hold the biggest risks for the institution. By refining the risk measurement of well-established transactions, instead of attempting to learn as much as possible about the new ones as quickly as possible, institutions are guilty of the corporate equivalent of looking at second base while the ball is going to first.

Prediction: Thus the measurement process is really a model-building process, attempting to predict the risk inherent in a transaction. By modelling the performance of an asset, a position, or a transaction under a variety of conditions, the institution develops an expected relationship between the causative factors (the independent variables) and the risk (the dependent one). In lending, this modelling would be the stress analysis we discussed in Chapter 5. In trading it would be the performance modelling of the instruments to be traded.

Although modelling seems relatively straightforward, and it is, far too few institutions do it. That is primarily because modelling requires a rigorous discipline—you can't model performance unless you understand the causal relationships involved. You can't begin to predict the price performance of a mortgage-backed security, for example, unless you have some understanding of what causes mortgage prepayments. Although there is plenty of verbiage around about such subjects, not much of it stands up to empirical analysis.

A workable model is a combination of a priori and empirical factors. A priori factors are derived from logic, such as the fact that, as GNP growth rates drop, delinquency rates on consumer debt rise. Empirical factors are derived from observation, such as the fact that dropping home values can bring the collateral value on a home mortgage down to where the homeowner cannot refinance, even though interest rates clearly call for it. Thus a prepayment model for mortgage-backed securities should incorporate both the positive impact of the rate drop that normally results from declines in GNP and the negative impact that results from a decline in home values, as well as the fact that those two causal factors are correlated. In the end, all a priori factors must be borne out by empirical evidence, or they must be changed to conform.

A model is best thought of as a mathematical equation, with the addition of Boolean logic. The nice thing about equations is that they can be run in either direction. Of course, most equations are easier to solve in one direction than another, but the reversibility of risk models allows the institution to get the maximum benefit from them—by running them "backwards."

If we think of running the equation "forward" as going from the causative factors to the results, we can see that, although there is only one result for each set of independent variables, there are an almost infinite number of actual results, based on the large number of permutations of causes. If we are concerned about avoiding the worst outcomes, we may have to run an inordinate number of simulations to find the ones we are looking for.

Instead, we may be able to run the model "backwards," going from the result to the causative factors. Because of the nature of such models, we may get many combinations of causes for each result, but those combinations of causes will at least give us a range to work with. By eliminating the causal factors that we view as extremely unlikely, we can identify those factors which have a much higher possibility of happening. Finally, by determining the range of causes which will give rise to the worst possible result, we can focus our attention on the combination of causes we need to be watchful for. If no combination of causes will give us a negative result, a result which we know to be possible, it means we haven't found the right structure for the model yet.

Management/Prevention: The final use of risk models is in the management and/or prevention of risk. In a typical risk model there are two kinds of causative factors—controllable and uncontrollable. Controllable factors are such things as the amount of credit or size of position, the structure of the asset, and covenants in a loan agreement. Uncontrollable factors are such things as general economic conditions, changes in the borrower's market, and major unfavorable developments, like lawsuits or natural disasters.

Having run a risk model backwards, having determined which causative factors would give the most negative results, having determined which of the uncontrollable factors are most likely to occur, the institution can then determine what effect changes in the controllable factors will have. In some cases, this kind of analysis can show that the effects of changing controllable factors can be counterintuitive. For example, incrementally stepped interest rates and debt service requirements over the life of a loan can build in the near-certainty that the borrower will default at some point in the future, while encouraging the lender to make the loan because the borrower can carry the early payments. Only a risk model, run backwards, will point out counter-intuitive risk correlations like this.

Advisory Risk

People do not normally associate financial advisory businesses with risk. At first blush, it is hard to identify a large risk component to such things as portfolio management, corporate finance, personal financial planning, or mergers and acquisition advice. The fact that it generates fees without appearing to expose the institution to risk is what makes this kind of business so attractive.

In fact, the advisory businesses do not incorporate the kinds of risk that the processing/execution or principal businesses do. There is, however, one risk they do incorporate—liability risk. And, while liability risk initially appears smaller than other kinds of risk, it may in fact be bigger. That is because while liability losses occur much less frequently than other kinds, they are usually larger, less predictable, and often surface long after other kinds of losses.

In addition, while lending risks depend on the ability of a borrower to repay a loan, and trading risks depend on price movement, liability risks depend on the decision of a judge or a jury, on a dispute perhaps many years old, which the institution thought was long since settled. Not only are judges and juries notoriously unpredictable, the review and appeal process almost ensures that liability risk has a very long life.

Managing liability risk begins with understanding that it generally arises from damages to someone, either because of the effects of good advice or because of the effects of bad advice. In the case of good advice, the parties in opposition to the institution's client are likely to sue. Most of these suits are a result of merger activity, where the losing acquirer sues or the holders of a company's stock feel wronged by the merger process. In the case of bad advice, the plaintiffs are likely to be the institution's clients, who feel that they suffered some loss as a result of taking the institution's advice.

In both cases, objective analysis, based on a risk model, would surface the risk, but the methods of managing it would be different. Risks derived from good advice are usually dealt with through indemnification by the client, while risks from bad advice require a completely different approach. Here the institution must ensure that employees follow a rigorous discipline regarding the suitability of their advice. Astute banks are putting in place expert systems, which capture the intellectual capital the institution has accumulated in the advisory field, and which document the application of that expertise to the clients problem. While such systems don't entirely preclude the possibility of legal liability for advice, they greatly lessen the likelihood, and they assist in the defense process as well.

A special kind of liability risk is especially important in light of the fragile condition of the economy and the possibility that things could turn down at any time. This risk is the ability of bankruptcy referees to declare certain transactions effected prior to the bankruptcy filings null and void.

One form of this risk is embodied in the doctrine known as *fraudulent conveyance,* which was originally used by the courts to reverse transactions which served to remove assets from a financially troubled company which subsequently filed for bankruptcy. Recent actions by bankruptcy referees have raised the possibility that a leveraged buyout could be construed to be a fraudulent conveyance, if its effect was to leave the company in an insolvent condition. In cases of this kind, referees have declared advisory fees returnable, as well as loan commitment fees. In addition, the logical extension of the fraudulent conveyance doctrine would be to declare the tender of stock pursuant to a leveraged transaction null and void, which could have significant consequences for portfolio managers.

The second form of bankruptcy risk is known as *equitable subordination,* and is a little cloudier than fraudulent conveyance. Equitable subordination allows a referee to place a lender in a worse position vis à vis other lenders, if the referee finds that the prior lender's actions caused the borrower to become insolvent. Thus, if an institution saw trouble on the horizon for a company and advised a client/lender to take action to protect itself, and that action was deemed by the referee to have rendered the company insolvent, the referee could reverse the action and cause the client/lender's debtor position to be subordinated to other lenders'.

Managing Financial Risk

Once all the risks inherent in the finance business are identified, the real job begins—the job of managing them. Many managers think managing risks means eliminating or avoiding them, but that is not the job at all. There is no way to eliminate financial risk, except by getting out of the business. Risk management takes three forms, selection, compensation, and modification.

Selection

The first step in risk management is selection, or identifying the risks the institution wants to undertake. One aspect of selection relates to the class of risks the institution wants to undertake. Does the institution want to emphasize interest rate risk or credit risk? Does the institution feel more comfortable with trading risk or liability risk? In many cases, the class selection will be a function of past experience. Classes of risk with which the institution has had bad experiences are likely to be avoided, and those in which the institution feels expert are likely to be chosen. Unfortunately, this criterion may not be timely or appropriate, if the risk class the institution knows well is universally poor, while another class, less familiar to the institution, is much better. For example, how many banks go on lending to an industry whose market conditions have worsened, simply because there is a body of expertise on that industry, instead of developing a body of expertise in a more favorable industry.

The second aspect of risk selection is the specific risk or risks the institution chooses. For example, once an institution chooses a class of risks, like credit risks, the institution might opt for corporate acquisition debt instead of real estate debt. Or, if the institution opts for trading risk, it needs to determine whether it will concentrate on currencies, fixed income instruments, or derivative instruments. This is also a case where experience makes a difference, but because the nature of specific risks changes so often, research and the ability to sense those changes plays a larger role. Thus, an institution can accept a higher level of specific risk in a new area if it feels comfortable with its ability to predict changes in the specific area. It is important to recognise that change is a constant here, as it is in most business situations. Thus the bank must get used to assuming that, as soon as it feels comfortable with its understanding of a certain risk, its knowledge is already becoming obsolete.

Compensation

Selection is an important first step, but by itself it isn't enough to go on. The second ingredient in the management process is compensation, or how much the institution is payed to accept the risk. It is here that the ability to measure risk becomes vitally important. For compensation purposes, risk measurement requires two inputs: the amount of the potential loss and its probability. Measuring the amount looks easy, but it can be misleading. For example, many institutions regard loans and securities positions as very similar risks, but the potential loss on a loan might amount to all or most of the principal, while the potential loss on a security might be limited to changes in its market value.

It is the probability of loss, however, that is the most difficult to quantify. In attempting to put a number on it, the institution must recognize that there are two primary ingredients to the probability. One is structural and changes relatively slowly. The other is situational and can change quickly.

To understand the difference, let's look at a specific credit risk, that of aircraft financing for the airlines. Structurally, the airlines are not a good credit risk. Their business is cyclical, it requires a large capital investment, and the product, transportation from one point to another, is essentially a commodity. The up-and-down earnings and stock performance of the major airlines in the United States bears that analysis out.

As a result, most aircraft financing for the airlines has been done in the form of leases or equipment trust certificates, in which the financers and not the airlines, own the aircraft. That method allows the financers to provide for structural risk by shifting aircraft to another airline if one gets into trouble. But it does not address the situational risk, which represents a nightmare for aircraft financing. In this case situational risk is a widespread decline in airline traffic, which would generate a heavy oversupply of aircraft. Under those conditions, the safety afforded by an equipment trust certificate would be of little use, since so many financers would be offering aircraft into the market.

Once the institution has made itself comfortable with the quantification of its risks, it can relate that level to the compensation it receives. That compensation can come in many ways. It can be in the form of interest, commitment fees, service fees, securities prices, or many other forms. What is necessary here is to relate the compensation to the risk which generated it.

That is often difficult to do. How many times has your institution received compensation, ostensibly for rendering a service, which was really for undertaking a risk? How many times was your institution awarded a contract to be a merger advisor because the institution agreed to finance the acquisition? Or, vice versa, how many institutions have undertaken to lend money under conditions which they would never have accepted, but for other fees and business the customer had awarded in the past?

It is here that differential pricing of risks, as propounded by Fed Chairman Alan Greenspan, becomes so important. Banks who don't differentially price their risks face two problems. First, they lose an important discipline in their marketing effort, and second, they lose the least risky customers to those who do differentially price. However, as good as differential prcing sounds, there are times when it is virtually impossible to do, particularly when the risk has become popular or the market underestimates the risk. Two areas where this has been a particular problem are the latest hot lending area, and the other is the property and casualty insurance area. In each case, risk absorbers tend to chase after customers without regard for differential pricing, only to be badly burned later. In these cases, differential pricing can serve as a warning to exit the market, or at the very least conduit market your competitors risk products to those customers.

So the institution needs a method of determining what compensation it is receiving for what risks. Then, it must relate those risks to their compensations, in order to be sure that it receives the most compensation for the least risk. The simplest way to do that is to adjust the compensation for the amount of risk it took to obtain it. For comparison purposes, income received for taking on twice the risk would be cut in half. However, as we have already seen, maximizing income isn't really the objective, maximizing return on equity is.

Thus, some banks have followed the example of Bankers Trust Co. of New York, using a measurement they call "risk-adjusted return on capital" (RAROC). In this methodology, the projected return on equity, or capital, is adjusted for the projected risk. Businesses that have a high level of risk must have a high ROE before they make sense. As we saw in Chapter 6, capital is the scarce commodity in financial services, so the RAROC approach allows the institution to factor risk into the optimization process.

But RAROC, as utilized by Bankers Trust, isn't a foolproof method for managing all risks, as Bankers Trust found out recently. As one of the biggest trading banks in the world, Bankers Trust was active in an area known as derivative instruments, or those instruments whose performance is derived from some other instrument. Derivative instruments can be relatively simple, like treasury bond futures, or extremely complex, like leveraged interest-rate swaps. Bankers Trust sold large amounts of some of the more complex derivatives to several corporations, like Procter & Gamble and Gibson Greeting Cards. When market movements generated large losses for those corporations, several sued Bankers Trust, claiming that they were misled about the nature of the derivatives. At the same time, some regulators accused Bankers Trust of not exercising due diligence in marketing these products. As a result, Bankers Trust has learned that RAROC is a good risk-management tool for principal risk, but not necessarily for liability risk.

Modification

It is a fact of economic life that nothing stays the same for long. Markets mature, and profit margins narrow. Public opinion shifts, corporate fortunes ebb and flow, and the political environment swings from one extreme to another. All these events can affect the risk profile of an institution's business after all the contracts have been signed and sealed. Selection and compensation are certainly not enough.

So, for all that an institution can do about risk selection and compensation, there is at least as much it can do to modify the risk itself. Modification is particularly important because it is often the only thing an institution can do once a risk has been accepted and the compensation set.

Institutions can modify their risk in many ways. One is *diversification.* Not only can an institution diversify its holdings and businesses, it can diversify the holders of the risk it already owns. By finding participants for risks it holds, the institution can significantly modify its risk profile in midstream. The normal way of thinking of this process is of selling off a portion of a complete asset or a business, but there is another way. Often assets and businesses can be broken into component parts, with different risk parameters.

An example of this is the breaking of assets into senior/subordinated structures through securitization. Another process is the separation of an asset into short-term and long-term cash-flow pieces. For a commercial bank which is unwilling to accept long-term interest-rate risk, separating fixed-rate mortgages into a short-term piece (which it retains) and a longer-term piece (which it might sell to a pension fund) is an innovative way to modify its risk profile.

However, one area where splitting the risk is not an effective strategy is in the sale of investment products to retail customers. Some banks have tried to split this risk by hiring outside marketing organizations to sell these products. Unfortunately, this strategy often backfires, since the banks customers are just as likely to sue the bank as they would be if the banks own employees handled the sale, and the bank has lost some control over the sales practices by outsourcing the sales function. One of the best examples of this recently was NationsBanks experience in a joint venture with Dean Witter. When some of NationsBanks customers felt they had received bad advice from the Dean Witter brokers, they went after NationsBank, not Dean Witter.

Institutions can also modify their risk profile through *hedging,* or the acceptance of an offsetting risk. Because hedging often involves futures and options contracts, and the salespeople who populate those markets, a great deal has been published and said about hedging—only some of it realistic. Some outrageous claims have been made for hedging, and more than a few financial institutions have been burned when they undertook hedging programs that were unsuitable, or just plain stupid.

The first thing to remember about hedging is that it always involves accepting risk, either through listed contracts or unlisted ones. The idea of hedging is to match the hedge risk against the business risk, but there is always a cost to hedges, and a hidden risk that too few institutions see until it is too late.

The cost is often buried in the hedge itself. For example, institutions that sell bond futures contracts to hedge long-term assets will find that the value of the futures contracts has risen just enough by expiration to reduce the long-term asset's yield to short-term rates. Buying options to hedge risks is also expensive, since the premium paid is lost if the option expires unexercised.

The hidden risk is embodied in the fact that the hedge instrument is almost never tied directly to the risk instrument. Using bond futures to hedge short-term interest-rate risk assumes that long- and short-term rates will move in tandem, which only happens often enough to convince people to make a mistake. Using treasury instruments to hedge corporate debt rates assumes that corporate and treasury rates will move in tandem. Using a LIBOR-based interest-rate swap to hedge a bank's cost of funds assumes that the bank's CD rates will move in tandem with LIBOR. Maybe they will, and maybe they won't, but it is amazing how often the divergence seems to cost the institution an arm and a leg.

The final method of modifying risk is through modifying the business arrangement which gives rise to the risk. Of all the possibilities, this is the most versatile and reliable. The trick is to present the changes in such a way that they are palatable to others—not only to the customer, but to one's competitors and regulators. It sounds like a tall order, but no one ever said finance was easy.

The first instance of this kind of modification is in the renegotiation of a loan agreement. Renegotiations don't happen very often unless the loan is in default, and then they usually result in a worse asset for the institution. In fact, after a loan goes into default is the very worst time to enter into renegotiation. The borrower and the lender both know the alternatives to renegotiation, and they aren't very pleasant for either side. The question is whether the borrower fears the alternative more than the lender does.

The best time to renegotiate an agreement may be when the borrower's business is booming, not when it is declining. Growing businesses often have growing needs for all kinds of financial services, not just a growing need for credit. This is the time when a lender must take a hard look at the borrower's management, and its market. Booming businesses have a way of slowing down suddenly, as markets reach saturation, margins shrink, and customers become more knowledgeable about the product. Managements used to the problems of high-growth businesses may be completely unsuited to the tough competition of mature markets. Lenders who have the opportunity to renegotiate an agreement with such a borrower might seize upon the opportunity to limit their lending risk, and one way might be through participating out part or all of the loan.

Loans are not the only source of financial risk, so they are not the only arrangements that can be modified. Many execution/processing businesses incorporate error risk, or the risk that the institution will make an error in execution or processing the customer's instructions. For example, custodians who used to accept settlement instructions from customers by phone or fax have begun installing terminals in their customer's offices. Institutional investors can enter settlement instructions themselves, eliminating a major source of risk for the bank. The terminal will allow the customer to get immediate information on his or her holdings, and the institution will save money in the process.

These opportunities for institutions to modify business arrangements exist everywhere, just as financial risk exists everywhere. It is the changing nature of the finance business that gives rise to those opportunities, just as it gives rise to the risks themselves. The essence of risk management is looking for the risk, and the opportunities, when and where you would least expect them, and being creative in how you deal with them. The simple fact is that success in the finance arena is not a matter of risk avoidance, but of risk management. It is a matter of getting paid to take the risks you want to take, and laying off the rest. It is a matter of taking the risks that give you the best ROE and structuring them to make the best use of your capital. It is a matter of identifying the risks that bring with them the highest noninterest income and using your marketing skills to bring in that business. It is a matter of quality, in your people, your processes, and your assets. If it is beginning to sound like all these strategies come together, congratulations! You have almost reached the winner's circle.

9 | Controlling Costs

Any company in a business beset with excess capacity knows that a critical element in survival is controlling costs. That is particularly true if the company's product is perceived by the public as something of a commodity, because the lack of product differentiation precludes differential pricing. Costs are even more of an issue in a service business, because people make up such a large part of the cost structure, and people turn out to be an expensive component of production.

It should not come as a surprise to us that the finance industry has all of the above characteristics. There can be no doubt at this point that finance suffers from too much capacity, that the public perceives its products as largely undifferentiated, and that much of its cost structure is made up of personnel. If there ever was a textbook example of the need to control costs, banking is it.

That fact hasn't been lost on the industry itself. The drive to reduce costs is at the forefront of almost everything the industry is doing. The mergers which are becoming an almost everyday occurrence have as a primary emphasis the reduction of expenses. The new buzzwords in the industry are outsourcing, or the external acquisition of services previously done internally, and reengineering, or the redesigning of processes to make them more efficient. And it seems that every management team is looking for a better way to determine the profitability of products, departments, and branches.

With all the attention that has been paid to controlling costs, we might expect significant progress on that front, and although there was some in the early 1990s, there is considerable evidence that the progress has stopped and even reversed itself.

Current Practices in Cost Control

The inability of the finance industry to keep costs down should not surprise us, because finance is a service industry, and service industry costs are always hard to control. Recently, financial institutions have concentrated on four main methods of cost control: retrenchment, mergers, layoffs, and outsourcing.

Retrenchment

Retrenchment is the process of exiting a business or market because the institution thinks it should concentrate its resources in another business or market. It takes such forms as selling a line of business, like the institution's money management or brokerage subsidiary, selling a market franchise, like a branch network or a foreign affiliate, or closing down a department, like a trading or mortgage banking unit.

Retrenchment has become a popular strategy in the last several years, as institutions "get out of ancillary businesses in order to concentrate on core businesses." The problem is the ancillary businesses or markets are sometimes growth businesses or markets, even if they demand an investment, while the core businesses are often stagnant, even if they are cash cows. And there is a disturbing common denominator among institutions engaging in retrenchment—they are often getting out of businesses and markets which are profitable, in order to concentrate their efforts where they don't make much money. For example, Chemical Bank in New York recently announced that it was selling its branch network in New Jersey, in order to concentrate its retail efforts in New York City. One of the banks rumored to be a possible buyer is NatWest USA, a subsidiary of the large British bank. Perhaps it shouldnt surprise us that NatWest was one of the top ten banks in profitability in the United States during 1993, and that Chemical was no better than the middle of the pack. In fact, retrenching institutions don't look like strong, growing institutions—in a word, like winners. They often look like troubled, shrinking institutions that can't escape from the past—in a word, like losers.

Of course, there are retrenchments that make business and economic sense. In the 1980s many banks embarked on international retail expansions, reasoning that if they could serve one retail market they could serve them all. For almost all of them, the reasoning turned out to be fallacious, and most of them retreated to markets they knew better, and where they were better known. Only Hong Kong Shanghai Bank, Citicorp, and NatWest appear to have made a go of international retail banking, so retrenchment was a smart move for the rest, even if it meant admitting a mistake.

Mergers

During the 1980s, most bank mergers were combinations of institutions in different markets, called cross-market mergers. In the early 1990s, the trend has shifted to mergers of institutions which serve the same markets, called in-market mergers. By the mid-1990s, the emphasis has shifted back again to cross-market mergers, as Congress finally passed the long-awaited interstate banking law. The problems with interstate banking: are its implementation will be a long time coming and states can opt out of it, and the cost benefits of cross-market mergers have turned out to be extraordinarily hard to realize.

Early on, cross-market mergers were driven primarily by a need to expand the institution's market coverage, or to grow its business. More recent in-market mergers have been driven by the institution's need to eliminate excess capacity. In other words, some of the emphasis has shifted from controlled growth to controlled shrinkage.

A merger, under the best of circumstances, is an unsettling time, but there is an enormous difference between being acquired because you have an attractive franchise and being acquired because you have too many people. There is no doubt that cross-market mergers eliminated jobs, but that wasn't their main purpose. In-market mergers are a personnel wringer, pure and simple, which makes them extraordinarily difficult to pull off.

In Chapter 17, Making a Merger Work, I will look at the subject of mergers in detail, but it is sufficient here to point out that mergers accomplished largely for the purpose of reducing personnel expense have a disastrous effect on employee morale, and that often translates into poor customer service.

At the same time, the internal jockeying for departmental and individual survival can seriously impair the bank's ability to capture the best of both institutions. The fact is, there is no assurance that, just because two institutions in the same market merge, the resulting institution will be judged a success by any measure, and a great many which have been done in the recent past were not.

Outsourcing

One of the most popular subjects on the banking cocktail circuit is outsourcing, or the purchase (from an outside vendor) of a service that the institution previously did for itself. If we look at the three businesses of financial services, we can see that the profit dynamics of the execution/processing business argue strongly for economies of scale. Logic would tell us that, to the extent that those services can be standardized, all participants would be well-served by buying those services from a large provider instead of duplicating each others efforts.

There is no doubt that outsourcing processing functions can generate significant savings over the immediate future. However, those savings could cover a multitude of sins. If we look at data processing (DP) for a moment, we can see why. There are several ways one can outsource DP.

Its simplest form, most applicable to the smallest institutions, is the service bureau, where the institution's processing is run, along with that of other institutions, on a single hardware platform. A more complex transaction is outsourcing a data center, where the provider buys the institution's building, equipment, and perhaps networks, and provides the staff to run the computers and provide systems programming. A more complete outsourcing would also include application development, where the outsource would provide the new and updated older applications to the institution. Finally, the outsource could provide enhanced data and access, turning the DP function into a marketing and competitive weapon.

For many institutions, outsourcing is simply regarded as a way to reduce current costs, so they often select an arrangement that gives them the lowest current cost per transaction. These arrangements can be very limiting, if not crippling, to the institution as it tries to compete later on. Outsourcers who provide generic or undifferentiated services, and arrangements which run several years in length, can put the institution in a position where it has no ability to enhance its systems for a long time. Such an arrangement is clearly a case of mortgaging the future in exchange for lower costs today.

The Nature of Cost, Expense, and Expenditure

If all this leaves us with the feeling that something is amiss, we may be getting the point. The problem often begins with a basic understanding of what we are talking about. In particular, what is the difference between cost, expense, and expenditure?

Cost

Let's begin with cost, which is an *internal* measure of the offsets to revenue. Because it is internal in nature, cost can be whatever management wants it to be. Costs can be obvious, like the salaries and benefits of the people who work in a department. They can be allocated, like the salaries of the legal department. They can be intracompany, like the price of a good produced in the United States and sold to a European subsidiary. They can be imaginary, like the opportunity costs often used to set the performance bar for departments.

Costs can be structured in any way that management feels makes sense. Costs can be applied to products, to departments, to functions, or to geographical areas. They can be overallocated, underallocated, or not allocated at all. And they can bear a striking resemblance to other measures, or none at all.

Properly used, costs are a useful tool for both performance measurement and employee incentives, but they harbor a whole host of dangers.

Here are some:

❏ Because costs are allocated, they become an end in themselves. One of the easiest ways to improve internal measures of performance is to change the way costs are allocated. A manager, by having overhead costs reassigned from his or her department to another, can significantly improve his or her performance without improving the institution's.

❏ Because costs are short term in nature, they encourage short-term management. When departmental performance suffers, the first things that get cut are those which have long-term payoffs. By allocating such costs as research and development to operating departments, the institution is almost ensuring that its future competitiveness will suffer.

❏ Because costs are designed for and by management, they may have no influence on the company's performance in the market. When operating departments concentrate on a set of numbers that will be put before management, they may not spend enough time concentrating on the numbers presented to the stockholders. This issue is the genesis of the often-heard observation, "All our departments met their cost targets, but the earnings didn't reflect it."

Expense

Where cost is an internal measure, expense is an external measure of the offsets to revenue. It is expense that is subtracted from revenue in the annual report to arrive at net income. While costs are important to management, expenses are important to auditors and stockholders.

It is the auditors who have the most to say about expenses every year, in particular about expenses that are accrued. In order to recognize events that occur over a multiyear period and to smooth out what would be violent swings in earnings, the auditors allocate certain expenses over relatively long periods of time. A few of those can have a major impact on earnings, but are little understood by those outside the corporate controller's office.

One such expense is depreciation, particularly of computer equipment. In theory, equipment should be written down from the purchase price to residual value over its actual useful life. In some cases, the equipment is actually written down significantly faster than its real life, leaving the institution with a skewed expense structure. The earnings value of that equipment is understated early on, when its earnings impact may be the greatest, and is overstated later in its life, when its actual earnings contribution may be lower. Institutions using fully depreciated equipment may have a disincentive to replace it, even though there is good justification, because they are unwilling to begin a new round of depreciation.

The exact opposite case is one in which the institution depreciates equipment over a longer period than its useful life. Here the institution might also be disinclined to replace obsolete equipment, not because of depreciation considerations, but because the trade-in value of the equipment is below its current book value, necessitating a one-time loss in order to accomplish the upgrade. In addition, there is a tax implication to all this, since equipment is usually depreciated over a different life for tax purposes than for book purposes. All these depreciation cross-currents can have a significant impact on decisions about technology, and we will look at some ways to deal with them later in this chapter.

Even in the more basic and obvious expense categories, there is considerable misunderstanding regarding size and categories. For example, in 1991, a spokesman for MNC Financial Corp., the holding company for Maryland National Bank, was quoted in *The Wall Street Journal* as saying, "The salary line is the biggest piece of all our expenses." Of course that's not true. The biggest single expense item by far in a bank is interest expense. In most banks it exceeds total noninterest expense by a fair margin. It is just that most institutions regard interest expense as an uncontrollable item. It may be, but even a small ability to control interest expense can dwarf reduction efforts in other expenses.

Another large expense item, often larger than personnel expense, is bad debt reserves. This is another item that institutions may not think of as part of expense control, partly because they think it is covered under enhancing asset quality, and partly because it is thought of as an extraordinary item. The fact is, however, that time and effort spent in reducing bad debt reserves, and in facilitating the recovery of principal on distressed assets, can have an enormous impact on expense control. The lesson here is to make sure that management looks at every category of expenses, not just those that are well known.

Perhaps the most fruitful area for expense control is one referred to in a 1990 *Wall Street Journal* article entitled "Bank's Internal Turf Battles Are Costly." In the article, after stating that, "The turf battles may be costing the U. S. banking industry billions," author Craig Smith points out that "mining a bank's client base is . . . cheaper and easier than prospecting for new business among the accounts of rival banks." The point of the article is that in banks where turf battles and client jealousy prevent people from sharing marketing information, the cost of marketing and sales promotion is significantly higher, and its benefits lower, than it is where information is shared. Although this article was written in 1990, there is little evidence that many commercial banks have addressed this very large hidden cost, and one of the primary reasons is covered in detail in Chapter 15, Productivity[2] and Power in a Changing Bank.

Expenditure

While cost and expense are somewhat complicated concepts, expenditure is quite simple—it is money out the door, for whatever purpose. If institutions kept their books on a cash basis instead of an accrual basis, expenditure would be all the stockholders and auditors would care about. However, because the expenditure concept is so simplistic, it is correspondingly less helpful in managing the business.

Nonetheless, expenditure is important in this context for two reasons. First, although there are many expenditures which are not expense items in the current reporting period, they are often confused with expenses by those making operating decisions. A commonly used term, the "budget" is an example of this confusion. Often, departments have both operating budgets and capital budgets, and it may not be clear which expenditure goes in which budget. If items in the operating budget are expense items, and items in the capital budget are added to fixed assets, there is a very big difference between the two, as far as profit goes. But I have heard many department heads talk about cutting back on the capital budget because of current expense constraints. If such logic prompts a bank to starve an important effort, such as marketing a new product, it can be very damaging to the institution's long-term competitive position.

Cost/Expense Control Strategies

Understanding clearly which items are costs, which are expenses, and which are expenditures is a first step in controlling each, but to accomplish the task, the institution needs a strategy or strategies. It is important to note here that I am not talking about reducing or eliminating these items, but about controlling them. There is a big difference. The fastest way to eliminate costs is to stop doing business, and we see many banks doing that in a micro way whenever they retrench, but that is clearly not the recipe here. It is crucial for management to understand that controlling expenses is a way to *grow* business and profits, not a way to preside over its demise. So what strategies can we employ to control expenses?

Relate Expenditures to Return on Equity

In the abstract, the purpose of spending money is making money. In theory, a rational businessperson would never spend money in order to reduce net profit. But reality is often very different.

As a business grows, money is inevitably spent for things that do not contribute to higher profits, not to mention a higher return on equity. Many expenditures develop a life of their own, with an assumed necessity that careful analysis would disprove. There are people in comfortable jobs whose employment appears to depend on these expenditures; vendors whose salespeople have convincing arguments in favor of them; and there are those in management who see the expenditures as necessary, under the "If it ain't broke, don't fix it," management philosophy.

But you can't just chop away willy-nilly. What is needed is a dispassionate look at the institution's business and profit dynamics. What are needed are answers to the following questions: What function does this expenditure perform? How much profit would the institution forego if the expenditure was done away with? Is there some other way to perform this function, one which could significantly increase ROE? Would our customers or our stockholders notice if we obtained this product, service, or process from outside, or dropped it altogether?

This is all part of a philosophy that says that every dollar the institution spends, like every person it employs and every process it uses, should have some impact on ROE. Expenditure dollars represent scarce resources and they must be allocated so as to maximize ROE. Let me hasten to point out that there are two important caveats to this blanket philosophy. The first is that the relationship between expenditures and ROE might not be immediately clear, as in cases like legal advice or some forms of research and development. Thus, I am not advocating that all expenditures which cannot be traced directly to maximizing ROE be eliminated, but that those where the connection is tenuous or invisible should be scrutinized carefully.

The second proviso is that, in the case of many expenditures, their connection with ROE may change over time. Certain projects that looked well-related to ROE in the beginning might become much less clear as time goes on. In that case, the whole purpose of the project, and the attendant expenditures, should be carefully reviewed. Stopping a project, and its expenditures, part way through may look like bad business, but it is infinitely more sensible than pushing to completion something that will never have a chance to pay off in a changed environment.

Perhaps the best example of this kind of thinking, or the lack thereof, is some of the work being done in retail branches. Some banks have spent a lot of money on decor, location, and branch automation, in an attempt to make their branches the best place for the customer to do business. However, research has shown that only about 20 percent of all retail financial assets are generated in branches, with 80 percent being generated outside of the branch system. In addition, it is doubtful whether the typical branch staff will ever be able to use much of the technology that their management is planning for them. In other words, many of these expenditures may never have any significant impact on ROE.

However, there is even a caveat to this example. Over the last two years, many banking consultants have done this exact kind of analysis of branch systems and have concluded that branch expenditures do not impact ROE and should be curtailed. As I point out in Chapter 14, Looking beyond Branch Automation, branches play a critical role in such successful companies as Fidelity Investments, Merrill Lynch, and IDS. The difference is, although they spend money on their branch systems, they have a different view of what a branch is for, and they *do* relate their branch expenditures to ROE. It isn't that banks should abandon their branch systems, they need to make them more relevant.

Have People Do Only Those Things That Only People Can Do

Among the assets that a financial institution has, the most expensive is its people. If the average employee costs $50,000 per year (including benefits), and the market interest rate is 8 percent, the capitalized value of the average employee is $625,000. If the institution's return-on-investment target is 15 percent, each employee must generate $93,750 in profit, which means in excesss of both the personnel and support costs, to justify his or her continued employment.

These expensive assets cannot be assigned mundane tasks. In the first place, people are much too expensive to be used for pushing around pieces of paper. In the second place, people are much too error-prone to do routine, repetitive jobs. If an institution must do twice the volume of business, through the same size balance sheet, with half as many people to be a winner, then each of those people must be responsible for four times as much business as they are currently.

In addition, people in a financial institution are often a barrier to customer satisfaction, even when they have the best intentions. When bank officers have to execute a money transfer or process a securities transfer, they are in effect delaying the transaction, increasing the risk of error, and making it less effective. When customers have a method for entering those transactions into their own accounts, they get faster service, they get better information about their account status, the possibility for error is reduced, and the institution saves money.

The scale of wasted human resources can be astonishing to bank management. For example, a research study showed recently that about a third of the platform officers' workday was spent preparing documents. That, by itself, isn't too startling. But over 90 percent of those documents were forms. Credit memos, debit memos, reversals of previous transactions, payment instructions, receipt instructions—all are examples of things a person shouldn't be doing at all. In fact, if you spend three days observing carefully what your employees are doing throughout your institution, you will be amazed at the amount of time they spend performing unnecessary tasks. Those three days could be the most productive time you spend this year.

If you do that, you will have inadvertently embarked on something called *business process reengineering,* one of the most productive exercises an institution can undertake. In management consulting, process reengineering is big business, and as such, attracts all kinds of practitioners. Some are very professional, and some are not, so reengineering can have results that range from spectacular to disappointing. In fact, Mike Hammer, the father of business reengineering, estimates that about 70 percent of reengineering projects fail to achieve measurable bottom-line results. This subject is covered in more detail in Chapter 13, Business Process Reengineering, but here are some fundamentals to help you achieve a successful reengineering.

The effort must be driven by objectives, not processes. If you begin reengineering by studying the current process in detail, there is every likelihood that you will make the current process better, but not achieve much of a breakthrough. If you begin by determining the business objectives you want to accomplish, you have a much better chance of achieving both savings and improved quality.

There is nothing so misguided as doing well that which you shouldn't be doing at all. Process reengineering is most effective when it eliminates whole steps or entire processes. Checking with the accounting department before selling a security could be made more efficient, but it isn't necessary at all if the portfolio manager already has accurate, current information on holdings. It isn't necessary for accounting to supply that information if the portfolio management system, where the trades originate, updates its records before its sends them to accounting.

Customers are often happier doing things for themselves instead of having you do them for them. The most powerful questions in process reengineering are, "Why don't our customers do this?" Why don't the customers transfer funds themselves? Why don't the customers enter custodial instructions themselves? Why don't the customers authorize payments themselves? Why don't the customers get our rate quotes for themselves and execute the transactions themselves? When these questions become routine throughout the institution, countless opportunities to simplify or eliminate processes appear.

Reengineering ideas can come from anywhere. Reengineering is a creative process, and you can never predict where creative ideas will come from. Customers' questions can trigger them. Employees' observations can trigger them. Someone's frustrations can set off a spark. But two things must happen. First, employees must be encouraged to be creative; this is done by offering them monetary rewards and recognition. Second, everyone must be trained to ask, "What are we trying to accomplish here?" not, "How does this process work?"

Since objectives and processes always change, reengineering is a constant job. There are always more ways to simplify what you are doing. There are always more ways to combine efforts and eliminate steps. There are always new levels of technology, new methods of communication, new demands by customers. The institution that believes that it has completed the reengineering job is a sitting duck for its competitors.

Structure Acquisitions of Fixed Assets in the Most Cost Effective Way

After all the analysis has been done to determine an expenditure's impact on ROE, and after the institution's people have become as productive as they can be, there remains one additional cost-control strategy.

As more and more of an institution's business depends on its technology, the institution must make larger and larger investments in fixed assets. In times past, those fixed assets were almost entirely computers, but the collection of technology assets, the technology "infrastructure," is now much more polymorphous. Today, a technology infrastructure is made up of a wide variety of hardware, including such things as mainframes, midranges, workstations, check sorters, communications controllers, and ATMs; software, including such things as operating systems, local area network (LAN) and wide area network (WAN) managers, database managers, applications programs, and programming languages; and a host of other items and services, such as fiber-optic cabling, systems integration, telephone switches, and systems design.

The purpose of this infrastructure is to enable the institution to perform financial services in the modern arena, but it is seldom viewed as a connected financial investment. Instead, it is viewed as a lot of small pieces, some of which are treated as fixed assets by the accountants, and some of which are not. In order to make proper sense of an institution's business, all the parts of an infrastructure that have a multiyear life should be treated as fixed assets and depreciated over an appropriate economic life.

This means that integration services the institution might have paid for in developing a trading or ATM infrastructure should be considered part of the cost of that structure, and should be depreciated over the life of the system. Many institutions treat hardware as a fixed asset, but may treat software as a short-term asset, to be expensed over one operating period. They may also treat integration and design services as pure expenses, instead of including them in the cost of the system.

This distinction becomes important because many banks are subject to the alternative minimum tax (AMT). In essence, the AMT requires an institution to figure its federal income taxes two ways: once the normal way, with the normal tax rate, and then with some deductions added back in, at a lower tax rate. Two of the "add-back" deductions are interest on municipal bonds and accelerated depreciation of fixed assets. Because many financial institutions hold investments in municipal bonds, they are not able to use accelerated depreciation for tax purposes.

They can, however, take lease rental payments as a full tax deduction, which means that institutions subject to AMT may well want to lease their fixed assets, instead of owning them. To the extent that the lessor can finance the assets (including such things as software and services) at an attractive rate, and can make use of accelerated depreciation where the institution can't, a lease transaction can make a significant difference in the perceived cost of fixed assets.

Another kind of acquisition strategy could involve the treatment of the equipment being replaced. In many cases, equipment which has been depreciated-fully for tax purposes will have significant value in the market. The institution usually needs to recoup that value in order to make the acquisition of the new equipment feasible.

If the institution sells the old equipment in the market, it will generate a taxable profit on the sale and will owe the IRS some portion of the proceeds. However, Section 1031 of the Tax Code allows a taxpayer to carry the tax value, or basis, of the old equipment forward to the new equipment if he or she exchanges the old equipment for the new instead of selling it. What this means is that structuring the transaction as a trade-in, instead of a sale and purchase, could save the institution a significant portion of the purchase price. It is important to note that, under Section 1031, the equipment exchanged doesn't have to be identical.

Finally, the most cost-effective acquisition strategy might not be an acquisition at all. For the past few years many institutions have been examining the possibilities of outsourcing as a way of reducing costs. However, the acquisition decision can effectively incorporate an outsourcing decision. This is particularly true if the data center occupies a building that has a higher market value than it has on the institution's books.

In that case, the institution can use all or part of the profit on the real estate to significantly reduce the cost of the equipment. The institution must decide how much of such a profit it wants to add to its capital base, and how much it wants to use to reduce its costs. An ingredient in that calculation is the fact that the value of the real estate that is used to reduce the acquisition cost need not represent a taxable profit.

Cost Control as a Philosophy

Controlling costs has been in the management repertoire of most financial institutions for many years, but it always seems to be an on-again off-again approach. The finance business, like many other businesses, has its cycles. For a while things go well, spreads are good, and cost control seems to go to the back burner. Then everyone discovers that there is too much capacity, competition heats up, profit margins shrink, and everyone scrambles to reduce costs.

This "accordian" approach has had a very bad effect on the finance industry. When people get used to the cycles of expansion and contraction, they lose sight of the basic requirement for continuity. When people come and go within departments, when institutions enter and exit businesses, and when they expand and contract their balance sheets, both bankers and customers lose sight of what makes good business sense.

Certain financial institutions have demonstrated long-term profitability and staying power and have adopted cost control as a philosophy. For example, large banks like KeyCorp and Shawmut have embarked on personnel reduction programs in the midst of the best two years banks have seen in a long time. But even these measures do not necessarily show the adoption of cost control as a philosophy, often they represent a constant application of the old, ad hoc, approach.

Instead, banks need to incorporate cost control into their pursuit of the other winning strategies. In good times and bad, whether the business is growing or stagnant, banks must recognize that expenses, like body fat, are easy to put on and hard to take off. They must relate every dollar of expense and expenditure to ROE. They must make sure their people are always as productive as they can be. Like world class athletes, these organizations must stay in shape year-round, even when others are taking it easy. Then, like world class athletes, they will be perennial winners.

10 | Putting It All Together

Now that we have completed a detailed examination of the six winning strategies, it is time to put them into practice, to mold them into a winning combination. In order to do that, I will have to spend some time on the problems associated with managing a financial institution, managing during periods of change, and the special problems that arise from mergers.

First, though, I want to bring the winning strategies together in a cohesive, logical way, because they are much more powerful as a philosophy, or a way of looking at your institution, than as a set of distinct rules. Let me express this as a progression of observations.

1. *Winning is the new objective for all financial institutions.* With the current level of excess capacity in banking, and with the changing laws covering interstate banking, the number of banks in the United States will probably shrink to about half the current number by the year 2000. In such an environment, consolidation will be accomplished by the stronger institutions acquiring the weaker ones. So survival will be a matter of being stronger, more aggressive, more profitable, with a larger market capitalization.

   The world of banking is already in the process of sorting itself out into a group of winners who will most likely be the survivors, and a group of losers who will most likely not survive. It is important to understand that strong is not synonymous with large, nor weak with small. Instead, strength is measured in terms of return on equity, regulatory capitalization, and price/earnings ratio. In markets with excess capacity, the strong tend to get stronger and the weak tend to get weaker, until enough of the weak disappear to eliminate much of the excess capacity. In banking, the future belongs to the winners.

2.   *Winning institutions will understand the nature and scope of financial services.* Financial services naturally fall into three categories, based on their profit dynamics. Execution and processing businesses depend for profitability on volume and efficiency. Principal businesses depend for profitability on risk management and pricing. Advisory businesses depend for profitability on applied intelligence and marketing.

     Although each category of business has its own profit dynamics, they are most profitable when they are combined. For example, execution/processing businesses generate large amounts of information which can be turned into benefits in the other businesses. Or customer relationships which stem from principal transactions can be leveraged into the advisory business. In order for these things to happen, there must be the opportunity and incentive for different departments within the bank to work together.

3.   *Winners can be identified by how they relate to their products, to their competitors, and to their customers.* The likely survivors will understand that markets always change, and will use change as a weapon. They will be innovators or opportunists in new markets and new products. They will be predators, looking for any sign of weakness on the part of their competitors. And they will be marketeers, utilizing feedback from the marketplace to shape their competitive strategies.

     The implications of being an innovator, a predator, and a marketeer will be reflected in the actions of every employee of the institution. Institutions which inculcate a winning approach will inevitably affect the lifestyles and performance of their employees, partly by example, partly by self-selection, and partly by attrition. Winning institutions start and end with winning employees.

4.   *Winning institutions will build their businesses on a good foundation.* Certain business principles apply as much to financial services as they do to manufacturing or transportation. Winning institutions will be focused on maximizing return on equity, the most basic and universal measure of performance. That focus will extend to every employee in the institution.

     Winning institutions will make a determined effort to incorporate quality as an integral part of everything they do, and that process will begin with the customer, who is the final arbiter of quality in financial services. Winning institutions will make the most of their people, since people are the most expensive, and potentially most productive, asset the institution has. And winning institutions will constantly seek to grow their business, since those who stop growing will already be shrinking.

5. *Winning institutions will maximize noninterest income.* Institutions that manage their balance sheets superbly will make enough money to become a good acquisition target. The income boost, which will elevate ROE enough to make the institution an acquirer of other businesses, must come from noninterest sources. This means that the institution must focus its attention on something other than selling space on its balance sheet.

    In order to maximize noninterest income, the institution must determine the businesses it is good at, the markets in which those services are most popular, and match the service to the market. Then the institution must deliver the marketing message on those services to the right customer set. Finally, the institution must constantly expand its service offerings by building upon those services it already does well and upon those customers it already serves well. The process involves offering new products to current customers, and current products to new customers, instead of offering new products to new customers.

    By far the most rewarding, and riskiest, process is developing new sources of noninterest income. Here the institution will have to look outside the traditional bounds of commercial banking for opportunities. By using a process called market-driven product planning, the institution can reduce the risk of new product introductions significantly. This process incorporates information about customers, competitors, and the institution itself, and results in a product strategy, an implementation plan, and measurement of the results.

6. *Winning institutions will enhance the quality of their assets.* The other side of the income coin from noninterest sources is balance-sheet sources. While selling services is difficult, the risk component is low. Selling the balance sheet is much easier, and more seductive, but it is the source of the risk that has plagued the banking business for years.

    As institutions strive for higher income, they are often tempted to turn from noninterest sources to balance-sheet sources, and in doing so they inevitably degrade the quality of their balance sheets. Thus the first step in enhancing asset quality is lessening the pressure to generate income from the balance sheet.

    The second is to incorporate additional information into the loan underwriting process, information about the borrower's marketplace, and the impact on the borrower of possible economic events. This information is incorporated into a stress model, which highlights the sources and extent of the borrower's financial risks.

The third is to structure the asset so as to maximize its quality, both from the institution's and the customers' points of view. And, since conditions change all the time, it often means restructuring an asset so that it better serves both parties.

Finally, the institution must put as much emphasis on monitoring assets as it does on creating them. Management must emphasize asset monitoring as a career path, and it must stop the practice of providing people incentives to create assets without providing them incentives to close them out. Monitoring assets can actually be turned into a source of noninterest income, but not by institutions that think only of creating assets.

Enhancing asset quality really depends on embracing two philosophies: the balance sheet isn't there to be tied up, it's there to be turned over; and the balance sheet isn't there to generate income, it's there to generate business. Assets that are created to be sold will conform to a higher quality standard than those not subject to market disciplines. And, by emphasizing the use of the balance sheet to generate other businesses, the institution will be doing all its business with a better class of borrower.

7.   *Winning institutions will optimize their use of capital.* Under the risk-based capital guidelines which took effect in 1992, capital has become the limiting factor in much of financial services. To complicate matters, there are actually three forms of capital: accounting, stockholder, and regulatory. Regulatory capital determines how much business an institution can do, stockholder capital determines whether an institution will remain independent, and accounting capital is the conduit by which the institution's auditors affect net earnings.

Because it limits the amount of business an institution can do, maximizing regulatory capital is the institution's first concern. Aside from the relatively unattractive alternative of selling common stock, the only ways to increase regulatory capital are retained earnings and monetization of hidden assets. Monetization normally involves the sale of hidden or undervalued assets such as data centers or mortgage servicing. The sale of these assets permits telescoping future income or savings into present value on the balance sheet.

Maximizing the efficiency of regulatory capital involves both asset selection and asset turnover. Asset selection requires that the institution construct its asset holdings in order to generate the maximum net-interest flow from each dollar of capital. Asset turnover requires that the institution utilize the capital markets as a source of liquidity as much as possible, allowing it to substitute other people's capital for its own, while still retaining the servicing responsibility and income.

Optimizing accounting capital requires that the carrying value of assets be managed, especially in light of the proposed FASB requirement that financial assets be marked to market. This requirement, if implemented, would provide incentives for an institution to revalue assets in concert with market revaluations of its liabilities in order to manage its capital and income stream.

Stockholder capital is a function of the market price of the institution's stock, so it is primarily affected by the institution's earnings, both in amount and stability. For that reason, a winning institution will minimize its dependence on principal transactions for income, and strive much more for both execution/processing and advisory sources.

8. *Winning institutions will know how to market their services.* Selling is getting the customer to buy the product, while marketing is getting the product the customer will buy. In adopting a marketing approach, institutions need to keep several things in mind. Markets are made up of customers, competitors, and the institution. Markets are always changing, usually to the detriment of the producer. As markets change, they always segment, and it is the bank's competitors who cause that segmentation. Products always have a predictable life cycle. Customers view products as linked. And the most important ingredient in marketing is good information.

Marketing financial services requires some specialized approaches. Most financial products have a short life cycle, so they must be aggressively promoted as soon as they are introduced, and rapid market segmentation must be anticipated. In addition, there are several marketing strategies which have special appeal to financial institutions.

Target marketing allows the institution to create and aim products for a specific market segment. The information necessary for effective target marketing is often available as a result of the institution's processing business. Conduit marketing allows the institution to offer its customers an array of products far larger than its resources would ever allow it to produce itself. Electronic delivery allows the institution to maintain more frequent contact with a wider range of customers, and allows customers to sell themselves more of the institution's products whenever they want to buy, instead of when the institution is able to sell. And cross marketing allows the institution to turn one transaction into many transactions, not by relying on its employees to detect the opportunity, but by using the banks technology to monitor the customer's transactions, looking for triggers to opportunities.

9. *Winning institutions will manage their financial risk.* Essential to managing risk is understanding that risk is about the unknown, and there will always be some unknowns in financial services. The nature of the unknowns is determined by the nature of the businesses, so risks can be categorized by: the events that cause them, the effect they have, or by the transactions which generate them. The following table shows this categorization.

Transaction	Cause	Effect
Lending	Interest rate	Income
Trading	Credit	Capital
Underwriting	Market	Opportunity
Asset/Liability	Performance	Legal Liability

Identification, while a crucial first step, is only that. The next step is measurement. Because risk is about the unknown, it is not measureable in the strict sense of the word. In this case, measurement doesn't mean an absolute determination of the potential for loss, but a bounding and comparison of the losses an institution could possibly suffer from each event or cause. Measurement allows the bank to compare risks and to monitor them in order to see if its measurement models are conforming to reality.

Prediction, the next step, is subject to the same limitations as measurement in dealing with the unknown. Here, however, modelling techniques can help the institution determine the sets of conditions which could cause significant losses, as well as making some determination as to the possible amount. Most predictive models are designed to go from causes to effects, but the type needed here must be able to give useful, if not precise, results when they are run from results to causes.

Finally, the institution needs to alter some of its business processes so as to manage the risks it has identified, measured, and predicted. Having isolated the uncontrollable causative factors, the institution must manipulate the controllable ones so as to give it the best risk profile. But the most important risk management technique is *monitoring,* determining if uncontrollable factors are playing out as predicted, and determining if the risks are evolving as predicted. Any risk management program, no matter how sophisticated, will fail if it does not have a significant component responsible for monitoring. It was the lack of this component which contributed to the large losses suffered by Orange County, California in late 1994.

10. *Winning institutions control their costs.* As competitive pressures get worse, many institutions concentrate their efforts on reducing costs, often through retrenchment, in-market mergers, and outsourcing. These avenues, while they may reduce costs, might not have much positive impact on ROE, because they might not address the all-important relationship between costs and revenues. The first step in effective cost control is understanding the difference between costs, expenses, and expenditures.

The second step is relating expenditures to ROE, not only new or potential expenditures, but established or ingrained ones as well. Those expenditures that can be directly related to ROE move on to the next step in the approval process, but those where the relationship is tenuous or absent should be dissected carefully.

The third step is making sure that your employees only do what only they can do. Using your people to perform tasks that a machine or your customer should do is wasteful and probably results in a lower-quality service. This step involves business process reengineering, which is covered in detail in Chapter 13.

The last step is structuring acquisitions of fixed assets in the most cost-effective way. Sloppy financing of major expenditures and acquisitions can severely impact their effect on ROE. The tax and accounting treatments of acquisitions and expenditures are so important that nothing significant should be bought or paid for unless the finance unit of the institution has looked at it, not from an approval sense but from a structuring sense.

When we look at the winning strategies, it becomes apparent that there are several common themes which are so important I want to call them out specifically here.

Competition and Winning Are the Name of the Game

In every aspect of these strategies is imbedded the fact that only so many institutions will survive the current consolidation. Being strong, both financially and organizationally, is an absolute prerequisite. Predators may not be the most popular animals in the forest, but they have the best chance of survival. Not everyone loves a winner, but everyone respects a winner.

The Road to Success Leads Away from the Balance Sheet

Strong institutions will get more of their revenue and more of their profits from selling their services and their brains, not from selling their balance sheets. Institutions that use their balance sheets to generate income will lose to those that use their balance sheets to generate business. Employees who are compensated only for creating assets will not generate consistent income and their institutions will not have high P/E ratios.

Winning Institutions Will Build from Strength to Strength

The safest method of building business is to sell more of your current products to your current customers. Next safest is selling new products to current customers. Next safest is selling current products to new customers. Least safe is selling new products to new customers. If you aren't making the most of what you do well, and of whom you serve well, you are inviting your competition to poach in your preserve.

Customers Are Often Happiest Helping Themselves

Whatever your product or whoever the customer, think first of how he can sell it to himself. Self-service and self-sales are cheaper for you, more responsive to the customer, less error-prone, and often perceived as higher quality. The customer who has made himself happy will often thank you for it, and will invariably buy more. All he needs is choice and convenient access.

The Most Underutilized Asset in Financial Services Is Information

In the final analysis, a financial institution's real product is information—processed, enhanced, delivered, combined, and stored. Information is an institution's lifeblood—without it the institution dies. But, like blood, it is often overlooked until something goes wrong. By maximizing the value of this hidden asset, information, a financial institution can put itself in an impregnable position, and eliminate or absorb its competition. Making the most of your information may be the most important winning strategy of all.

III | Making the Strategies Work

As important as a set of winning strategies is, it is only the beginning. Remaining an independent company and winning the competitive struggle require much more than having strategies—they require that someone execute them. Games are won on the field, not in the locker room.

Executing winning strategies requires the commitment of all the institution's employees. Executing requires a constant and strenuous effort on everyone's part, as well as teamwork, where everyone knows not only his or her job but the jobs of those he or she depends on. But most of all executing requires *leadership*.

Over the last 10 or 15 years, leadership in business has been overshadowed by management, to the extent that some people might think that the two words are synonymous. On the contrary, they are very different.

Management focuses on administration, while leadership focuses on inspiration. Management is about budgets and performance plans and personnel reviews; while leadership is about excellence and profits and winning. In the words of the late Navy Admiral Grace Hopper, "You can manage a business, but you must lead people." So the first step in making the strategies work is to understand how to recognize leadership in business. There are four components which make up leadership:

Leaders know where they are going. The first component of leadership is understanding the objectives. It is knowing what is attainable and what is not. It is seeing the market in which the institution sells its products and how that market is evolving. It is having a vision of what the institution can be, as well as what it is.

Leaders know how to get there. The second component of leadership is understanding the mechanics of the business. It is knowing what has to be done and who has to do it. It is knowing what tools are available and which ones the institution will have to make as it goes along. And it is knowing the cost of all the effort, as well as the payback.

Leaders can get others to follow. The third component is variously referred to as communication, charisma, or charm, but it boils down to convincing people that they can exceed even their own expectations. It means getting others to accept the leader's vision of the future, as well as his or her determination to shape it. It means getting employees to rely on each other, cover for each other, and demand the best of each other. And it means sharing the credit for all the leader's accomplishments.

Leaders listen to their followers. The fourth component is the most difficult one for leaders to attain. It derives from the fact that no one is so smart or farseeing that he or she can detect or predict everything. Leaders don't dictate actions, they meld them from the diversity of their people. The best measure of leadership isn't how many good ideas you have, but how many good people you produce.

In implementing the winning strategies, leaders will need to avail themselves of some management methodologies. In Part III of this book, I will examine three of them. The three methodologies are:

Critical path analysis
Strategic alignment
Business process reengineering

11 | Critical Path Analysis

It goes without saying that real success in business is elusive and ephemeral. Few indeed are the businesses and the business people who attain real success, and fewer still are the ones who maintain it over a long period of time.

In financial services, the selectivity of success is more intense, and the absence of success is more penal, than in many other businesses, largely because of overcapacity and the commodity nature of many financial products. Banks and other financial institutions that expect to achieve significant and lasting success will have to overcome more and larger obstacles than companies in many other businesses.

If you doubt that last statement, just take a look at one measure of success, the one the stock market uses: price/earnings ratio. The P/E ratio is the stock market's favorite measure because it treats the past (the earnings) as history, and only reflects the market's view of the future. Companies with high P/E ratios are regarded by the stock market as having a rosy future, while those with a low P/E are not thought to have much of a future. At the end of 1994, *Business Week* published its annual investment survey, which looked at all kinds of investments. The average P/E ratio for the stocks they surveyed was over 20. The average P/E for the banks they surveyed was 10, and the average for the biggest banks was about 8. What the stock market is telling us is that it thinks banking will be a struggle for many years to come.

In that struggle to win, financial institutions will discover that certain factors will be critical. Some will be decisions, some will be events, some will be alliances, some will be products, some will be internal, some will be external, but all will share a common characteristic—they will have an overarching impact on the institution's success. Clearly, one of the first requirements will be to identify these critical factors, and most of this book has been devoted to that.

There is, however, another, higher-level requirement, that of bringing these critical factors together into a successful enterprise. That requirement is often thought of as *integration,* which is defined in *Webster's Dictionary* as "forming or blending into a whole." Although that is certainly part of the job, a much larger part involves making the whole more than the sum of the parts.

That is the job that team sport coaches attempt to do, and that good coaches do effectively. Team coaching involves more than putting the team together, more than assigning positions, more even than coming up with the game plan. It involves getting the most from each player by finding unique ways to motivate him or her. It involves matching players with each other, so that one player's strength compensates for another's weakness. And it involves instilling an intensity and desire that culminates in a stretch drive that puts the game in the "win" column.

In a financial institution, the players aren't always people. In the banking business, people are the first of the critical factors, but there are five more. The six critical factors are:

People
Information
Products
Alliances
Events
Decisions

The Critical Factors

In order to see how the critical factors play together, I have placed them in Figure 11.1. There is no hierarchy shown in this figure because there is none among the critical factors. The essence of these critical factors is that they relate in unstructured, and often unexpected ways. When you have seen how these factors relate to each other, then see how they relate to employee enhancement in Chapter 16, Employee Enhancement as a Competitive Differentiator. But first we will look at the factors individually, and then we will see how they relate to each other.

People

There is no shortage of management literature that emphasizes the importance of people in any enterprise, so it is not my purpose to do that here. Nor will I discuss the kind of people an institution needs, since I did that in Chapter 3. Here I want

Figure 11.1
Critical Factors

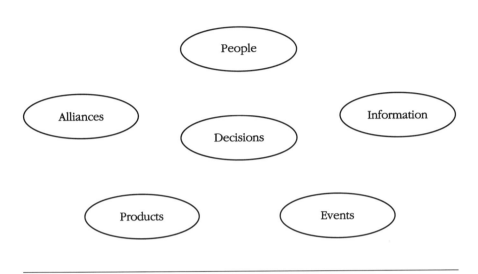

to focus on people in the corporate environment, and how to maximize their value to the corporation.

Assuming that you have hired good people, the next requirement is that you provide them with the tools they need to do their job. That is a simple statement, but it covers a lot of ground. Different people work differently, even when they are doing the same job, so the tools you give them must be flexible enough to make them as productive as possible. That is especially true of computers, which have become both immensely powerful and easier to use.

The next requirement is that you give them an environment in which to be productive. That is often thought of as "empowerment," in which the ability to make decisions is dispersed throughout the organization. Empowerment is a seductive, but dangerous, concept. In organizations where incentive compensation plans, or motivations, are highly compartmentalized, empowerment runs the risk of generating centrifugal competition, so that individual parts of the company are deemed productive, but the productivity is never channeled in one direction, and the better performance never gets to the stockholders.

As I mentioned in Chapter 3, cross-compensation plans can significantly raise the true productivity of individual departments and people. Another method of increasing total productivity is by increasing horizontal and vertical communication. Across all industries, organizations which have above-average performance have above-average communication. But people will not communicate the really important things unless they have the motivation to do so. Building those motivations is a crucial function of leadership.

Information

After people, this is the other major hidden asset of every financial institution. But I must be very precise in what I mean by information. I do not mean the numbers and words stored in the institution's transaction records. These are data and data have almost no value. It is only when data are enhanced that they become information and have value to the organization.

Enhancement can mean many things. Data can be sorted, compared, combined, graphed, filtered, and distributed. *Then* data become information. Throughout this book I have given many examples of data being turned into information to be used in marketing, asset enhancement, income maximization, and countless other ways.

The important thing to remember is that no one can predict the exact enhancement needed to turn data into the information required at a particular point. No one can predict what combinations of data the institution will need to look at, how data will need to be sorted, filtered, compared or distributed. Anyone who attempts to predict how information will have to be enhanced is simply misleading himself and the institution. Thus, flexibility of design in the institution's computer systems becomes paramount. The key to making the most of the critical information resource is its easy availability to the critical human resource.

However, most computer systems are not designed for flexibility. Because of the historical need for rapid access to the massive amounts of data that banks must store and protect, most banking systems have rigid structures, and are self-contained. Such systems are poorly suited to the sharing of information between computers or programs, and to the ad hoc requests for information that the current environment requires. Thus, the systems designers for the finance industry will have to balance the structured needs of the transaction processors against the unstructured needs of the marketers and managers.

Products

In other parts of this book, particularly Chapter 4, I have spent significant time on the importance of products. I covered product planning, product design, and, in Chapter 7, product delivery.

Here I want to look at products differently and to think about them as a collection of attributes, among which customers choose. In this case, the product isn't *what* the customer buys from you, but *why* the customer buys from you.

Of course, customer choices are governed by different things for different business lines, but there are some commonalities within the three lines of business we identified previously.

Execution/Processing

Here the basis for customer choice has been shifting for several years. Previous to this shift, the priorities were low cost, accuracy, and reliability. Now those attributes are assumed by everyone, not evaluated by the customer. The new priorities are access and flexibility. Whether it is an ATM or a custodial service, customers assume it will be accurate, reliable, and low in cost. What they really want is access to more information and the flexibility to do more things with it.

Principal

Here the overcapacity in the finance market has driven spreads and profitability down. Commercial banks have all but disappeared as lenders to large corporations, with the exception of a few remaining leveraged buyouts, and trading profitability has eroded in all of the more established markets.

The trend is toward financial engineering, where transactions are combined, broken down, and reformed so as to respond to the ever-changing financial needs of the customer. New instruments, new versions of old instruments, new customers—they all represent the profitable parts of the principal businesses. But, in order to bring the new products to the new customers, the institution must be able to move quickly and be flexible. Finally, in financial engineering there is increased risk, for both the bank and its customers, so the last, and probably biggest, requirement in the principal product line is a good understanding of the risks involved, by both the bank and its customers.

Advisory

This is the business where information has always played a tremendous part. In the advisory business all you have to sell is what you know. But there is more to it than that; it isn't just what you know, it's what you know that benefits the customer that brings in the fees.

Whatever the form of advice, whether it is portfolio management, corporate finance, personal financial planning, or cash management, success is a result of applying an array of financial information to the customer's individual situation and turning that information into benefits for the customer.

So we can see a pattern developing. To be successful, products must be defined in terms of value to the customer, and most of that value comes from information. The demands of the business require that information be enhanced, and the enhancements require both access and flexibility. And it is the people in the institution who make all this happen.

Alliances

With the resource pressures and demands for ROE that currently assail the industry, and with the limitations on capital and other resources that banks have, the key to winning may well lie in making the right alliances. Many companies in other industries have begun to wrestle with the concept that their success depends in no small way on teaming up with other companies. These alliances can be broadly or narrowly based, very temporary or relatively permanent, rigidly or loosely structured, all depending on the desired outcome.

But, although it is easy to see how important alliances are, it is not so easy to see how to make them work. In fact, several banks have recently found out how hard it is to make an alliance work. One such example is NationsBank, which formed an alliance with Dean Witter, the brokerage firm, in order to allow Dean Witter brokers to sell securities products to NationsBank customers. The alliance did not allow NationsBank executives enough oversight of the Dean Witter brokers, and several NationsBank customers sued the bank when the securities they had been sold declined in value. So, forging a successful alliance, difficult as it is, is extremely important.

The first step in forging successful alliances is understanding clearly what an alliance is expected to accomplish. Many alliances fail because the objectives are either poorly defined or inherently unattainable. The next step is the selection of alliance members. Here the most common mistake is selecting members who have such conflicting corporate cultures that the participants spend all their time defending themselves, and no time advancing the alliance.

The next step is structuring the alliance, so that every participant has an incentive to make it succeed. Proper structuring will prevent the formation of alliances which are doomed for a variety of reasons, one of which might be that the members have different agendas. One such alliance occurs when one member has the hidden agenda of sharing some of the costs of developing a product for its own use, a product that has a limited market appeal or that they might later be disinclined to sell.

Finally, the alliance must be monitored, to ensure that it continues to serve the needs of all participants. This may involve changing the structure of the alliance at some point, to reflect the changed priorities of one or more of the members. It may involve changing participants, if one of the participants drastically changes its priorities, or proves unable to fulfill its commitments. And it may involve terminating the alliance altogether, if it has outlived its raison d'être.

The monitoring function is both crucial and delicate. Most alliances which fail do so because the monitoring process doesn't work, either because everyone assumed that the objectives and incentives of all the participants were cast in stone, or because everyone is afraid to reopen a negotiation process that had been difficult originally.

Events

The term "events" can be extraordinarily vague, but in this context it means things that happen between the institution and the market, with the market made up of the institution, its customers, and its competitors. One large class of events is comprised of things that happen between the institution and its customers, logically called customer events. Another large class of events is comprised of things that happen between the institution and its competitors, and is called competitive events. Finally, there is a class of events made up of things that happen between the institution and its alliance partners, called alliance events.

Customer events are the most familiar ones, but the category is wider than it may at first appear. Obviously customer transactions are included, even though they may only become critical in the aggregate. However, there are other customer events, such as the introduction of new products; modification of old products; changes in delivery methods or emphasis, such as branch or ATM location changes; or marketing events, such as advertising campaigns.

Like all events, the results of customer events are sometimes within the control of the institution. Some customer events depend on other customer events, and some depend on competitive or alliance events, but very few customer events stand alone, especially with regard to their results. However, many banks know little about their customer events and even less about their results.

This is because customer events have another important characteristic—they are often in the hands of the institution's least experienced, and often worst compensated, employees, if they are in the hands of employees at all. Most bank managements are aware that tellers often represent the bank to its customers, just as waiters represent a restaurant or sales clerks represent a store. Astute managements go to great lengths to provide tellers with incentives to represent the bank well, and that is good as far as it goes, but many aspects of customer events do not involve tellers.

For example, 24-hour help lines are usually staffed by part-time employees who may not have a strong feeling of corporate responsibility. Credit applications are often handled by lower-level employees, as are many of the bank's clerical services, like custody. The point is that many customer events occur far from the corner offices where the strategic and tactical thinking is done, and far from those who may think of themselves as responsible for the institution's success.

Competitive events are usually thought of as the chess game of product introduction and pricing that makes up the competitive arena. To use a military analogy, competitors are usually thought of as the enemy, and everyone in the institution, from the generals to the privates, strives mightily for their downfall.

But the military analogy is not particularly apt here, and the institution needs to take a more enlightened approach to its competitors. The first step in that enlightenment is determining exactly who the competition is. If we refer back to Michael Porter's competitive model, we can see that our competition can come from almost anywhere. Other industries and our customers themselves represent two sources of competition which we need to keep an eye on. The fact that banks regarded their competitors as other banks exclusively until only a few years ago is largely responsible for the banking industrys loss of market share.

The second step in the enlightenment is learning about and from our competition. In Chapter 2, I described Professor Liam Fahey's framework for analyzing competitors. That analysis should generate a wealth of information which can be used to improve your own performance, as well as to predict the actions of your competitors. Here again, banks need to concentrate on those competitors outside the bounds of the banking industry. Banks unwillingness to do that is one of the reasons they have been unable to reverse the loss of market share I just alluded to.

The third step is looking for acquisition possibilities among your competitors. The first thought, of course, is the acquisition of an entire institution, but that is only sometimes the best alternative. Another alternative is the acquisition of branches, and another is the acquisition of lines of business. Here again it pays to look outside the banking industry, but in order to do that the bank needs to keep its market valuation, and its price/earnings ratio, high. Remember, the consolidation process will largely consist of the stronger absorbing the weaker, often a piece at a time.

Finally, the competitor can become an ally. This is particularly true when it competes with you only in one market area or business. Many businesses in many industries are forming alliances with competitors, particularly where there aren't enough resources to support everyone in every business. The recent alliance between IBM and Apple Computer is a classic example of two companies that competed fiercely but have come together so that they both can do better. It is also an example of how difficult it can be to make alliances between competitors work.

Thus, competitive events can become alliance events. So, in fact, can customer events. Alliance events have the potential for more benefit, and more danger, than any other kind, because alliances depend for success, not on structure and documentation, but on incentive and motivation. Organizations, and states and people, ally themselves because they have common goals. More and more, in modern business, organizations will have to ally themselves with other organizations to succeed.

But alliances, like politics, are slippery things. Motivations can change, just as politics can change. Markets can change, customer desires can change, regulations and statutes can change, and technology can change. Institutions that enter alliances without a clear and skeptical view of their purposes, or that assume an alliance is forever, or who expect anything but self-interest from all parties, will certainly be disappointed.

Decisions

The last of the critical factors is decisions. Here I am referring only to the decisions made within the institution, not those made by customers, competitors, allies, or regulators. Those other decisions are important, and might be influenced by the institution, but they are too heterogeneous to be covered here.

Decisions are most commonly thought of as being "handed down," implying that they are made at or near the top of the organization, and disseminated throughout. That, too, is a part of the military legacy that haunts the business world. The "chain of command" reporting structure that many institutions incorporate is part of that legacy as well.

But the first thing we can say about the military legacy is that, whether or not it applies, it isn't necessarily being properly implemented, and that comes through clearly in the area of decisions. Military/hierarchical structures are specifically designed to counteract the chaos of the battlefield, where all kinds of decisions have to be made on the spot, far away from the generals or the command post. Those decisions have to be made on the basis of very limited information, and many battles have been won or lost on the basis of such decisions. The military model recognizes that such battlefield decisions are necessary and provides the latitude for them.

That need is very much the same in business. In most organizations, decisions need to be made at all levels of the organization, often on the basis of partial information, and the demands of business are pushing businesses more and more in this direction. The difference between well-run organizations and others is that decisions in well-run organizations are made on better, more complete, information, and with a clearer understanding of the decision's impact. The key to modern business success isn't just pushing the decision point downward in the organization, it is pushing the information and strategies downward as well. Empowerment, the buzzword of the 1990s, will be a disappointment, and will pass rapidly from the business lexicon, if all that happens is a dispersal of decision points. It will represent a business breakthrough if both information and strategies are dispersed as well.

The Critical Paths

Like the winning strategies, the critical factors appear at first to be separate things. Like maximizing noninterest income and enhancing asset quality, people and information have different definitions. Like optimizing capital and controlling costs, events and products look like they have different purposes, and different effects.

However, like the winning strategies, the critical factors are interwoven in the success story of a financial institution. Each of the critical factors relates to the others, but the relationships are essentially fluid and somewhat unpredictable. The problems many institutions experience in dealing with these factors are often a result of trying to relate the factors to each other by a rigid formula.

Let's look at some of the relationships between the critical factors. Since there are 21 of them, I won't deal with them all. I will start with some of the lesser known ones.

Events and Alliances

Although it might not appear so on the surface, there are clear causal relationships between events and alliances, and they run in both directions. Events like customers' rejection of a new product can prompt the institution to form an alliance which allows it to introduce a better product to the market. Or an alliance currently in place which goes awry can prompt an institution to abandon a product or market to the competition.

In general, competitor events can prompt alliances and alliances can prompt customer events. The establishment of an alliance can cause competitors to take action, which can result in a series of customer events, like a price war, or a series of new alliances. The point is, *alliances serve to change the face of the market,* and can either come as a result of one or more events, or can cause one or more events. In the shifting world of alliances, the astute management keeps its eye on the unfolding events.

Products and Decisions

Decisions are normally thought of as the independent variable in the business equation; it is a part of this logic that decisions determine everything else. Certainly that is the conventional wisdom regarding products. (Remember that here I am talking about a product as a collection of attributes from among which customers can choose.)

But products can influence decisions. For example, how many banks have withheld certain investment products, with their attendant noninterest income, from the market because it was felt that they would draw funds away from the retail deposit base? Or how many poor loans were made, with the approvals heavily influenced by the attractive fees offered by the borrower? The fact is, many of the bad decisions banks have made were based on an incomplete or erroneous understanding of their products and their competitors'.

People and Products

The conventional wisdom in a service business is that the business begins and ends with people, that the people are the product. Thus it is easy to conclude that the customer is really buying (or perhaps renting) your people. But financial services customers buy a lot of their products without coming into contact with any of the institution's employees at all. With the advent of direct deposit, ATM networks, and electronic funds transfer at the point of sale (EFT/POS), much, if not the majority, of the actual depositing and withdrawal of funds by retail customers is accomplished without involving the bank directly, let alone an employee. With credit cards and overdraft facilities, the same holds true for a growing portion of retail loans. Finally, with the introduction of the telephone voice response unit (VRU) many customers now communicate frequently with the bank without ever talking to an employee.

The corporate side of the business is becoming equally dehumanized. Many corporate transactions are becoming more automated, like the movement of securities in custody accounts, and the transfer of funds into and out of corporate demand deposit accounts (DDAs). These trends are changing the way the people at a financial institution relate to its products. Instead of delivering the products, the people are designing, evaluating, and overseeing them. Although customers might see less of the bank employee, the employee can see more of the customers, by observing their patterns of financial behavior and how they react to the institution's product offerings. This changing relationship is one of the most important keys to success in the 1990s, but it requires a different kind of bank employee with a different set of skills.

This brings us to some of the more obvious relationships between critical factors.

Events and Information

Events generate data. Deposits, withdrawals, securities purchases and sales, loan takedowns and repayments, ATM accesses, rate changes, money transfers—all these transactions and events in the institution's marketplace make up most of the data it keeps track of.

But these data aren't information until they are enhanced. Patterns in customer behavior, connections between transactions, price elasticities of demand, marketing opportunities—these are simply data, often generated by events, which have been turned into valuable information.

Turning events into information is partly a job for people and partly a job for computers. Computers can remember vast amounts of data, recall data in an almost unlimited number of formats, perform complex math on data, and present the results in tabular or graphical form. But people must decide which data, what format, what mathematics, and what presentation. Finally, and most important, people must determine what it all means. Turning events into information is a challenge for both human and machine, working together, but the results can be spectacular.

Alliances and People

Perhaps nothing has brought more uncertainty to the business world in the past few years than the growth in both the number and complexity of business alliances. This phenomenon has all but taken over much of the industrial world. The auto companies have begun manufacturing cars and parts of cars for long-time rivals. The airlines service each other's planes. But nowhere has the alliance boom been more in evidence than in the technology field.

Software, hardware, and services companies join forces and split up again with confusing speed. Manufacturers who used to make computers out of other people's parts go into the parts business, and parts manufacturers start assembling computers. Arch rivals team up in consortiums to try and establish standards, and then go their own way. As a result, the customer has a huge array of attractively priced choices, but very little way to make those choices work together.

In the finance business, the alliance boom is just beginning, but there are unmistakable signs of it. A classic example of the alliance trend is ATM networks, where banks and thrifts provide competitors with access to their machines in order to stay in touch with their peripatetic customers. Some banks—Citicorp is the most prominent—have resisted the networks, but even Citicorp has joined recently.

The advent of alliances will have a profound effect on the people in the industry—on how they work, on what they do for a living, and on who they might work for. In some cases, alliances will open market opportunities for providers of financial services, creating jobs for some people, and making the jobs of others more secure and lucrative. In other cases, alliances will amount to outsourcing, where an institution buys a product component or service instead of producing it internally. These cases will serve to eliminate jobs and significantly alter how some remaining employees work.

Alliances will also have an impact on how people view their relationship to the organization they work for, as well as to other organizations. In his recent book, *Power Shift,* Alvin Toffler talks about "power-mosaics," referring to the shifting relationships between people and organizations. This is what Toffler says about power-mosaics:

By tracing information patterns in a power-mosaic, we gain a clue to where real power and productivity lie. For example, communication flows might be densest between a parts supplier and a manufacturer (or more accurately between a specific unit of each). The shipping operation of one and the stock-intake operation of the other form, in effect, a single organic unit—a key relationship. The fact that for accounting purposes, or for financial reasons, one is part of Company A and the other is part of Company B is increasingly divorced from the productive reality. In fact, the people in each of these departments may have more common interest in and loyalty to this relationship than to their own companies.

As alliances proliferate throughout the finance industry, the questions of loyalty and interest will become ever more important and immediate. As the motivations and objectives of financial institutions shift, in reaction to changes in market forces, the motivations and objectives of the people in the industry will shift, and there is no guarantee that the institutions and people will shift at the same speed or in the same direction. It is management's challenge to keep those changes under control.

People and Information

This critical path has been under public scrutiny for many years. It has become almost an axiom that people, and the decisions they make, are only as good as the information they have access to.

Countless volumes have been written on the subject of the value of information and how to use it in business. Computer companies, as well as software developers and technology consultants, spend a lot of time educating finance people, especially senior managers, about the importance of information in their businesses.

And yet, few people in the finance industry, especially senior managers, appear to take that education to heart. Financial institutions still process a tremendous number of transactions, generating a tremendous amount of data, without turning much of that data into information, let alone into more profitable business. Given that these senior managers are not stupid or intransigent, why is so much information wasted?

The primary reason is that creative people and computers handle information in different ways. Computers are structured and rigid in the way they handle information. Although a computer can remember a single transaction forever, it can recall it only if asked for it very specifically. If a customer has several accounts with a bank, the computer might not be able to determine that those accounts represent the same person or household or company.

People, on the other hand, handle information in an unstructured and associative way. This approach is ideally suited to leaps of reasoning, but not to remembering details or processing large amounts of information. A person may be able to recognize that the tax laws suggest that credit-card customers pay off their balances from their home-equity line, where a computer could not, but it takes a computer to identify which customers could use that opportunity.

The question is, how do we bring the associative thinker (person) together with the structured processor (computer)? Part of the answer lies in new kinds of software, which make computers appear more like people in the way they operate. But another part of the answer lies in teaching people to anticipate the structured approach of the computer. The meeting in the middle generates tremendous benefits for people and for the institution as well.

Critical Path Analysis

Figure 11.2 shows the same critical factors as Figure 11.1, but here they are connected by a series of critical paths. This illustration represents an abstract reality, and, as such, runs the risk of being misleading, but the concept is powerful. In a nutshell, the concept is that *each of the critical factors has a logical relationship with the others, and those relationships are direct, not funneled through some control point.*

Figure 11.2
Critical Factors

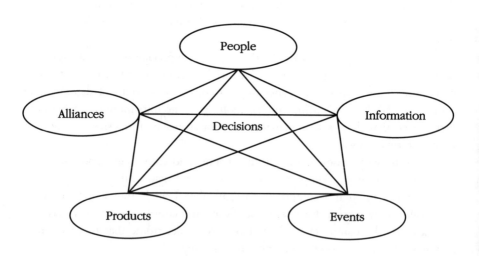

For each institution, the nature of the critical factors will be different, and the critical paths will be different, but here are some rules of critical path analysis.

1. *The correct paths are logical.* Given the institution's strategy and its understanding of its markets, the right relationships between the critical factors have to make sense. If the wrong people are in charge of designing a product, or if the product is being designed with the wrong or missing information, the results will fail. If the wrong people are building an alliance, or if the alliance is set up with the wrong objectives in mind, the relationships should appear illogical. But logic is sometimes a matter of perception, and what may appear logical to someone directly involved with the relationship might appear illogical to someone viewing the matter at arm's length. Thus it is essential that the logic of the critical path be clear to everyone. In many cases, this will require that management commit these relationships to paper, so that they can be looked at by everyone.

2. *Decisions are at the center of the process, but not necessarily at the center of the institution.* Making decisions has become the prerogative of management, the mace and orb of modern business. The more important the decision, the more important the person designated to make it. But that approach flies in the face of enlightened business logic. The prerequisites for making a decision are an understanding of three things: the objectives, the constraints, and the impacts of the alternatives. There is no assurance that management has all those ingredients when it makes a decision, or that management is ideally suited to weigh them.

    The new paradigm of management will be that *the best one to make a decision is the one best suited to do so.* Being suited means having access to the necessary information and having the clearest judgment about the results. And the best "one" might not be a person at all. With the development of expert systems, many decisions can be made by a computer better than they can by a human. Of course, humans are loath to turn anything so critical as decisions over to a mere machine, but the smart humans have begun using computers to check their decision making

3. *The paths must add value.* The only reason to connect the critical factors is that the connection adds value. This may seem obvious, but too many institutions add paths and connections that do nothing to add value, and often detract. This happens most often with people, probably because people are the most plentiful resource in the industry.

    For example, many customer events work better when the institution's people are not involved. Customers often know what they want and are even able to combine products to suit their needs without help. Adding people often makes the process more cumbersome, and less satisfying to the customer. However, there are other paths which may not add value. How many alliances, which didn't serve to enhance the products they were designed for, have been imposed on other products in order to justify keeping them alive? And how many decisions have been based on information that wasn't vital but was readily available and supported someone's position?

Gradually, business is moving away from a maximalist approach toward a minimalist approach. Instead of involving as many factors as possible in every event, business people are learning to involve only those factors that are essential. This refers equally to people, information, allies, decisions, products, and events. Instead of asking, "Should we include this factor?" businesses are beginning to ask, "Do we really need this factor?" That minimalist thinking is the first step toward more efficiency and higher profits.

4. *The paths are not hierarchical.* Just as the arrangement of the factors isn't hierarchical, neither are the paths. Value can flow in either direction, and any factor can have an impact on any other. It is tempting to view both the factors and the paths as hierarchical, with people at the top, but such thinking limits both the value of the factors and the strength of the institution.

For instance, information can be both an ingredient and a result of an event, and both can occur without the interference of people. Products can contribute to alliances and can result from them. Decisions can stem from events and can cause other events. If you want to think of the critical paths in Figure 11.2 as arrows, remember that each one runs both ways.

5. *The paths are flexible.* The key to success in a rapidly changing environment is to stay flexible. The institution that doesn't actively pursue change and doesn't use change as a competitive weapon will find its position eroding. The only thing we know about any successful strategy is that it is already on the way to becoming obsolete.

Although the critical paths have specific implementations, they are in fact a philosophical approach. The idea of identifying those factors which are critical to your success, and the idea that those factors are connected along critical paths, are relatively constant, but the implementation of those ideas will require flexible rules of behavior, flexible relationships, and flexible thinking.

So, how does one integrate flexibility into a corporate structure without losing focus? That is the subject of the next two chapters: Strategic Alignment and Business Process Reengineering.

12 | Strategic Alignment

Over the past several years, there has been a significant change in the leading-edge thinking about management. For about twenty years, from the beginning of the 1970s through the 1980s, the best minds at the best business schools in the country focused on the strategic approach to management. Corporations were urged to have a corporate strategy, often based on target markets, to have a strategic combination of products in their portfolios for those target markets, and to give each business unit a strategy of its own. The common thread running through all of this was the concept of management by objectives.

Although it might not have been expressed this way, the strategic approach was based on some rather important assumptions. One was that the management of a corporation could, to a greater or lesser extent, control that corporation's destiny. That assumption made sense in a time when the United States appeared able to control its own economic destiny, and when economic growth was the order of the day. Plans to grow a business made sense and were easy to implement when demand exceeded supply, and the only problem management had was to produce enough.

However, the economic boom which began at the end of World War II has recently begun to run out of energy. Economic growth in the United States and Western Europe has been slowing for years, and is now down to a crawl. Even the Far East, and particularly Japan, long a wellspring of growth, has started showing signs of a long-term slowdown. Mexico, until recently a phenomenal success story, has not realized the benefits it expected from NAFTA, and only a few countries in South America, most notably Brazil, continue on the growth path. Even the newly emergent communist countries, like Russia and China, have run into growth roadblocks, just a few years after everyone hailed their economic rebirth.

What is important about all these countries is that their slowdowns have started to coincide, no matter what part of the business cycle they were in. Large-scale layoffs are becoming a fact of life from New York to New South Wales, corporate restructurings are announced every day in the business press from London to Hong Kong, and voters are turning the "ins" out from Washington to Rome to Tokyo. It remains to be seen if the Kondratiev business cycle has finally begun to kick in, but there can be no doubt that the economic mood has turned decidedly sober.

Managing in a Stagnant Economy

One of the implications of an economic slowdown is a change in management thinking. Instead of the emphasis being on long-term planning, it is now on survival. Instead of planning for new products and markets, companies of all kinds are thinking more about exiting markets and selling off product lines. Instead of building juggernauts, companies are downsizing, getting back to core competencies, and depending more on alliances. Instead of books on building a well-oiled corporate machine, we are reading books about thriving on chaos.

Is all this just another iteration of the management consultants' *issue de jour*, or has something fundamentally changed? The management facts of life are that difficult times require an entirely different management philosophy than good times do. They are, in fact, much harder. One of the first things I learned when I went to work on Wall Street was, "There is a world of difference between brains and a bull market." Just as traders fall into the trap of assuming that because they were able to earn trading profits in an up market they are good traders, so can businesspeople fall into the trap of assuming that because their businesses prospered in periods of growth they have the secret to management in any environment.

All of the above applies doubly to the finance industry, because it has so much excess capacity. The pressures on profits that are currently being felt by the industrial sector are being felt even more by the finance sector. The general inability of the regulators, Congress, the administration, and the industry to find the right prescription is partly a function of the difficulty of the problem and partly a function of a memory of better times, when the banking system existed in a protected environment.

But the new banking environment is not protected and everyone involved—the regulators, Congress, the administration, and the industry—must act accordingly. Bankers cannot expect help from any quarter. In spite of the passage of interstate banking legislation, and a new Congress that promises to be more sympathetic to business in general, bankers cannot stake their futures on more enlightened legislation or more enlightened regulation; they must save themselves by their own actions.

Strategic Alignment

In such an environment, no resource can be wasted. Every person, every department, every business unit, and every division must work in concert to achieve success. Everyone must have a strategy that shows which road to travel and all the strategies must serve to make the institution a winner. This is the essence of strategic alignment, that all of the institution's strategies must work together to make it a success.

"Wait a minute," you say, "that seems obvious." It may be, but the obvious isn't always reality. One doesn't really think of a bank as being made up of parts working at cross purposes. Whether we are talking about departments like loan production, credit research, and marketing, or about business units responsible for different products, most people imagine the parts working together for the greater good of the bank.

It would be nice if that were true, but most of the time it is not. In all too many cases, the people who work in adjoining departments, either horizontally or vertically, see themselves as having little responsibility for each others success. Part of this phenomenon is due to corporate politics, particularly in banking, where most employees see that there are only so many jobs within the industry, and even a colleague can be a competitor. But part of the cause is bound up in the strategies each department is following.

It is important to note that a strategy is more than a vision—the "Where do we want to go?" part of leadership. A strategy also contains the methods—the "How do we get there?" part. In some cases, different parts of an institution can have the same or similar visions, but quite different methods. In other cases, even the visions can be different. There are often very understandable reasons for these differences, but the fact that the reasons are understandable doesn't make them right.

Let's look at some of these reasons.

Different Market Conditions

This reason applies most often to business units that have products in different market environments. Figure 12.1 is the Boston Consulting Group's market analysis which we saw in Chapter 2. Here, though, we are going to use the matrix to identify the strategy for products in each category.

Figure 12.1
Boston Consulting Group Anaysis

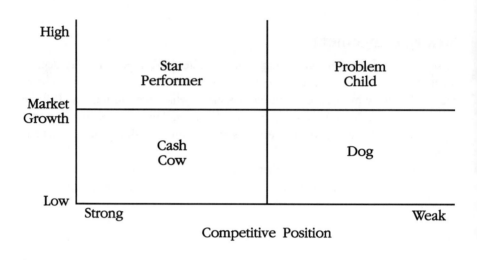

The Cash Cow and the Star Performer

Let's start with the lower-left quadrant, the cash cow. Here the institution will defend its market position to the death. People with a cash cow don't want anyone talking to their customers about anything, especially not about a competitive product. Cash cows are regarded by senior management as funding other product development, so they are considered sacrosanct. Even if the cash cow's customers could be more profitable if they were shown other products, they are often kept in the dark and may feel that the institution is ignoring them.

Many of the older banking products and many of the balance-sheet products fall into this category. Checking accounts, commercial-paper backup lines, securities custody, credit cards, and travelers' checks all fall into this category. Although a few cash-cow businesses are growing, in most cases the growth is slow, and one or two banks have established dominant positions in each market. Not only will they resist competition from outside the institution, they will resist internal competition as well.

In the upper-left quadrant, the star performer is hungry for new customers. He's not thinking about protecting turf, he's looking for markets to conquer. In most cases, people with star performers know that the window of opportunity is limited, and that someone will establish a dominant market position soon. When that happens, it may be too late to for those who miss the boat, so the star performer isn't about to let anyone stand in the way of success, and senior management, knowing how important the star performer is to the bank's future, may be his biggest cheerleader.

In banking, the star performers are likely to be newer products, and those which generate noninterest income. Mutual funds, corporate cash-management services, financial engineering, securitization, and even travel services are the kinds of things which are, or soon will be, star performers. These are the kinds of services that visionary management sees as the key to the industry's future, and the kinds of services that customers welcome enough to pay well for them.

So what happens when the cash cow and the star performer collide? What happens when the aggressive salespeople from the mutual-fund department start siphoning off deposits from those checking accounts? What happens when the financial engineers show the corporate treasurer that he or she really doesn't need that commercial-paper backup line? There is a clash of strategies, followed by a heated argument in the executive vice president's office, followed by one side or the other being instructed to step aside. It doesn't take too many such confrontations before the institution becomes polarized between the star performers and the cash cows—or between the hotshots and the good old bankers.

The Dog and the Problem Child

In the upper-right quadrant, the problem child needs lots of attention and that usually means money. Problem children always have lots of promise and success always seems to be just around the corner, but some problem children never seem to mature. In the lower-right quadrant, the dog is just hanging on. Perhaps this was a cash cow whose market has gone into a decline, or a brand new product that will never make it before the market passes it by, but the prognosis isn't good. The problem is that both the dog and the problem child demand scarce resources.

What to do? The logical step is to eliminate the dog. Sell the product, close the department, and free up the resources. The problem is, there are people in that department who have made a commitment to that product, and they have a strategy for making it a success. Not to mention the customers the product has gathered, even if they are relatively few, as well as the commitments that might be left to honor.

And does the institution redirect the resources to the problem child? What if it never pans out; will those resources, generated by killing off the efforts of a department, be wasted? On what grounds does such a decision get made? Since success lies in the future for both products, how does the institution determine which should live and which should die?

In all instances where strategic differences come from market differences, the resolution is largely a function of market analysis. However, that market analysis *must be done from the point of view of the customer, not the institution, and it must incorporate the kind of competitor analysis that I covered in Chapter 2.* It must answer questions like: Which product would the customer pick, if given a choice? In which direction are customers moving, and how fast? And, finally, what are the customers likely to be offered by my competition?

That last question is the key to resolving market-based strategy differences, because the one sure bet is that, if you don't satisfy customer demands, both current and emerging, someone else will. The old marketing adage is that it is better to compete with yourself than to let someone else do it for you. If you think the logical conclusion to this reasoning is that you must cannibalize your own successful products, you are absolutely right, and you have made a leap of reasoning that few bankers can acomplish. All companies which enjoy long-term success in competitive situations have learned to cannibalize their successful products; it remains to be seen if bankers can learn how to do it.

Different Perceived Functions

The age of corporate specialization has left us with departments, within all kinds of companies, which appear to have no functional relationship to each other. In a manufacturing concern, for example, certain departments are charged with the responsibility to develop new products, others to sell them, others to produce them, others to deliver them, and other to keep track of the rest. Within those departments, people may feel that they have no stake in the success of another department, a feeling which can be exacerbated by competition among department heads for promotion within the corporate pyramid.

This kind of psychological separation can also be exacerbated by compartmentalized measurement and compensation schemes. Departments which are measured by minimizing financial risk may not feel much incentive to maximize customer satisfaction. Those who get paid to keep costs down may find themselves at odds with those who get paid to keep sales up.

This kind of contention has been thought to be healthy for a corporation, just as a system of checks and balances has been thought to be healthy for our federal government. The problem is, contention fosters parochial thinking and that fosters conflicting strategies. In the end, these conflicting strategies will make the company less successful, not more.

A particular form of functional-strategy misalignment relates to the use of technology. For many years, the purpose of a financial institution's computers was to process transactions and keep the bank's records. That meant the so-called "data processing" department was a cost center, charged with processing the data at the lowest possible cost. In addition, partly because the information in the computers was so sensitive, and partly because technology had gotten so complex, the computer departments insulated themselves from most of the other parts of the institution.

Over the last ten years, an institution's ability to compete—in fact, its ability to win—has been a function of its ability to turn data into information and information into money. The problem is, the information is the responsibility of one department and the money is the responsibility of another. In many cases, the people who take care of the information have little or no knowledge of the environment in which the people who make the money work. Not too surprisingly, the people who make the money often know little about the people who handle the information. A natural outgrowth of this separation is a polarization between the money,—or business—side of the organization and the information—or technology—side. Because making money is what it is all about, the primary result of this separation has been the growth of an entire set of computer systems controlled by the moneymakers, or the "users."

In many financial institutions, this separation has led to technology strategies largely unrelated to, or at odds with, the business strategies. In the winter 1991 *Business Quarterly,* Professors Jon Henderson and N. Venkatraman wrote about this issue in an article entitled "Understanding Strategic Alignment."

In the article, the authors propose a strategic alignment model, which deals with the relationships among four components: business strategy, organizational infrastructure and processes, information technology (IT) strategy, and IT infrastructure and processes (Figure 12.2). The authors point out that relationships that run along the vertical axes (strategic fit) are more common in the business environment than those that run along the horizontal axes (functional integration), and that both these relationships are much more natural than those that run along the diagonal axes (cross-dimension alignments).

On first examination it is easy to understand how the business strategy could impact the organizational infrastructure and processes, but it is startling how often those two business components are out of alignment. I will say more about that later in this chapter. It is also easy to understand how the IT strategy (if there is one) could impact IT infrastructure and processes, but here, too, the relationship is less frequent in reality than in theory.

However, some of the functional integrations are at least as apparent, and perhaps more empirically evident than the strategic fits. For example, the advances in computers (IT infrastructure and processes) have been known to affect the way individual jobs get done (organizational infrastructure and processes) for years, and the business strategy clearly affects the IT strategy for many institutions.

However, the cross-dimension alignments represent breakthrough thinking for many people in the finance industry. The idea that changes in hardware and software capabilities could impact an institution's business strategy, while appearing logical in the abstract, is almost unheard of in practice. Even rarer are the instances where changes in the business strategies of an industry have caused hardware and software developers to change courses on products under development.

Figure 12.2
Strategic Alignment Model

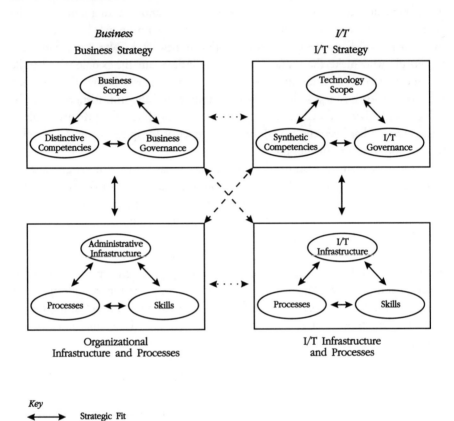

Henderson and Venkatraman then identify four ways, or "perspectives," in which these strategies are often related in the real world. They are:

❏ *Strategy Execution*—where "a business strategy exists and is the driver of both organizational design choices and the definition of IT infrastructure."

❏ *Competitive Potential*—"essentially a strategic management process that explicitly considers how IT may be used to enhance strategy and ultimately enable transformation of the organizational infrastructure."

❏   *Service Level*—"this view focuses on the ability to deliver IT products and services to the organization."

❏   *Technology Potential*—where "the focus is now establishing strategic fit for IT."

As you look at the authors' strategic alignment model, the subtle but profound wisdom is that the arrows run in both directions. In other words, any of the four strategies can each have an impact on any of the others. In winning financial institutions, understanding that simple fact alone can add millions to the bottom line.

Different Organizational Levels

Nothing has contributed more to a loss of corporate focus than the stratification of the corporation. Organizations in which people at different levels are thought to have different missions, different frames of reference, and different compensation systems should expect a wide divergence of strategies across those different levels.

Like vertical compartmentalization, horizontal stratification appears to have a grounding in good business sense. In both cases, the foundation rests on specialization, the economic theory that traces its beginnings back to Adam Smith's *Wealth of Nations*. The idea is that people produce more when their responsibilities are narrowed. People who install carburetors should install carburetors, those who sell should sell, and those who arrange financing should arrange financing. It all makes good logical sense.

That same concept has found its way into the hierarchical structures of corporations, including financial institutions. The perception is that the people at the lowest level of the organization have the narrowest impact and those at the top have the widest. The people at the bottom have the least complex jobs, and those at the top have the most. The jobs at the bottom have the smallest impact on profits, and those at the top have the largest.

Somewhere in that last paragraph, a warning bell should have gone off in your head. By the bank following this line of thinking, it is easy to see how the people at the bottom of the organization could conclude that they live by a different set of rules than those at the top. It is easy to see that the ground-floor dwellers might march to a different drummer than the folks in the penthouse. (To understand how powerful an impact this thinking can have on a bank, read Chapter 16, Employee Enhancement as a Competitive Differentiator.)

There are several factors which contribute to the impression that there are large inherent differences between the top of the organization and the bottom. First, there is compensation. Almost universally, as you move up the corporate ladder the incentive part of the individual's compensation package gets larger and more dependent on profitability. This is one of the main reasons why many lower-level employees have the feeling that their jobs, and the way in which they do them, have little or no impact on profits.

And yet, that is completely at odds with the truth. Most of the customer contact is handled by lower-level employees. Most of the sensitive processing is handled by lower-level employees. And there are so many more lower-level employees that, although any one of them may not have a large impact on the corporation's profits, taken together they are crucial. In fact, if all the lower-level employees did their jobs superbly and the senior management stayed home, the institution would probably make a lot more money.

But knowing how to do their jobs better is almost impossible, because of the second factor, the fact that strategies are imposed from the top down. What is much worse, because business-unit strategies stem from corporate strategies and because departmental strategies stem from business-unit strategies, most strategies are written to be read by the person above the author, not the people below. The words and sentiments in a strategy are often a reflection of the words and sentiments of the boss, not the words and sentiments of the customer. As you move down in the organization, getting further from the boss, the strategies look less and less like the corporate strategy, until it seems to disappear entirely.

But it would be a fallacy to assume that at the lower levels there is no strategy at work. Down where the rubber meets the road—where the company meets its customers, and its competitors—there certainly is a strategy at work. It just might not be the same one that is in the notebook on the shelf in the chairman's office.

This misalignment between the abstract strategy at the top of an organization and the concrete one at the bottom represents both a threat and an opportunity. The threat is that the institution will meander through the market, without a clear focus on its business (or perhaps many clear focuses), losing momentum and market share to competitors. The opportunity rests in the fact that a proper melding of the two approaches often represents a powerful competitive weapon.

For example, by combining the teller's practical knowledge of the customer's changing desires, and the platform officer's knowledge of the shifting landscape of the market, with the chairman's vision of where the institution wants to go, the different levels of an organization can build from each other instead of clashing or diverging. If the de facto strategy which those on the firing line have adopted can be combined with the de jure strategy from the corner office, the combination can be extremely effective. If, on the other hand, a strategy is pushed down from the top, it runs the risk of not only disappearing, but of casting management's credibility in doubt.

Loss of Contact with the Market

One of the reasons there can be differences across organizational levels is that the strategy adopted by all levels of the bank can be out of line with market conditions. Most bank managements would bridle at the suggestion that they would devise a strategy that was at odds with the market, but it is more common than you might think.

Generally, corporate strategies begin with a mission statement referring to providing the best quality banking services, while maintaining profitability. There isn't much chance that the mission statement would be out of alignment, but there isn't much substance in such a mission statement either. It is when the institution gets more specific that the strategy has more value, but that is also where the alignment problems with the market surface.

The first alignment issue often arises in selecting the target market. Whether it is retail or wholesale customers, or it refers to geographical concentrations, the target market must need the things the institution does well. In addition, the target market must be the right size for the institution, and the competitive structure must be conducive. There are lots of examples where financial institutions chose to target market segments that needed a different product, or a different delivery method, or were well-enough served by another institution to make market penetration almost impossible. For example, a bank which has a well-developed branch system, with friendly tellers and platform officers, but not much of an ATM network or EFT/POS network, would probably not find much success targeting the yuppie market, but there are plenty of examples of banks who have tried.

Another market issue has to do with covering customers across most, if not all, of their needs. The breadth of coverage can apply either to geography or product. Trying to service a customer by offering a narrow product range could lead to frustration for both the institution and the customer. Both individuals and businesses tend to combine transactions, and often want service across those transactions from the same firm. Retail brokerage firms have responded to that desire by combining stockbrokerage with money-market mutual funds, financial planning, and even insurance.

On the wholesale side, investment bankers have combined corporate finance, trading, merger advice, and even portfolio management, in order to keep the corporate customer in-house. The banking industry must provide, as much as regulation will allow, a comprehensive package of financial services, even if it must deliver some of those services through alliances. The same holds true geographically. On a global basis, most large U.S. banks have been retrenching recently, abandoning foreign markets to the local banks, in an effort to conserve capital. These retrenchments may appear to strengthen these institutions in the short run, but they only serve to weaken the banks' hold on their corporate customers over the long run.

Finally, alignment with the market can be lost if the institution doesn't stay in close touch with its customers. At first glance, that sounds obvious. Staying in touch is what the branches and wholesale sales force are supposed to do. But staying in touch means more than saying hello in the teller line or calling on a company and asking for business. It means keeping tabs on their fortunes, as individual customers and as an industry. It means knowing when the profit dynamics of their business changes. It even means learning what your competition is doing by hearing it from the customer. And it means turning all this intelligence into better products, better delivery systems, and even better strategies.

Aligning the Institution's Strategies

Knowing if an institution's strategies are out of alignment is the first step in the process, and knowing why is the second. The third step is bringing them into alignment.

As important as aligning strategies is, however, there is a larger underlying issue; the relationship between a written strategy and the actions of the people who are expected to follow it. There are countless instances of strategies in existence, especially at the business-unit level, which appear to have no bearing on how people do their jobs. When this is true, it makes no difference how apt or aligned the strategies are; they might as well not exist.

In most cases, the primary reason for this discontinuity relates to the way people are compensated and, to a lesser extent, how their careers advance. If a written strategy stresses providing a quality service and growing the unit's business, but the management gets compensated based on near-term profits, it shouldn't surprise anyone if strategic projects with extended payoffs get short shrift. If the written strategy addresses running a lean organization, but people tend to get promoted and paid based on the sizes of their fiefdoms, management will tend to act as if the written strategy never existed.

A particularly common case of this kind of discontinuity occurs when the written strategy incorporates cooperation among business units, but compensation packages are determined by the performance of each unit separately. This compartmentalized kind of compensation system has the effect of encouraging internal competition among business units. Competition of this type isn't inherently bad, but it can be counterproductive when the success of the institution requires cooperation. In such cases cross-compensation packages, which allow employees to be compensated for helping other units be successful, can often bring the strategy and the actions rapidly back into alignment.

Specific Methods of Strategic Alignment

Focus the Strategy on the Customer

There is a strong tendency when you are running a business to focus the strategy on the needs of the business. That kind of focus leads to product-oriented and misaligned strategies. For example, a strategy to be the lowest-cost processor of credit-card transactions, or to be the most profitable foreign exchange trading desk talks about what the *institution* derives from its achievements, but not what the *customers* derive from it. In addition, the needs of each business unit will differ somewhat, so internally-focused departmental strategies are almost certain to be out of horizontal alignment.

On the other hand, strategies which focus on the customer will probably be aligned across multiple lines of business, as long as the customer set is the same. Thus, a strategy to enhance the profitability of corporate customers through improved financial management, or to enhance the financial position of retail customers, contributes to a customer focus that will make subsidiary strategies more consistent.

Of course, since a strategy is more than a mission statement—it is a whole series of specifics—the focus will have to be maintained as the management makes the strategy more granular. As strategies become more specific, there is ample opportunity for their focus to change from the customer to the business, so management must be vigilant for signs that the pressures of running a business unit are changing the strategy focus from the customer to the business.

And the pressures will surely be there. It is difficult for bankers in the heat of the competitive battle to equate customer service with profitability, but history has shown that delivering a high quality, on-target offering is the best way to make money. Even in highly competitive markets, customers will differentiate between service providers based on quality. But what if that isn't the case? Most often, if the market appears not to respond to a customer focus, the product in question is in the declining part of its life, and the real opportunity is in replacement products. Only a strategy focused on the customer will allow you to take advantage of those opportunities.

Design the Strategy as a Working Guideline

It is easy to find the corporate strategy in most financial institutions: it is on a shelf in the chairman's office. And it is easy to find the departmental strategies as well: they are in the offices of the executives who oversee the departments. Such corporate strategies are often the result of an expensive management consulting engagement. The consultants present the strategies to the board of directors, and perhaps to the management committee. Everyone nods agreement, and then they get on with business.

Periodically, senior management instructs departmental management to prepare their own strategies, to be presented to the management committee. Miraculously, the departmental strategies are a reflection of the corporate strategy, sometimes word for word. Management nods agreement, and everyone gets on with business.

But very often no one who meets the customer in the marketplace has ever seen the strategy, has had any input to it, or buys into it. The people on the firing line are usually too busy dodging incoming artillery, or keeping the enemy off the ramparts, to worry about something as distant as a strategy. And besides, whoever wrote the strategy obviously never had to work on the firing line.

Does that sound familiar? If it does, you need to think about how you formulate your strategies. Are they designed to be read by the management committee, or by the mail room? Do the strategies enumerate lofty corporate goals, or do they address the real problems of doing business? Here is an acid test: *Could you take your strategies to a teller, or a note clerk, or a receptionist, and have them understand what is expected of them?* If so, you have good reason to be proud. If not, perhaps you need to reformulate the strategies.

Make Sure Your Strategies Reflect the Realities of the Marketplace

There is something very American about reaching for the stars. Somehow, we think that if we set lofty goals, perhaps unattainable ones, we will try harder, do better, and surprise ourselves with our success. In the business world, however, establishing excessively optimistic goals often engenders a very different result.

When the employees see a set of goals put forth by management which appear to be more a dream than reality, their first reaction is often not determination but despair. Setting revenue, profit, or market penetration objectives that would take a miracle to achieve doesn't usually stir up enthusiasm; it usually stirs up resentment.

Management must set goals that are clearly attainable, with open-ended incentives for exceeding them. With this kind of structure, the effort level actually increases when the bar is passed, instead of flagging.

There is a positive side to this issue. Strategies that recognize the institution's strengths and its competition's weaknesses are a powerful stimulus to effort and accomplishment. When management is cognizant of its weapons, as well as those of its competitors, it can allocate resources where they do the most good. Everyone knows the adage that success breeds success, but there is another truism which must be just as old: soldiers fight harder when they think they outnumber the enemy. Entering the fray when you think you are at a disadvantage can occasionally produce extraordinary effort, but it most often produces a retreat.

Make Sure You Use All Your Resources

Winning the competitive struggle is difficult enough when you are wearing all your armor and are carrying all your weapons; to try it half-armed is foolhardy. The strategy you design, the products you offer, and the market segment you target should all make the most of your strengths.

In doing this, it is important that everyone be as objective as possible about the institution's resources. In terms of people, reputation, culture, and tradition it is easy to assume that "we are better than those guys across town," but what *you* think is much less important than what the *customer* thinks. This is one place where the competitor analysis that we outlined in Chapter 2 can pay handsome dividends. The kind of steely-eyed examination that analysis requires goes a long way toward making sure you have an objective view of your resources.

And some of those resources might not be so obvious. One that is often overlooked is information. By processing a blizzard of transactions every day, a bank gets a look at a blizzard of data—about itself, its customers, and its competitors. It must turn that data into information about where its retail customers use their ATM cards and where they use their credit cards. It must see which of its corporate customers have positive cash-flow and which do not. Of course, it takes some work to determine all that. Whether or not you actually look at it is up to you.

By implication, another resource is the bank's technology. The computers and the software that banks use to run their businesses range from antiquated to state-of-the-art. As a result, systems can range from being a competitive engine to being an anchor. In order to align the strategies, it is necessary to know your own technology, of course, but your strategies can be much more effective if you know your competitors' technology as well.

If you know that your statements are virtually error-free, while your competitions' are late and prone to mistakes, there is a strategic opportunity to emphasize the quality of your retail account products.

If you can determine which are the top 10 percent of your customers in terms of cash flow through their accounts, and you can relate their average credit-card balance to their home-equity line, you can offer them financial management products no one, not even their stockbroker or insurance agent, can match.

Finally, one of your most powerful resources is your processes. That's right, the way your institution does things can be the kind of resource that has a huge impact on strategic alignment. If your processes are properly designed—efficient, flexible, and timely—they will lead you into the right strategies. But how do you know if they are properly designed and how do you redesign them if they aren't? That's the subject of the next chapter, Business Process Reengineering.

13 | Business Process Reengineering

In the last decade of the twentieth century, no line of business will be more competitive than banking. There will be no industry in which profit margins will be narrower, no environment which will be harsher, and no workplace which will demand more of the worker. The rule for survival in banking is simple: *You will have to process twice as much business through the same-sized balance sheet with half as many people.*

And yet no industry appears less able to grapple with these conditions. For hundreds of years, banking has been a matter of taking money in one window and lending it out another. For hundreds of years the image of a bank has been the branch, with a line of tellers along one wall, and the platform officers along the other. Many years ago they had celluloid collars and dipped their pens in inkwells. Today they wear button-down collars, and tap away on keyboards. But, other than that, not much has changed.

The fact is, banks will never make it simply by accelerating the same work. Whether it is in deposit accounting or portfolio management, whether the people are tellers or traders, whether they have a corner office or a cubbyhole, doing the same thing with half the people is not the answer. Pushing the same papers, generating the same reports, and filling out the same forms are all examples of the real problem with the industry—by and large, the processes have not changed with the market demands.

That is not to say that a lot of time and money hasn't been spent in the name of "efficiency." Somewhere in every bank is at least one study of work flow, showing literally hundreds of ways in which things could be done faster and perhaps more accurately. Millions of dollars have been spent on computers and software, in some banks equipping every officer and teller with a personal computer, and probably linking those computers into some sort of a network. In many ways, banks can now be looked at as well-oiled machines.

What Is Reengineering?

The problem is, the machine is still doing the same old job. Officers and tellers use their personal computers to do the same things they used to do with pen and paper: look up account balances, enter debits and credits, record payments, and so forth. Every morning someone from the "data center" probably sends out a bunch of electronic reports, which chronicle yesterday's transactions, overdrafts, balances, and perhaps the profitability of the branch. And every morning, people all over the bank bring those reports up on their screens. Everywhere one looks in the bank, people are busy with their computers.

But what are they doing? And much more important, why are they doing it? For that is the key to reengineering the finance business. In the July/August 1990 issue of the *Harvard Business Review,* Michael Hammer published what is now regarded as a watershed article entitled "Reengineering Work: Don't Automate, Obliterate." In it, he points out that "heavy investments in information technology have delivered disappointing results—largely because companies tend to use technology to mechanize old ways of doing business. They leave the existing processes intact and use computers simply to speed them up."

What Mr. Hammer is getting at is that all our business processes must be adapted to the demands of the market and to the capabilities of both people and technology. The way he puts it, "Reengineering strives to break away from the old rules about how we organize and conduct business. It involves recognizing and rejecting some of them and then finding imaginative new ways to accomplish work." That definition is fine, as far as it goes, but reengineering is still in its infancy, so it probably doesn't go far enough. For our purposes, let's say that reengineering is *redesigning and reworking our business processes so as to maximize attainment of our business goals.*

There are several important words in that definition. The first is "redesigning," because it implies that our processes were designed in the first place. But, according to Mr. Hammer, "Many of our processes were not designed at all; they just happened." As a business was built, needs arose. They were dealt with on an ad hoc basis, and the work got passed along from person to person as the demands of the moment dictated. But that no longer suffices. Just as manufacturing processes have to be designed to be effective, so do business processes.

The second important word is "reworked." Redesigning a business process is challenging and perhaps intellectually satisfying, but it has no value unless the process itself is reworked. For a couple of reasons, which I will discuss later, reworking processes is not nearly as satisfying, or as much fun, as redesigning them.

The third important word is "maximizing." Redesigning and reworking processes are not only hard work, but dangerous. All changes involve some risk, and wholesale changes involve big risks. Unless the new process is designed to maximize something, its eventual success will be a hope instead of a probability or a certainty. Furthermore, maximizing something by changing a process assumes that there is a relationship between the process and that something, that you know what the relationship is, and that you can determine how much you have improved the something. None of those assumptions are trivial.

The last important word is "goals." Everyone in the organization needs to know what the business goals and strategies are. In the last chapter, I discussed keeping those strategies in alignment. In this chapter, I will discuss how to move closer to the institution's goals by re-engineering its processes.

What Is a Business Process?

The first step in reengineering is understanding what it is you are working on. In manufacturing processes, the definition is usually relatively straightforward, but that isn't quite so in business processes. As a working definition, let's use *a series of connected business events that occur for the purpose of accomplishing an objective.*

Once again, there are several important words in the definition. The first is "series," which implies that a collection of things is done, probably one after another (although several could, and perhaps should, happen simultaneously). By this definition, one event isn't a process; several events that are connected (a series) constitute a process. The second key word is "events," which can cover a wide variety. Events are normally thought of as occurrences caused by people within the organization, but we will need to expand that concept to cover people outside the organization, as well as occurrences not caused by people. Another key word is "connected," because the way in which the events are connected is a crucial aspect of process reengineering. Finally, the word "purpose" indicates that there is a reason for the process, if not for each event, which means that each event will have to be judged in light of that purpose.

I'm comfortable with that definition, but it leaves one question unanswered: Where does the process begin and end? Depending on how all-encompassing we make the purpose, we could be facing a relatively small process or essentially everything the organization does. Defining the beginning and ending points of the process is much more than a philosophical exercise. In most business situations, events and processes are heavily intertwined and dependent. Choosing an inappropriate point as the beginning or ending of the process can render the reengineering effort invalid, either because it doesn't account for events that occurred before and weren't reengineered, or because it makes no provision for its effect on later events that are dependent on it. In other words, reengineering a single process in the middle of a larger business is like changing one line of code in a large computer program. Your work may look fine to you but when you turn on the machine, hold your breath!

Understanding Processes

Clearly, the first step in reengineering a process is to understand what the process is, and there are three levels on which that understanding can occur. The first is procedural, the second is strategic, and the third is financial.

Procedural Understanding

Procedural understanding requires that you know exactly what happens in the process. This is normally thought of as codifying, on paper or electronically, the events that occur and how they are connected. Who does what, from whom do they get the necessary ingredients, and to whom do they deliver the product of their work? Who depends on whom and how long does each event take? Perhaps most important, how long does the process take between events, when essentially nothing is happening?

There are two ways to approach procedural understanding. The *transactional approach* treats each event in the process as if it were a process of its own. Each event has a "vendor" who supplies what is necessary for the event to occur and a "customer" who accepts the result of the event. On the other hand, the *flow approach* treats each event as part of a continuum. In this approach, the "vendors" enter the flow at various points (but especially at the beginning), and the "customers" take delivery of output at various points (but especially at the end). Within the process, all the events are regarded as inseparable parts of a flow.

Each of these approaches has its advantages and disadvantages. On the plus side, the transactional approach makes very clear where the hand-offs are, the extent of the periods between productive events, and the justification for each step. On the minus side, this approach runs the risk of obscuring the impact of the process as a whole, the synergy of the events, and the part the process plays in the institution's strategy. The flow approach makes much clearer the impact and strategic fit of the process as a whole, which is how many outsiders view it, but it makes it more difficult to determine the value and dependencies of the individual events. In the end, the best approach is probably a combination of the two.

Strategic Understanding

Strategic understanding is the method by which you determine what strategies, if any, gave rise to the process, what the strategy of the process itself is, and how that process aligns itself with the institution's or the business unit's overall strategy. It involves asking certain questions: Why did we begin doing this process in the first place? As the process has evolved, has it kept pace with changes in the underlying strategy?

In addition, what strategies governed the design of the process? Why do people, and perhaps machines, do what they do? What do people think they are accomplishing?

Finally, how does this process advance the business unit and the institution as a whole? Does this process serve to accomplish our goals, and does it fit with the way we want to do business? Is it a reflection of a corporate culture in which we are comfortable, and is it appropriate for the market environment?

Financial Understanding

Strategic understanding begins to tell us whether the process needs reengineering, and perhaps gives us clues regarding how it needs to be reengineered, but the necessary final step is financial understanding. This step recognizes that there is a financial aspect to every process. There is a cost and a benefit, whether you look at the process transactionally or as a flow. Some costs are fairly obvious, such as the salaries and occupancy expenses of the employees who perform the functions, but there are other, less obvious, costs as well. Processes which delay the receipt of revenue, for example, must carry the time value of that money as a cost.

Attributing a financial benefit to a process is often more difficult than attributing costs. Processes that result in a deliverable to a customer generate a measurable revenue, but perhaps not all that revenue is attributable to that process. Attributing revenues is a common problem in determining the profitability of various parts of an institution, since every part will attempt to claim as much of the revenue as it can. The simplest method of revenue allocation is a pro-rata method, based on costs, so that each event has a pro-rata "profit." Unfortunately, this allocates the most revenue to the most costly events, which might fly in the face of the whole idea of process reengineering.

A final method of financial understanding is to price the performance of the process by a third party. This provides a cost benchmark, as well as some input as to the financial efficiency of the process. In some cases, adjustments will have to be made for the fact that an outside entity would perform the process differently, perhaps better, or perhaps worse.

Assessing the Process

Up to now we have been on a purely fact-finding mission; now we must apply some judgment to our findings. In other words, after understanding the process, we must assess it. We must determine whether it is essential, efficient, and well designed. The result of an assessment will be a determination to eliminate a process, reengineer it, or leave it alone.

Assessment requires that we make comparisons and judgments. We need comparisons because we need standards against which to judge, and we must make judgments because we must make decisions, even if the decision is to do nothing. In order to make decisions, we need a methodology to ensure that we are making the decision with all the information we can accumulate.

The first step is to determine *necessity*. At its most basic, necessity refers to the process itself. The question is, should we be doing this process at all? But we need to be more objective than that. We need to ask, would our customers or stockholders notice if we never did this again? Lots of other groups might notice, but those are the two that really matter. Processes that don't impact either the customer or the stockholder are clearly candidates for elimination.

One example of such a process is the entry of securities-movement information by employees of a bank's custody or safekeeping department. Many such departments receive securities-movement information by telephone, telex, or fax. Upon receipt of the instructions, employees enter the information in the control program, which issues the instructions to send or receive the securities.

Several major custody banks have begun installing data-entry terminals in the offices of the major money-managers who execute the trades that result in the securities movement. Now, as soon as a trade has been executed, the customer enters the information directly, bypassing the bank's employees. Not only is the process cheaper, it has fewer errors, and customers regard it as being of higher quality, because they have direct access to their securities-movement information. Thus, determining that this process wasn't essential improved both the banks performance and its customers.

At another level, the necessity question revolves around who performs the process. Here, the institution wants to know whether customers and stockholders would be better off if someone else performed it. In many cases, this kind of question is already being asked. Mortgage servicing, credit-card transaction capture, and mutual-fund accounting are three examples of processes that many banks farm out, often without their customers or stockholders needing to know about it.

The assessment of the necessity of performing the process must be objective, but it is more than a financial decision. There are lots of opportunities to be subjective about how well an institution performs a process, especially if the institution competes heatedly in that arena. That is why it is essential to get an outside opinion regarding whether the process might better be done by someone else.

However, there are good reasons not to base that assessment completely on performance benchmarks. One reason is that other processes may depend on this one, and if you farm out this process you might be less able to perform another one. An example would be the outsourcing of mutual-fund sales, which could leave the bank less able to provide financial-planning information or advice to its customers. Another reason is that some processes keep you in contact with customers, and farming out those processes can sever your connection with the source of other business. An example of this would be the sale or outsourcing of mortgage servicing, which gives another financial institution, potentially a competitor, free access to your customers. In the end, however, the institution can often find examples of processes that it currently performs which are better performed by someone else.

Another aspect of assessment is determining whether a process is *efficient* and *well designed.* Efficiency refers to whether the process accomplishes as much as possible for the resource used, and design refers to how well it fulfills the banks objectives. In order to make both assessments, we need to depart from an understanding of the process to an understanding of the objectives.

Like processes, objectives come in a variety of forms, depending mostly on whose they are. Individuals have objectives and so do departments, business units, and institutions. As we found out about strategies, objectives can vary within any of these groups. So the first step is to let everyones objectives surface.

The diversity of objectives within even a small process may surprise you, but it will probably go a long way toward explaining those aspects of the process that appear irrational. In many cases, objectives will be expressed from the point of view of management or some other department. "We produce this report because the credit department needs it," or "We assemble this information because the manager began asking for it six years ago."

A better method of expressing objectives is in terms of the two constituencies you serve, the customer and the stockholder. When departments and employees have to couch objectives in those terms, obvious inefficiencies and design flaws surface. For example, it makes no sense to say, "We receive money-transfer instructions by telephone and process them manually because our customers don't want to enter the instructions themselves."

On a larger scale, departmental objectives are at least as prone to misapplication as individual ones. In Dr. Hammer's article, he cites a now-classic example of reengineering for the Ford Motor Company's accounts-payable department. The department employed about 400 people to keep track of the paperwork generated when Ford ordered parts, when the parts were shipped, when they were received, when the bill for them was received, and when they were finally paid for. Based on what was being done, one could surmise that Ford's objective was to produce paperwork.

When Ford took a close look at the objective, it determined that it should be *to obtain the necessary parts and pay for them in the most efficient way.* Based on that objective, Ford designed a process that captures the payment information when the parts are ordered. This information is stored and is searched when the parts arrive. When the receiving department matches the ordering information to the receiving information, it authorizes payment for the parts. By matching the process to the objectives, Ford reduced its accounts payable staff from 400 to five.

Reengineering the Process

With a clear understanding of the objectives, the institution can begin to reengineer processes. This is where the job really gets ticklish. You have now embarked on making changes, some of them sweeping, which can make or break your business.

Now the the novelty has worn off the process-reengineering game, some of its negatives have begun to surface. Professor Hammer has publicly said that approximately 70 percent of all reengineering projects fail to deliver bottom-line impact, which means that, in the most objective analysis, they failed altogether. For a program which arrived with such high hopes, that is a very bad statistic. Professor Hammer has several explanations for this failure rate. I have summarized a few among them: 1) failure of senior management to publicly throw its weight behind the effort, 2) hidden resistance in the ranks of middle management, 3) using reengineering as a sub-rosa way of introducing downsizing, which prompts those who would be downsized to work against it, and 4) scoping the reengineering effort so low that it can never achieve the expected results.

When you look at them, all of Professor Hammer's reasons revolve around achieving (or not achieving) universal support for the effort. There are, however, many more reasons why reengineering fails. One has to do with the institution's programs for enhancing employee performance, which is covered in Chapter 16, Employee Enhancement as a Competitive Differentiator. Another has to do with organizational resistance to change, and this is covered in Chapter 15, Productivity^2 and Power in a Changing Bank. Another has to do with processes which cross department lines, where the departments strategies are out of alignment, and these are discussed in Chapter 12, Strategic Alignment. Whatever the possible reasons for failure, here are some guidelines for succeeding in the reengineering process:

1. *Design the process as if you were a customer/stockholder combined.* As you wend your way through the levels of processes, it is easy to lose sight of the purpose(s). However, the common themes running through everything the institution does are service to the customer and value for the stockholder. Sometimes those themes synergize and sometimes they conflict, so you will have to balance them. The most effective way to do that is to take on the role of a customer who is also a stockholder. In that role, you can effectively ask yourself, "What would I like the bank to do in this situation?"

For example, look at the process of processing retail-loan applications. For current customers of the bank, that process is almost universally frustrating since it involves filling out forms with information the bank already has. From the stockholder's point of view, the process of collecting information is essential in order to manage the credit risk, but the reactive, versus proactive, process most banks use doesn't do a particularly good job of collecting that information.

What both the customer and the stockholder would applaud is a process that minimizes the time spent collecting credit information, but maximizes the value of that information. In addition, the stockholder would value a process that proactively selects the best credit risks.

The solution is a process that uses credit screening as a marketing tool. By determining the profile of the ideal retail credit customer, and then selecting those current customers who fit that profile, the institution can prescreen the customers to whom it will offer the loan first. The customers appreciate not having to fill out forms, and the institution can maximize the kind of assets it wants to originate, at a relatively low marketing cost. Both the customer and the stockholder come away from the reengineering feeling better.

2. *Think of each component of the process as having a cost/value dichotomy.* In every process you will use components: people, information, communications, equipment, etc. Each of those components has a cost associated with it. It obviously costs money to employ people and buy or rent equipment, but it also costs money to send and receive communications, as well as obtain and store information.

The objective is to get the most value from every component. We often think of this requirement in terms of getting the most from employees, or perhaps from computers, but the requirement applies to all the other components as well. If you are sending information from one office to another, are you getting the most value from the communications component? Are you communicating all the right information, or only part of it? Are you communicating the same information in several ways? Are you sending it by the most efficient method?

Here is a simple example of that. Fax machines have proliferated because they are convenient. They are used to send information, both intercompany and intracompany, much to the delight of the telephone carriers. However, if you carefully watch two fax machines at work, you will see that the receiving machine spends a great deal of its time printing, during which time neither machine is receiving or sending data. However, the telephone lines are in use and being charged for during the process. Think about how much money is wasted if you use faxes for intracompany communications versus E-mail or some other, more efficient process.

The reengineering process will require you to evaluate the cost/value dichotomy for all of the process components, and to design the process so it maximizes the overall value received from all the components. In some cases that will mean purposely receiving lower value from one component, which might have a much lower cost, in order to maximize the value from a costlier component. Sometimes it is worthwhile to represent graphically the cost contributions of each component to the process in order to see obvious disparities in the cost and usage of components.

3. *Most modern processes extend beyond the enterprise itself.* In an age when alliances proliferate, and when the connection between the institution and its customers must be closer, thinking about a process as entirely internal is a great mistake. Institutions which expect to win the competitive struggle will have to forge alliances of many kinds, and will have to forge close links with many kinds of customers. In some cases, entities who are customers for one process will be allies in another.

This approach, known as intercompany process reengineering, is one of the most powerful tools and one of the most difficult to perfect in the bank's reengineering arsenal. By reengineering another company's processes so that they work better with the bank's own processes or products, the bank greatly enhances its marketing efforts and can often shift much of the risk and cost to a customer, vendor, or alliance partner. But make no mistake; this form of reengineering is more difficult. The bank has no direct control over many of the people in the process, many of whom have different agendas and objectives, and another company will be reaping many of the visible rewards. In the end, though, intercompany process reengineering will become the new standard for forming business alliances.

As I said before, alliances are by necessity impermanent relationships. Time will change market dynamics, entities will restructure and change strategies, and both regulations and accounting can be expected to change. As a result, processes that have rigid implications about alliances and/or customer relationships will require constant reengineering, with constant disruption as a result, unless a certain amount of flexibility is built in.

For example, capital and accounting pressures have provided banks with incentives to originate loans for sale, as opposed to originating loans for retention. In order to facilitate that process, open communication between the originating bank and the purchasing entity will have to be established. However, the information to be exchanged can be sensitive, so safeguards will have to be arranged to protect the borrower. In addition, more than one purchasing entity will probably be involved, so borrower information may have to be shared. As long as the customer and the stockholder are being served, the process that does that will work.

But change is a fact of life, and the bank may occasionally want to shift its relationship from one purchaser to another. Thus, there will need to be clear guidelines on who owns the customer-credit information, who originates future business, and who has rights to the information resulting from past transactions. Extending such a process beyond the walls of the institution has tremendous potential, but it also carries significant risks.

4.   *The most difficult component to reengineer in any process is people.* Although a good job of process reengineering will be applauded by the institution's customers and its stockholders, it may not be applauded by all of its employees. Even in the best of times, employees dislike disruption. They are most comfortable and contented when the job goes on as before. So, a group of process reengineers is not necessarily what the employees want to see.

In the banking business, this feeling is exacerbated by the fact that there are still too many people in the business, and there isn't enough growth forecast in the business to absorb them. Thus, in banking the process reengineer is universally regarded as a hatchet person, who has come to eliminate jobs. It is difficult to get cooperation from a group of employees who regard every question you ask as the prelude to a pink slip.

And don't make the mistake of assuming that this psychology applies only to lower-level employees. One thing to consider—there are too many managers in banking. As processes become more streamlined, and as fewer employees are needed to perform them, fewer managers will be needed to manage employees. In fact, fewer executives will be needed. It is not too difficult to see reengineering coming to be regarded as the culprit in a growing pool of unemployed bankers.

It is important in dealing with this phenomenon to be as open and objective as possible with the employees involved. If it is an unavoidable fact that banks will have to reduce employment in order to survive, there are two ways to do it. The most common has been to reduce the employees and keep the processes essentially unchanged. That concept is now universally discredited as a method of survival. As the service quality fails, customer satisfaction falls off, customers depart, and another round of layoffs is mandated.

The second way is by using process reengineering as a method of downsizing. In this way, the institution can accomplish something more than reducing head count. It can make the remaining personnel more productive. The only way people in the banking business can earn more money is by becoming more productive, and that will require reengineering. It's a little like going to the dentist. No one likes to do it, but fixing a toothache, however unpleasant, is far better than just waiting for the pain to go away.

IV | Succeeding in a Changing Environment

Throughout this book you can see the underlying factor of change in the banking business. Whether it is consolidation, the financial needs of customers, the rules of the business, the channels of communication, or the design of products, change is everywhere in the business, and it is accelerating.

Many books and articles have been written about business change in the last five years, ranging from half-time oratory about getting in there and winning through organizational schema like matrix management to academic analyses of the process of organizational change itself. Much of this literature is exploratory in nature, the sort of "thinking out-loud" that probably has some real nuggets in it if you can extract them. Some of it is breakthrough thinking, but not necessarily all that applicable to the banking business. And some of it is just plain rubbish, churned out to capitalize on a popular topic and a difficult ongoing problem.

In the last part of this book, I will discuss four issues of change within the banking business, and postulate some ways of dealing with it.

Chapter 14, Looking beyond Branch Automation, addresses the perplexing issue of the branch as a retail-delivery channel. The orthodox wisdom in banks is that branches are unsuitable as a channel—too expensive and out of line with customer preferences. But that thinking doesn't explain why two of the most successful nonbank financial institutions in the United States, Fidelity Investments and Charles Schwab, have been opening branches all over the country. This chapter looks at the driving forces in retail banking and derives a possible approach to making branches into the engines of retail of retail business.

Productivity[2] and Power in a Changing Bank, Chapter 15, addresses one of the reasons why organizational change has been hard to effect in almost every business, but particularly in banking. It utilizes a four-box matrix to examine the relationship of productivity and power within individual employees and within organizations, and draws some conclusions about how management can enhance an organization's change capability.

Employee Enhancement as a Competitive Differentiator, Chapter 16, looks at the perplexing issue of how banks can differentiate themselves from other banks and nonbanks, what are the influences of employee performance, and how the enhancement of employee performance can be incorporated as a permanent part of the bank's corporate culture.

Chapter 17, Making a Merger Work, addresses the apparent lack of success in many of the in-market mergers which the industry has seen over the last several years, particularly when measured by the price/earnings multiples of the merged banks. It identifies the important tasks necessary to a successful merger, and discusses some ways to make sure they are accomplished.

14 | Looking beyond Branch Automation

There is probably no subject which has received more coverage in the banking press, or more attention from bank managements, than *branch automation*. Virtually every banking publication has had articles that list the advantages of branch automation and branch-automation products. Numerous market research studies invariably show that a preponderance of banks expect to commit significant resources to branch automation over the next several years. Not unexpectedly, those plans have generated a lot of offerings in the area of branch automation products.

But there is something vaguely unsettling to many people about the concept of branch automation, and it begins with the words used to describe the concept. Automation itself began on the shop floor, as a method of increasing the productivity of manufacturing workers. Its early manifestations involved the mechanization of repetitive tasks, and necessitated the replacement of people with machines, which in itself gave automation a bad name. As a result, one upshot of the automation wave was a rebellion by the shop-floor employees, which led, among other things, to the union movement which swept American and European industry.

But automation has certainly had its advantages. In manufacturing it initially allowed the mass production of *standardized products* at low prices, and then allowed the mass production of *customized products* at low prices. Years ago Henry Ford could make any kind of car, as long as it was a black Model T; today Ford Motor Company assembles a dizzying array of cars on one assembly line, as computer-controlled parts come together at the right spot as if by magic. However, the nature of the work the people on the assembly line do hasn't changed much. Although manufacturing automation has made great strides in becoming a customer-focused process, it has not yet become very employee-focused.

Automation in Financial Services

The concept of automation is at a very different stage in services than in manufacturing. The application of automation is a much less mature science in services, so it is more often being used to produce standardized offerings than customized ones. In services the people are pretty much the product, so automation has to be applied in a different way.

It would be best at this point to define branch automation. As with most business concepts, there are really two definitions—the ideal and the practical. The ideal definition is "the redesigning of the business processes which occur in a branch so as to make them more efficient for both the customer and the employee." The practical definition is "the incremental improvement of branch processes which reduce both cost and customer waiting time." The ideal definition is most often used by bank managements and technology vendors, while the practical definition is most often used by branch personnel and, if they were asked, customers.

The problem with this approach to branch automation is that it doesn't adequately address the changing nature of retail banking as a business, the changing market for retail-banking services, and the changing structure of retail-banking institutions. If branch automation is viewed within the microcosm of a branch, it makes sense. If it is viewed within the macrocosm of the retail financial-services industry, it may not. In order to understand the pivotal role of the retail bank branch, one has to look beyond branch automation to the business of retail banking as a whole.

The Foundations

The first step in understanding retail banking is to bring together some business fundamentals, some *foundations* of the retail-banking business. Although some of these facts have been covered in other parts of this book, in this case we will look at their impact on the bank branch.

1. *Banks are losing market share in their traditional businesses to other kinds of financial institutions.* On both sides of the balance sheet, banks have been losing retail market share (as well as wholesale market share) for years. On the liability side, the banks' share of the retail transaction-deposit business has been falling into the hands of mutual funds, credit unions, and brokerage money-market accounts. In addition, their share of savings and time deposits has also been falling. On the asset side, all kinds of asset holders have been making inroads into the banks' turf. Among the many reasons for this erosion are the banks' cost structures and their lack of flexibility in responding to changing customer demands.

2. *Consolidation in the banking industry will probably not lead to higher base profits.* Contrary to popular belief, there is no empirical evidence that the current consolidation of the banking industry will lead to higher profits in banking's traditional businesses. In fact, my research supports the argument that as a banking system consolidates, net interest margin falls about twice as fast as overhead does, putting increased pressure on profit margins. That leaves nontraditional income sources as the main hope for maintaining profitability.

3. *Customers tend to regard large banks as unfriendly and unresponsive.* The overwhelming body of evidence, gathered mostly from mergers of small banks into much bigger ones, shows that customers who perceive a difference between the service quality of small and large banks feel that larger banks are less responsive and not as easy to do business with. Not only do market observers see this, bankers do as well, which explains the number of de novo institutions which have been set up by former employees of merged small banks. It also explains the immediate market appeal of those de novo institutions.

4. *Branch automation, and technology in general, have not been perceived as adding to profitability.* At bank after bank I hear the refrain from management that the money spent on technology hasn't done a thing for the bottom line. This is a part of a larger debate about what, if any, improvements there have been in services productivity, but to bankers it strikes very close to home. A large part of this issue is understanding that technology does nothing about the market conditions under which an institution operates. If an industry has excess capacity and margins are being forced down by competition, automation may only serve to keep the profit shrinkage from being even more drastic than it would otherwise be. However, there is a legitimate question as to whether the current incarnation of branch automation will make a significant bottom-line difference to a majority of banks.

5. *Branch personnel regard themselves as especially vulnerable to the downsizings that result from mergers and consolidations.* Customer service and morale are a function of not only perceived job security but perceived job importance. In virtually every in-market merger, the management and the press focus immediately on the closings of redundant branches and the resulting reduction in workforce. As long as the branch employees do not see themselves has having a significant impact on profitability, they will think of themselves as pawns in the consolidation game, and customer service will suffer.

The Conclusions

Each of these foundations might look like a separate issue, but, when they are viewed as a part of a total picture, they allow us to draw some conclusions about retail banking as a business. All of these conclusions relate to the difference between being *customer-focused* and being *product-focused*. The definition of customer-focused is that you know as much about your customers as you do about your products. If you know more about your products than your customers, you are product-focused.

1. *Generally, banks have been more product-focused than customer-focused.* This is not an especially startling conclusion, because most businesses are product-focused, and they become more product-focused as their business matures. The more competitive a market is, the more customer-focused the businesses in it become. For a long time, banking was an uncompetitive business, and, although it is rapidly becoming more competitive, it is still a lot less competitive than other businesses.

2. *The larger a bank becomes, the more product-focused it becomes.* This conclusion may not be intuitively obvious, but my observation of banks from both the inside and outside shows it to be true. The primary reason has to do with the control that is necessary to run a large organization. When any organization exceeds a certain size, the structure necessary to keep all its parts moving in the same direction forces the organization to turn inward. This fact is readily apparent in most of our major corporations, such as IBM, GM, Sears, and AT&T. In many cases, very large organizations have taken one of two approaches to dealing with this issue: either decentralization or retrenchment.

3. *Customers are more attracted to a customer-focused institution than a product-focused one.* This conclusion *is* intuitively obvious, but its implications may not be. Product-focused companies think a lot about selling things, while customer-focused companies think about satisfying customers. Product-focused banks measure quality by internal standards, while customer-focused banks measure quality by customer standards. In a product-focused bank, the employees feel that *they* are the reason *you* are there. In a customer-focused bank, the employees feel that *you* are the reason *they* are there. Customers can tell the difference.

4. *The current implementation of branch automation is often a good incarnation of product focus.* To the extent that branch automation is the streamlining of typical product-focused branch functions, it is the reinforcement of product-focused thinking. To the extent that the purpose is to speed up customer transactions, it is all about productivity. To the extent that it is about getting

the customer out of the branch quicker, it acknowledges that he or she doesn't want to be there in the first place. Of course, most bank managements would protest that this isn't how they view the business, but it might very well be the way branch personnel view the business.

5. *Branch personnel will become more valuable, to the bank and to themselves, only to the extent that they become more customer-focused.* In this arena, the difference between product-focus and customer-focus may be subtle, but tremendously important. Product-focused employees view customers as potential buyers of a product, while customer-focused employees view produc ways to satisfy customer needs. Product-focused employees are smiling ones you see seated beneath the banners advertising cial products, while customer-focused employees are inv   . with the customer, perhaps at the customer's place of h   g out how to deal with his or her financial needs.

Odd as it may seem, the customer-focused empl   are the ones who get the customers to buy more products. They are the ones who generate longer-term multiproduct relationships with customers. By knowing as much about their customers as they do about their products, they generate more value for both the customer and the bank.

6. *Investments in technology will only pay off when they help personnel become customer-focused.* This issue is much more complicated than it first appears, and only part of the complication relates to technology. The rest of the complication rests with measuring productivity. In particular, it is extraordinarily hard to measure services productivity and the contribution of technology to it. Clearly, a great deal of work still remains to be done in understanding services productivity, but the feeling that advanced technology has done little to promote productivity is so pervasive that we have to give it some credence.

Technology, by itself, contributes nothing to profitability. Machines don't make money, people make money. There is a saying in the computer business (not often repeated within earshot of the computer buyer) that advanced technology will allow a well-managed company to grow faster, and a poorly-managed company to go broke faster. But what is less obvious is that technology is a wasted resource if it only enhances your product focus.

If your computers are used only to determine the profitability of your products or branches, they contribute almost nothing to increasing that profitability. If they simply allow your employees to process business faster, they may do nothing about getting more of that business, or the right kind of business. It is only when your technology allows you to give your customer better service, or when it allows you to reach him wherever he goes, or when it allows you to learn more about his needs, that it really starts earning its keep.

The Concepts

From these conclusions it becomes apparent that successful retail banking has to adopt a different paradigm from the "large bank with lots of interchangeable branches" concept. The new paradigm must make both the branch and its employees customer-focused, which means making the bank's technology customer-focused. And, the incentives to do this must come from the bottom up, not the top down. This all gives rise to new concepts about retail banking. Although these concepts appear revolutionary, they have in fact been proven by some very profitable retail banks.

1. *The fundamental business unit of the retail bank is the branch.* This concept says that the driver of retail-banking profits is not a product department but the branch. It says that profits don't come from developing new products but from getting new customers. And it says that the business model of a retail bank isn't a large business with numerous outlets, but a group of small businesses with a common back end.

2. *The defining denominator of the retail branch is its customers.* This is perhaps the most revolutionary concept of the lot. Branches tend to be defined by their location, or by their balance sheet, but not by their customers. Thus, the success of a branch is often measured by the number of transactions done in the branch, or by the volume of loans and deposits on its balance sheet, instead of the volume and quality of business done by its customers, wherever in the bank that occurs. As a result, branch management is often disinclined to offer profitable financial products to its customers because these products will drain balances from the branch.

3. *The branch has to be organized so that its personnel view the branch as a small business.* There is no doubt that the productivity of branch personnel is a major problem for many banks. It is a well-documented fact that workers in any business tend to be more productive when they have a stake in the success of the business. This is one reason why management buy-outs almost always arrange for an equity interest in the company for its employees. The same business sense applies to services businesses, and especially to financial-services businesses.

    Under the right branch structure, each employee will be able to see clearly that his or her efforts have an impact on the success of the branch. It is

important to understand that the measures of branch success, and their relationship to the measures of individual success, must be essentially the same
across the branch and at all levels of the organization. This means that incentive-compensation plans which focus exclusively on individual or small-de-
partmental performance are likely to result in centrifugal efforts instead of
cooperative ones. Pooled compensation systems or cross-compensation systems are more likely to generate the team efforts necessary to make a branch
a success.

4. *Branch profitability is the best measure of a branch's success as a business unit.*
    Perhaps the most troubling aspect of establishing the branch as the primary
    business unit is attempting to measure its success. If branches are thought of
    as cost centers, their measure of success is likely to be some version of cost
    control. If branches are thought of as retail outlets, success is likely to be
    measured in terms of traffic, or volume of transactions. If they are thought
    of as balance-sheet entities, success is likely to be measured in terms of bal-
    ance-sheet size, such as the volume of loans and/or deposits.

    However, if a branch is thought of as a business unit, then the appropriate
    measure of success would be branch profitability. Although that might be an
    alluringly simple concept, its realization is not nearly so alluring, or so sim-
    ple. Because of the risks inherent in banking in general, and lending in
    particular, bank managements are often loath to give branch managers the
    kind of latitude that is necessary in order to manage to a profitability stand-
    ard. However, the demands of the retail banking market are such that the
    winning financial institutions of the future will have to solve that dilemma.

5. *Branch profitability will have to be a function of the business that its customers
    do throughout the bank.* In order to maintain and enhance customer-focus,
    branch personnel must focus on every relationship the bank has with the
    customer, no matter where in the bank it occurs. One way to accomplish
    that is to measure branch profitability on the basis of customer business, no
    matter where in the bank the customer interacts. Obviously, such an ar-
    rangement carries its own set of issues. For example, how does one branch
    provide incentive to another branch to go out of its way to serve its cus-
    tomer? Or how do product organizations, like credit-card departments,
    measure their success with customers? These problems will all have to be
    addressed.

6. *The best model for addressing all these issues is probably a modification of the
    structure that has worked for Marriott, MacDonald's, Ford, and CBS.* The ideal
    structure for dealing with the demands of modern retail banking will allow
    the branch the freedom necessary to respond to its local market conditions

while affording the bank the necessary control to manage its business. Although such conflicting demands appear new to the banking business, they are common problems in retailing, as well as the hotel business.

These businesses have evolved the franchise system to meet their market needs. Individual outlets are independently owned, but are tied to the parent organization by a franchising agreement. The agreement gives them an exclusive representation in a particular geographic area, in exchange for adherence to standards established by the parent. The profitability of each outlet is a function of its relationship with its own customers, and outlets often follow sharply divergent marketing strategies, but the public often views them as relatively homogeneous parts of a larger whole.

The Issues

Thinking about retail banking this way, while potentially beneficial, opens up a Pandora's box. Specifically, there are issues relating to control over risk that bank managements feel they must have; to potential and implied changes in organizational structure; to regulatory requirements; to internal accounting; to stockholder valuation. All of them will have to be addressed if banks are going to stop their long decline as retail financial institutions.

These are some of the major issues to be resolved in going beyond branch automation.

1. *The branch needs to be able to track the business its customers do with the bank, wherever in the bank it occurs.* Account numbers are often assigned by the business unit, so the branch might assign a customer an account number for traditional banking relationships while the trust department might assign its own account numbers for trust accounts. Active customers who do business with many parts of a bank might have account identifiers in all those areas and no common identifier for the bank as a whole.

    This problem is particularly difficult for banks which have disparate processing systems for the various parts of their business. Checking account records might be on an older, mainframe-based system with a flat-file structure, while the mutual-fund account records might be on a newer, client-server system with a relational database. The bank might think that it is too risky or too expensive to scrap the checking-account system, which is doing an adequate job for its purpose, because it doesn't integrate well with a newer system that supports a much smaller, although more profitable, business.

2. *The accounting system must be able to recognize the branch as a profit generator, and handle cost accounting in that way.* Cost accounting is a well-defined

science in manufacturing businesses, but it is more of an art in services businesses. Because so many services costs are "soft," assigning them appropriately under a traditional structure can be difficult. For example, the costs of credit-risk management, which are extraordinarily important to the health of the organization, may not find a welcome, or perhaps even justified, home in any of the bank's profit centers.

In the examples of franchise-based organizations I used earlier, much of the cost allocation is accomplished through transfer pricing. That approach can work in parts of the banking system as well, as long as the pricing is done at market levels. However, because cost accounting tends to have a large impact on incentive-compensation plans, management should take extra pains to ensure that the accounting system encourages the activities throughout the organization that management and the stockholders want.

3. *The change in focus, process, and structure needs to be accomplished in a controlled, cost effective way.* Under the best of conditions, fundamental change in an organization is difficult to accomplish. When an industry is under profit pressure, the risks of change are compounded. As a result, this kind of corporate transformation must be accomplished in a multistep, multiyear progression which uses early benefits to pay for later efforts.

Figure 14.1 shows such a multiyear plan to transform a retail bank. The first step is the establishment of baseline measurements to determine effectiveness and profitability. Each bank must choose the measurements appropriate to

Figure 14.1

	IMPLEMENTATION		
	Year 1	Year 2	Year 3
Funciton	Branch process reengineering and employee training	Branch-to-branch and branch-to-parent linkages	Corporate-wide structures, incentives and technology
Benefit	Cost reduction and customer retention	Business growth and product positioning	Branch and corporate profitability

its market and strategy, but there is no shortage of measurements to choose from. The first year's efforts are focused within each branch, and are tailored to generate measurable benefits in both cost reduction and customer retention. The efforts in the second year are focused on the connections between the branches and other entities; these efforts generate benefits in terms of business growth and product positioning. (Proper positioning increases the profitability of products by increasing the hit ratio and decreasing marketing and sales expense.) Efforts in the third year are aimed at enterprise-wide transformations, including structural changes, incentive compensation programs, and changes in base technology.

4. *Branch personnel need to be able to concentrate on customers, not on products or processes.* This is perhaps the most difficult transition to accomplish, because it requires a change in the way people approach their jobs. Much of this change has to do with how comfortable the branch's employees are with their knowledge of products and processes. When they are knowledgeable and are confident of their knowledge, they can concentrate on the needs of customers and how those needs can be addressed. When they are less knowledgeable, they tend to spend more time and effort making sure that they get the right product or process. In the end, this issue revolves partly around training and partly around incentive systems. The bank can provide part of the answer, but also the employees must provide part. I have covered this issue in more detail in Chapter 16, Employee Enhancement as a Competitive Differentiator.

5. *Bank-wide incentive systems will have to reflect the branch-based structure.* This focus on the branch as a business unit will require many parts of the bank to change their incentive programs. For example, support functions within the bank will have to have some portion of their incentive plan reflect their ability to serve the customer through the branch connection, and some portion reflect their own profitability. In order to reflect proper pricing and profitability, various departments may have to "sell" their offerings to the branches at cost plus a departmental profit margin. In other cases the branch may have to pay an internal "commission" to units which perform a function, or specified units may have to pay a "commission" to the branch. Here, as well, creativity will stand management in good stead.

6. *The connection between the branch-based structure and bank profitability must be obvious to everyone, especially the bank's stockholders.* One of the biggest problems with the modern corporation is the lack of connection between individual and departmental efforts and the overall results of the company. The commonly heard refrain is, "Everyone made his profit targets, but the company as a whole didn't."

This often occurs because of overlapping and overcounting of revenues and the underallocation of costs. In order for the branch-based structure to work for the bank and its stockholders, such under- and overcounting must be eliminated. In addition, a portion of most incentive compensations must be a function of the overall performance of the bank.

There is no doubt that these issues are real and that they will require a concerted effort to solve. They are solvable, and working through them may be the most important work retail bankers do over the next few years. Not only will bankers' futures depend on it, their banks' futures will as well.

15 | Productivity[2] and Power in a Changing Bank

One of the most frequently discussed topics, in the boardroom as well as in the newsroom, is the evolution of organizational structures in response to rapidly changing market and economic conditions. And yet, as constant as external change is, corporate change remains extraordinarily difficult to accomplish, even in situations where it is clearly warranted. Virtually every banking executive can point to his or her own experiences regarding personal resistance to organizational change. Among the many reasons why banks appear resistant to change is one which has to do with the relationship between *power* and *productivity* in any enterprise. Understanding that relationship is an important component to enlightened management.

Defining Terms

In most banks, the concepts of power and productivity are poorly defined, and even more poorly implemented. And yet, both power and productivity play a major role in determining both how successful a bank is and how well it adapts to a changing environment. Thus, our first step should be a clear definition of what we mean by the terms power and productivity, particularly because they are often ambiguous or misused.

Power means the ability to command resources, whether those resources are financial, temporal, or human. It is the ability to spend the bank's money, to hire and fire people, and to allocate their time. There are two kinds of power within banks, visible and invisible. In most banks, visible power comes with a set of trappings, including compensation, perquisites, title, and prestige. Invisible power comes largely from affiliation with or influence over those with visible power. As an illustration, bank presidents have visible power, and their administrative assistants or advisors have invisible power.

Productivity has traditionally meant output per work-hour; the concept of "getting the widgets out the door." Output is usually measured in either physical or financial terms. That concept has a major flaw—it does not usually recognize the changes in quality that accrue to a product over time, meaning that productivity gains are often understated. In addition, because output can have many meanings in services, the concept of output per work-hour has a difficult time dealing with productivity in services. For example, an engineer might be thought of as producing engineering plans or new products, so his or her productivity might be thought of in terms of more plans or better products. However, in this case I will assume that the definition of productivity has been agreed to for a particular business, and refer only to the improvement in such output, which I will call *productivity^2*, or the productivity of productivity. At the risk of mixing mathematical metaphors, this might be called the first derivative of productivity. This distinction is important because academics and business observers routinely confuse the concepts of productivity and improvement in productivity. Productivity^2 is both a contributor to and a product of change.

In every bank, every participant exhibits both power and productivity^2 to some degree. Power can range from very little, in which the person must obtain approval to make even the smallest commitment on behalf of the bank, to almost absolute, in which no one within the bank is in a position to question the person's decisions. In recent years, banks have attempted to move power down the organizational structure and spread it over a wider number of participants, in a process known as empowerment. Although empowerment is a worthwhile objective, some recent empowerment efforts have foundered for one of two reasons: either the employees weren't given the tools with which to make the proper decisions, or intermediate levels of management were reluctant to surrender control.

Productivity^2 is also exhibited in degrees. People exhibiting the lowest levels of productivity^2 can be antagonisitc to change, whether it comes from within or without. These are the people whose watchwords are, "If it ain't broke, don't fix it," or who express the view that, no matter how bad the situation looks, the bank will weather the storm and get back to the "good old days." At the other extreme are people who actively seek to improve aspects of their jobs and the bank's processes. They are always saying, "Why are we still doing that?" and "Wouldn't this process work better if we did this?" At the opposite ends of the productivity^2 scale, people tend to regard each other as either troublemakers or place-holders.

Combining Productivity^2 and Power

Things really begin to get interesting when we combine power and productivity^2 in the same person. In order to do that, I have prepared the Productivity^2/Power Matrix in Figure 15.1. The vertical axis measures power, from low to high, and the

Figure 15.1
The Productivity^2/Power Matrix

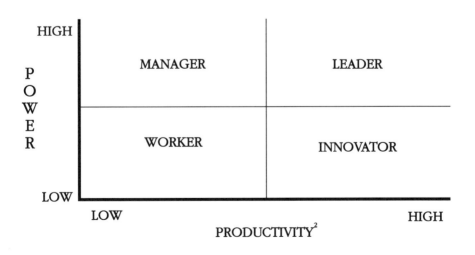

horizontal axis measures productivity^2, also from low to high. The risk in using such a matrix is that the reader will assume that it is possible to measure such things as power and productivity^2 numerically and precisely. Of course it is not, but the matrix gives us a framework for thinking about the relationships.

I have divided the matrix into quadrants, not because there are only four possible combinations, or because there are sharp breaks in the gradients at some point, but because it provides a convenient way of looking at the relationships. Obviously, reality is a matter of varying shades of gray, not abrupt changes from black to white. However, the matrix allows us to look at the general characteristics of four kinds of participants in a bank. One additional point—the words used to describe each of the quadrants were chosen carefully and should be read for their denotative, or exact, and not connotative, or implied, meanings. There is no emotional or value content to the names.

Let us first look at the lower left-hand corner of the matrix, where both power and productivity^2 are low. In this quadrant we find the vast majority of the work force. They perform tasks defined for them by someone else. Their primary, if not entire, focus is on the job at hand, not on change. As a result, I have called these people "workers."

In the upper left-hand quadrant are people who exhibit more power but not much more productivity^2. These are people who are charged with overseeing the production process; who make sure that schedules are met, budgets are not exceeded, procedures are followed; in a word, productivity. They have the power to hire and fire, to buy and sell, and to schedule, but they do not see their mission as expressly improving the process. I have called these people "managers."

In the lower-right quadrant are people who have little power, but who exhibit higher levels of productivity^2. These are the workers who constantly tinker with the process, seeking ways to improve it. In some cases, their job requires them to effect changes, such as engineers or software developers. In other cases, their personalities cause them to look for improvements. Not all their changes are improvements because they often have a narrow, low-level view of the general objective. I have called these people "innovators."

In the upper-right quadrant are those people who have significant amounts of power and exhibit lots of productivity^2. These people generate change in their banks partly by example and partly by requiring it. They are constantly remaking the bank and redefining the roles of the people in it. These people, like the innovators, are not always successful, and their failures are significantly more spectacular, because they often involve an entire bank. However, partly because of the force of their will and partly because of their power, they can change an entire bank. I have called these people "leaders."

Using the Matrix

One useful approach to this matrix is positioning the bank in it. This requires that you assess the numbers of people in the bank who fit in each quadrant, and approximately where in each quadrant they fit. This kind of analysis can yield a couple of possible results. One is a "blob" which represents the bank in its entirety, and is useful for seeing how disparate its members are with regard to power and productivity^2. The other is a "pinpoint," equivalent to a weighted average, and is useful in determining the status of the bank as a whole and how that status is changing.

Banks where the pinpoint is somewhere in the lower-right quadrant are those which are constantly in the process of remaking themselves, largely from the bottom up. Many software development companies fit this mold, although some, which are dominated by one or two leaders, might have the pinpoint just inside the upper-right quadrant. Banks where the pinpoint is in the lower-left quadrant are usually those focused on mass markets, such as America's Big Three auto companies. There is an interesting development to note here. As a banks market matures and the growth in employment levels off, the pinpoint in many banks tends to drift upward, particularly if it is on the left-hand side of the matrix. This is because many workers expect that they will naturally become managers over the course of time, and a reduction in the labor requirements often leaves banks with a plethora of managers. This situation can make it extremely difficult to streamline the bank, since the excess capacity is concentrated in those positions with accumulations of power.

Now we need to look at the relationships between the sectors. Each of these combinations of power and productivity^2 would make an interesting study by itself, but it is much more useful to see how they interact in an bank setting. There are many kinds of relationships between the various quadrants, but the ones I have chosen for this analysis are the relationships most likely to be impacted by organizational change. The labeled arrows show the value provided by one quadrant to the other.

The Manager/Worker Axis (Figure 15.2)

In this case, the workers provide *power*, among other things, to the managers, and the managers provide *protection*, among other things, to the workers. The manager's position, while important, is one which is vulnerable. Because managers do not "produce" things in the same sense that workers do, there is a widespread perception that banks should be able to function without them, or at least with fewer of them. Since the primary function of the manager is one of control and

Figure 15.2
The Productivity^2/Power Matrix: The Manager/Worker Axis

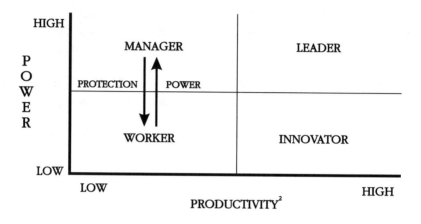

supervision, eliminating or downplaying his or her function would require alternative forms of control and supervision.

The traditional worker is not well adapted to such alternative forms, so he or she requires a manager to perform that function. At the same time, the presence of the manager function alleviates the requirement for the worker to be self-controlling and self-supervising. As we will see in examining other relationships, the worker depends on the manager for protection, not only from outside forces, but from forces internal to the bank. Thus the worker and the manager often have powerful joint incentives to slow, stall, or minimize the forces of change.

The Worker/Innovator Axis (Figure 15.3)

The primary difference between the worker and the innovator lies in the way they approach their jobs. Where the worker regards a job as something to be done, an innovator regards it as something to be improved on. Where the worker is concerned with productivity, the innovator is concerned with productivity^2. This difference can create tension between the two when the worker sees the innovator upsetting his comfortable applecart.

Figure 15.3
The Productivity²/Power Matrix: The Worker/Innovator Axis

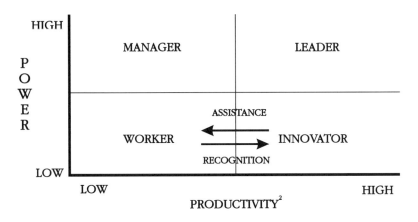

However, outside pressures for change can significantly alter this relationship. When market pressures force change on the worker, the first place he turns for *assistance* is often to the innovator. This is because the worker may perceive that the manager is ill-prepared to incorporate or deal with change, and because workers traditionally have little or no contact with leaders. The innovator, who often feels that he is laboring unheralded in the vineyard, and who often encounters hostility toward his innovations, suddenly finds himself a necessary part of the worker's world. This *recognition* may be a temporary event, based on the demands of imposed change, but the innovator may well use it to implement his favorite changes.

The Leader/Innovator Axis (Figure 15.4)

As much as the manager/worker axis is structured, the leader/innovator axis is unstructured. It is also more ambivalent than most of the others. On the one hand, the innovator represents the best hope for the melding of practical knowledge and vision in the workplace itself. On the other hand, he or she represents uncertainty, and the distinct possibility of a loose cannon on deck. The leader, who

Figure 15.4
The Productivity² /Power Matrix: The Leader/Innovator Axis

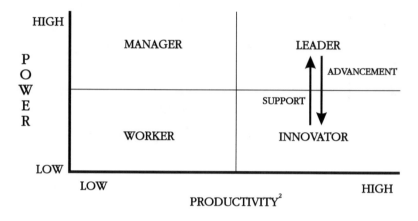

understands the constant need for evolution in the bank, also understands the constant specter of revolution.

The leader and the innovator must communicate by a back channel which may be both acknowledged and ignored by the other parties. The leader depends on the innovator for *support* in his efforts to shepherd the bank along the change path, and the innovator sees the supporting function as an avenue for *advancement*. Coordination of approaches comes, not through direct contact, but by careful reading of signals, and the leader must be careful not to let this communication disrupt the communication between him and the manager.

The Leader/Manager Axis (Figure 15.5)

Although leaders and managers appear to occupy the same world, full of corner offices and perks, their views of it are often diametrically opposed. The manager sees his or her responsibility as getting the work out; meeting schedules and budgets. This is productivity. The leader sees his or her responsibility as dealing with future change and competition. This is productivity². By necessity, the manager tends to concentrate on details, and the leader on the big picture. Thus the two

Figure 15.5
The Productivity^2/Power Matrix: The Leader/Manager Axis

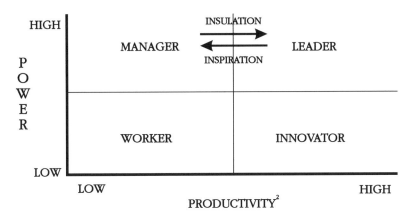

find themselves dependent on each other while their roles might appear in opposition.

By paying attention to detail, the manager *insulates* the leader from the bothersome aspects of running a bank, leaving him or her free to provide *inspiration* and direction. When they are properly matched and work well together, these two provide a powerful combination which makes the bank an awesome competitor. When they are in conflict, they can sap the bank of its strength and leave it ill-equipped to survive.

The Manager/Innovator Axis (Figure 15.6)

Of all the relationships, this is the most explosive, as well as the most potentially rewarding. As befits their positions in the matrix, these roles have the natural inclination to be totally opposite in their approaches to almost everything. The manager has the power to institute a great deal of change, but the inclination to keep everything the same. The innovator has almost no power to change things, but every reason to make change happen.

Under the best conditions, the manager recognizes the value of the innovator as an astute observer of the production process, and encourages his or her original-

Figure 15.6
The Productivity²/Power Matrix: The Manager/Innovator Axis

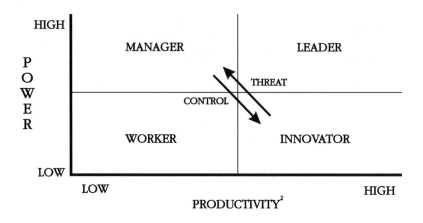

ity. Much more often, however, the innovator represents a *threat* to the manager, because innovation upsets the manager's ordered world. Thus the manager often takes steps to *control* the innovator's creativity, perhaps by imposing or enforcing operating procedures. This kind of relationship is almost never discussed openly within the bank, although it is usually acknowledged by both participants.

The Matrix under Stable Conditions (Figure 15.7)

When we look at the matrix with all the relationships included, we can see that they represent a complex kaleidescope where each of the participants must deal with at least two relationships, often with very different requirements and motivations. Managers must serve to insulate, protect, and control three different categories. Innovators serve as an assistance, support, and threat mechanism all at the same time. Some relationships are essentially synergistic, like the manager/leader axis, and the manager/worker axis. Others are essentially conflicting, like the manager/innovator axis. And some have the potential to go either way, like the worker/innovator and leader/innovator axes.

Under stable conditions, the pivot points are the leader and innovator categories. Everyone is fairly aware of the importance of the leader in this analysis, but

Figure 15.7
The Productivity^2/Power Matrix: The Matrix under Stable Conditions

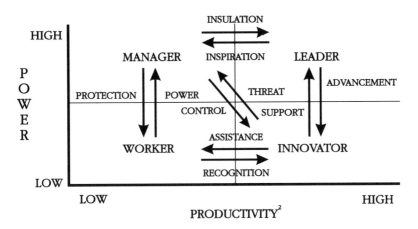

not many people are as aware of the role of the innovator. Because he or she has the potential to be a change agent, but is not perceived by most of the participants as a party to the decisions being made, the innovator can either facilitate and support those decisions, or inadvertently sabotage them. Thus, under stable conditions attention needs to be focused on the lower right-hand corner of the matrix.

Productivity^2 and Power in a Changing Bank

Once a bank begins undergoing change, whether that change is internally or externally fostered, many of these relationships change markedly. It is the difference between the static relationships and the dynamic ones which causes so much resistance to organizational change, and which perplexes both executives and academicians.

The first thing to understand is that under stable conditions the roles on the left-hand side of the matrix appear the most in sync with conditions, and the ones on the right appear the most out of sync. When change is forced on the bank, the roles on the right start to appear more in sync with conditions, and those on the left appear out of sync. Being in sync with conditions confers power with a role of its own, so the shift from static to dynamic conditions also implies a power shift from the left-hand boxes to the right-hand ones. Power shifts are generally resisted by those on the losing end, and it is no different here.

Thus, under conditions of change the relationships on the right-hand side of the matrix become more important than those on the left. The back channel by which the leader and the innovator communicate becomes more important, and perhaps more formal. The innovator's support becomes more important to the leader, and more visible, while the innovator's road to advancement becomes clearer to him and to everyone else in the bank. At the same time, the horizontal relationships change significantly, with more value flowing from right to left than from left to right. The inspiration and direction provided by the leader to the manager become more important than the insulation provided by the manager, and the assistance provided by the innovator to the worker becomes more important than the recognition provided by the worker.

As some relationships are enhanced, others are degraded, particularly those on the left-hand side. Change itself is most threatening to the worker, and only a little less so to the manager, so it serves to reduce the amount of protection a manager can afford a worker. As a consquence, the manager's primary power base is also eroded. All of this makes the diagonal relationship between the manager and the innovator very explosive. As the manager's traditional power is being eroded, the power and influence of the innovator is increasing, making him or her even more of a threat. As the manager's control over the innovator declines, he or she is faced with an apparently unresolvable conflict. Given the responsibility to make the production process run smoothly, the manager must deal not only with change forces from outside the bank, but even more with those from within. No wonder the manager can lapse into a defensive posture.

An even more difficult issue is the missing set of linkages; the ones between the leader and the worker. Those are not included in my matrix because they are most often accomplished indirectly. Instead of going diagonally, these linkages usually take a right-angle path, either horizontally first and then vertically or vertically first and then horizontally. For example, the insulation linkage between manager and leader often takes the place of a direct worker/leader linkage. In many cases, this is known as the chain of command, and is the orthodox and overt method of communicating. There is, however, another, unorthodox and covert method—through the innovator. Under static conditions, this linkage is less necessary and less used, but it becomes much more significant when change is forced on the bank. Communications between leaders and workers are a crucial aspect of organizational adaptation to change, and how they occur has great import. If managers are an effective impediment to that communication, then the opposite channel will open up, creating great tensions between managers and innovators.

Guiding the Bank through Change

The real value of this analysis is in helping banks cope with rapid change, whether that change is internally or externally generated. The first useful aspect of the analysis is simply a better understanding of why people play certain roles in banks. Workers will concentrate on business as usual and object to changes in their job descriptions if someone has told them to do so. In banks where change is regarded as a product as well as a business condition, everyone in the bank welcomes it. In banks where change is regarded as a necessary evil, workers and managers will view it with trepidation.

A corollary to that is an understanding of the linkages between the roles, and how those linkages transform under the stress of change. Certain linkages are particularly dependent upon a stable environment, like the manager/worker or the manager/leader axes. As the pressure for change increases, these linkages become strained and begin to break down. To the extent that the participants are aware of that, they can make adjustments before positions harden and people dig in their heels.

Overall, there are some general guidelines for leaders who want to use the productivity^2/power matrix to guide the bank through periods of change.

Understand the way relationships are altered by the threat of change. A bank at rest is an engineering marvel of forces in balance, much like a bridge. Just as an earthquake can bring down a bridge, organizational change can severely disrupt the balances of power and productivity^2. People who happily worked together may now see each other as threats. People who had comfortably structured relationships will have to forge new bonds, based on new requirements. Some people will lose power and prestige, and others will gain. Everyone in a bank will have to deal with new or altered relationships, but it is the leader who will carry much of the responsibility to assess the impact of change on the relationships, and to alleviate the stress as much as possible.

Move the bank to the right within the matrix. Some of the roles I have discussed have a natural antipathy to change, but people themselves often have a remarkable affinity for productivity^2. Given the opportunity and incentive, many people who appear entrenched in the left-hand quadrants will happily migrate toward the right. In particular, people at all levels of the bank can clearly see the need for improvements, but they may also perceive an antipathy or resistance on the part of their superiors. By instituting a structured program for thinking and talking about these improvements, leaders can break down those perceptions and begin moving the bank to the right. There is a very significant side benefit to such a program—it can serve as a reality check for the leader's own ideas.

Keep all the channels of communication open. Banks at rest tend to have formalized communications channels, and departure from those channels is often frowned upon, particularly by those people whose control of the channel gives them invisible power. But banks undergoing change require open, unstructured channels of communication, even at the risk of threatening certain people or relationships. The two most important participants in making organizational change work are the manager and the innovator, and yet they often appear, both to others and themselves, to be at odds. In such cases, the leader must act as both a filter and communications channel. If the leader can bridge the gap between the manager and the innovator, he or she will ensure that change will happen, that his or her model for the bank will evolve, and that the bank will be a success. And, after all, that is what leadership is all about.

16 | Employee Enhancement as a Competitive Differentiator

As competition increases in the banking business, a primary concern of management should be competitive differentiation—how do we make our institution look different and more appealing to customers? However, although there is ample research to indicate that competitive differentiation is a key determinant of long-term profitability, there is little evidence that bank managements give it a great deal of attention or that they can identify the most important competitive differentiators.

In 1993, Unisys commissioned some research into how bankers and bank customers viewed the business of retail banking. One of the questions posed to 300 or so senior bank executives was, "What are the primary things customers tell you they want from you?" The predominant response to the question was "better, more-personalized service from more-knowledgeable employees who are capable of providing sound advice."

We also asked, "To what degree has competition precipitated changes at your bank?" This question elicited three main responses, in order of frequency:

❑ Developing and offering more products

❑ Doing more with less in the way of staff

❑ More cross selling and better understanding of the customer

As I'm sure you have noticed, the things banks felt were important don't necessarily match up against the things that customers tell them they want. Although customers indicated that employees were the primary differentiator, banks appear to be de-emphasizing employees as a resource.

There is a logical explanation for this. Employees *are* a resource, but an expensive one. How expensive? If the average employee costs you $35,000 per year, with the current long-term interest rates of 7.5 percent, each employee is the financial equivalent of a piece of equipment costing over $450,000. When you look at it that way, it is easy to see why bank executives are trying to cut back on personnel expense.

So we have a quandary. Customers rank employees as a prime differentiator, but banks tend to think of them as an unaffordable luxury. The resolution to this quandary is both simple and subtle. It involves enhancing the bank's employees' performance, so that they become engines of business expansion. But that is easier said than done. Although bankers would like to enhance their employees performance, few of them would regard themselves as successful in doing so. I hear many reasons for this lack of success, but I believe the primary reason employee-performance enhancement is difficult is that performance influencers are more complex than people think.

Performance Influencers

Employee performance is influenced by a myriad of factors. These factors can be internal to the employee, external but under the employee's control (to a greater or lesser extent), or completely outside the employee's control. I have organized these influencers into eight major categories:

> Motivation
> Expertise/skills
> Tools
> Corporate culture
> Leadership
> Processes
> Communication
> Environment

Although these influencers interact, they have unique characteristics, so I will cover each of them individually.

Motivation

This category contains everything which prompts an employee to do things. There are two aspects to motivation: internal and external.

Internal motivators, or *personal goals*, are those things the employee values and is willing to work to achieve. They include monetary rewards, power, recognition, job security, personal excellence, and leisure time. Internal motivators may be well established in the employee when he or she first comes to work for an institution, but they can change over time and can be affected by external factors. For example, younger employees might value monetary rewards to such an extent that they take career risks to achieve them. Those same employees, later in life and with children, might place much more value on job security, particularly if economic conditions have deteriorated.

External motivators, or *incentives*, are those things which the institution places before the employee as rewards for job achievements. Often they are the same things as the internal motivators: money, recognition, power, and job security; however, there are two things employees evaluate about external motivators. One is the reward itself, and another is what performance is being rewarded. The old saw is that employees normally exhibit the behavior that they are rewarded for, and that is sometimes true. However, attempting to motivate certain kinds of behavior with rewards that are low on the employee's priority list may generate no response, or the wrong response.

Expertise/Skills

This category encompasses what an employee applies to his or her job. I have divided expertise/skills into four domains: job skills, education, interpersonal skills, and experience.

Job skills result from the job training that most employees receive, and cover what to do when presented with an expected requirement. When bank executives think about training, this is what they are usually thinking about.

Education is what most employees receive away from the job, and covers what to do when presented with an unexpected requirement. This is what employees fall back on when presented with situations outside the realm of job training.

Interpersonal skills allow employees to deal with other people. Some employees develop and hone these skills throughout most of their life, but some do not. Much of this domain involves listening and speaking skills, but creativity, content analysis, and conflict resolution also fit. Many corporate workshops focus on developing these skills, but few really do that over the long run. Most produce temporary results because the motivations that encourage or sustain change are wrong or missing.

Experience is just what you would think it is, the number and breadth of job situations the employee has experienced. There are two primary abilities gained from experience—the ability to deal with challenges either not covered or improperly covered in regular training, and the ability to predict the actions and reactions of other people.

Tools

This category contains all the things besides expertise/skills that an employee uses to do his or her job. As in any other industry, the bank employee's facility with his or her tools is an important performance influencer, and is heavily dependent on expertise/skills. Thus, we can begin already to see how the influencers interrelate. Tools come in two forms: concrete or abstract.

Concrete tools are those which the employee can physically touch. The primary concrete tools in the finance industry are technological, but they go beyond just computers. Peripherals, industry-specific tools (like item processing equipment), and networks are examples of concrete tools that are not be strictly computers.

Abstract tools are those which the employee cannot physically touch, but are equally necessary. Two closely-related primary abstract tools are software and information. Important quality determinants of these tools are their accessibility and usability.

Corporate Culture

This category contains those things which define the institution. Corporate culture exists at two levels: the official level, where the culture is published and acknowledged by the institution, and the unofficial level, where the culture is manifested by employees to each other and to customers. When the two levels are in sync, the culture is a powerful motivator and serves to attract customers. When they are not in sync, the cultural conflict acts to drain corporate energy and resources, and can serve to drive customers away.

Corporate culture has six aspects: mission, goals, policies, values, beliefs, and structure.

Mission is a brief, communicable, high-level statement that defines the institution's reason for being. However, high level does not mean vague. The mission statement should identify the business(es) the institution wants to be in, its target market(s), and the way(s) it plans to compete. But beyond these requirements, the mission must be an accurate reflection of the institution's position in the market. Most financial institutions already have a mission statement; the question is whether most employees understand it and believe it is relevant and achievable.

Goals are those things the institution intends to achieve, and are thus bounded by time, even if that time period is long. Goals must be measurable and as stable as possible, but they can be changed to reflect changes in the business and market environment. They can be financial, statistical, or perceptual. Financial goals are obvious, like revenue growth, return on equity, or even stock price. Statistical goals are less obvious, but encompass things like market share, error rates, or productivity. Perceptual goals are less obvious still, and these can include customer- and employee-satisfaction ratings or brand recognition.

Policies are the hard-and-fast rules of the institution. Policies can cover generic functions, like expense accounting, or more banking-specific functions, like loan origination. They can be written or unwritten, acknowledged by the institution or operating in the background. One significant question is whether the policies reflect the current needs of the institution and the current conditions of the market. In addition, most institutions have a plethora of policies, probably more than they need. A bank with too many policies leaves employees unable to react to changes in the market and potentially unable to maximize their performance.

Values are simply the things the institution places a value on, as evidenced by the measurement and reward systems. It is important to note that the values as expressed in corporate documents may be quite different from those implied by the measurement and reward systems. Some reward systems, especially financial ones, are quite clearly laid out, while others, like promotions, are much less obvious to many employees. Corporate values are often underemphasized when looking at performance influencers.

Beliefs are those things that the institution believes, about regulators, employees, competitors, and customers. One major set of beliefs revolves around how those people will respond to an institution's actions. This is another area where the institution's stated beliefs may not be reflected in the general beliefs of the employees. Of particular importance are the beliefs regarding what customers value and how customers will react to the institution's actions.

Structure refers to the way an institution is organized, both vertically and horizontally. In recent years, attention has been paid to how organizations are structured vertically, but of equal importance is how the institution is structured horizontally. For example, are distribution channels structured by the market served, by the product distributed, or by the technology used. Both values and beliefs are imbedded in structure, so the institution needs to make sure that its structure reflects the other parts of its culture.

Leadership

This category refers to the people who lead the institution. In many institutions, people think this refers to one person, the CEO, who dominates the institution. However, no matter how dominant the CEO, leadership is actually exhibited by many individuals within the institution, some who have positions of power and some who do not. It is important to understand what message the leadership is sending out and how cohesive that message is. There are four aspects to leadership: background, biases, style, and motivation.

Background refers to the leader's professional history. Previous job responsibilities and corporate affiliations are important here, as well as areas of expertise. In addition, leaders whose entire careers were spent in one institution may have a very different background and perspective than those who have worked in several institutions.

Biases are those values and beliefs that leaders intuitively embrace, and can often be traced to their background. Biases may or may not be acknowledged by the leaders themselves, but they are usually perceived by the employees. Because clashes of biases are unpleasant, CEOs often surround themselves with individuals whose biases parallel theirs. An astute leader seeks out those with different biases, in order to promote diversity of thought.

Style refers to the way in which leaders interact with others, and ranges from a high level to the most basic. Is the leader autocratic, or does he or she promote debate? Is the leader formal or informal, focused on details or the big picture, a delegater or a controller? Although subordinates cannot adopt a leader's background, and may not adopt his or her biases, they will often adopt the leaders style. In fact, depending on the leader's position and charisma, the whole institution may reflect his or her style.

Motivation has the same meaning for the leader as it does for the employee, but here the leader's motivations affect all those who are led. This is particularly important if the incentive programs for the institution's leaders are significantly different from those for the employees in general. If executive-incentive programs focus on profitability while departmental incentives focus on revenue, motivational conflict should be expected. Such conflict will probably not be overt, but it will surely be covert, and often it will affect customer satisfaction.

Processes

This category contains the ways in which the institution accomplishes tasks. Under our definition, processes encompass everything the institution does, including setting policy, designing new products, and entering new markets. As with culture, there can be two kinds of processes: those which are codified, and those which are not. In some cases, the actual processes differ from the codified ones because the codified ones are no longer appropriate. For the employee, two kinds of processes are important: those where he or she has direct involvement and those where involvement is indirect.

Direct involvement clearly covers those processes in which the employee plays a direct part. An employee can be directly involved in more than one process in his or her job, and as more processes cross corporate boundaries, employees are becoming directly involved in intercompany processes.

Indirect involvement covers those processes where the employee is a "vendor," "customer," or has some other kind of involvement. Indirect involvement surfaces when a process is changed from within and that change triggers a change or problem in another process. Employees are more often aware of indirect involvement when they are the customer rather than when they are the vendor.

Communication

This category contains the ways in which parts of the institution communicate with other parts regarding the institution's business, and the ways in which the institution communicates with outside entities, including vendors, alliance partners, and customers. It does not cover incidental nonbusiness-related communications. Among the aspects of communication are: channels, protocols, and expectations. As with other categories, these aspects exist in both the overt and covert forms. In addition, there are two forms of communication: internal and external.

Internal communication covers what goes on within the institution, and it occurs in three directions: downward, upward, and horizontally. In most institutions, the official forms of downward communication consist primarily of instructions, directives, and requests for information. Official upward communication consists primarily of performance reports, requests for resources, and conflicts to be resolved. Official horizontal communication consists primarily of requests for assistance, notification of opportunities, and communication incidental to the execution of processes.

External communication generally falls into four classes: communication with vendors, communication with customers, communication with alliance partners, and official communications with regulators. Many institutions have comprehensive policies about how employees carry out external communication, but, in order to facilitate business, employees often ignore or subvert these policies.

Environment

This category covers most of the working conditions which exist within the institution. One part of the environment is provided by the institution, and is normally referred to as workplace conditions. Another part is provided by the employees themselves, and is normally referred to as attitudes.

Workplace conditions include as office layout and furnishings, staffing levels, and general ambiance, as well as parts of other categories like tools and processes.

Attitudes cover the way employees feel about their work, each other, and their leadership, as well as how they feel about customers and the institution as a whole. Attitudes are contagious, which can be either positive or negative. In particular, employees who demonstrate leadership characteristics but are not part of the leadership structure can have a powerful impact on attitudes, as can employees who disagree with official positions, policies, or goals.

How Performance Influencers Interact

When you look at performance in light of these eight influencers, you can see some reasons why it is difficult to foster continuous performance enhancement. One of the most basic is that many managements either do not recognize, or choose not to address, some of the influencers. For example, although management may be aware of the influence its leadership has on the performance of the institution as a whole, it may be less aware of its impact on individual-employee performance. Also, there is often very little evidence of bank management's attempt to match individual-incentive programs to individual-employee motivations.

However, the real impact of these influencers lies in the way they interact with each other. To help you better understand how the influencers relate to each other, I developed the Corporate Wheel of Performance Influencers (Figure 16.1).

Figure 16.1
The Corporate Wheel of Performance Influencers

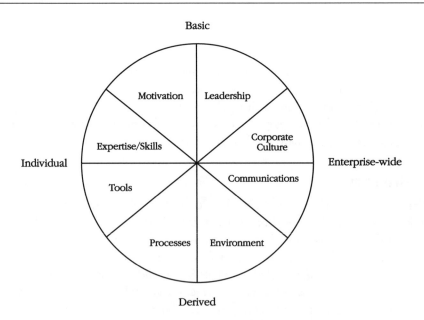

This wheel presents the individual influencers as parts of a cohesive whole, and begins to set out their relationship with each other. There are several points I want to make about these relationships. First, the wheel is divided vertically into two groups of four. This division is fundamental to understanding the relationships. The set on the left are applied to, and have most of their influence on, the *individual*. The set on the right are applied to, and have most of their influence on, *enterprise-wide*.

This means that you must apply, and undertake to change, these influencers in different ways, depending on which side of the wheel they occupy. For example, expertise and skills are developed in the individual. Therefore, no matter how enterprise-wide your development programs are, those programs must focus on, and adapt to, each employee. On the other hand, corporate culture must be enterprise-wide to be effective, so it must be built across the entire institution at once.

It is also true that, the lower you go in each semicircle, the less strict this interpretation is. Tools and processes must involve more than one person to be effective, and individuals have more influence on their environment than they do on corporate culture. In order for institutions to have continuous and effective performance enhancement, managers must recognize that each category has a different impact on individual employees.

The second point to be made is that, in each half of the wheel, each influencer is somewhat derived from the one above it. The top categories, motivation and leadership, are the most basic building blocks, from which the whole structure evolves.

This means that, for instance, banks which attract employees who are not motivated toward self-improvement, or banks which don't reward self-improvement, should not expect their employees to continually enhance their expertise and skills. Such employees are unlikely to embrace or effectively use the latest in tools, which might lead management to conclude that the technology is unproductive and that further investments in it are unwarranted. The resulting absence of advanced technology is the most common reason for antiquated, cumbersome processes, which further restrict both profitability and customer service.

The same causal chain works on the right side of the wheel. If the leaders of a bank spent much of their careers as controllers, they are likely to be biased in favor of cost control over marketing. Those biases can lead to a corporate culture which does not value the marketing creativity of individual employees, and which believes that customers will only respond to price competition. Communications both inside and outside the institution will probably reflect the importance of efficiency over marketing programs, which could mean that management may not be aware of the marketing impact of cost-driven decisions. Finally, the environment within the bank would probably discourage employee creativity, except to the extent that it reduced costs, and would probably reflect a low valuation of individual employees.

The final point is that, as we move around the wheel counterclockwise, beginning with motivation, we move from things which are almost entirely within the individual's control to those which are almost entirely outside it. As we go from motivation to expertise/skills to tools and so on, each category becomes a little less individual and a little more corporate.

This perception is usually shared by the employees themselves. As they view the influencers around the wheel, they see them as moving progressively out of their control. In all probability, employees have more control of many influencers than they believe they do, but they are usually right when they believe that they have little impact on the last two influencers. People who feel they have no impact sometimes withdraw from participation, which can also have a negative impact on how customers perceive both your employees and your institution.

Drawing Conclusions

Taking this rigorous, organized view of employee performance can explain a lot about why some employees and some organizations underperform against both expectations and peers, while others keep on improving. I have drawn some general conclusions about employee performance based on this analysis.

1. *Since there are so many influencers and interactions between influencers, a bank must take the time and make the effort to understand which ones are impacting its, and its employees', performance.* My analysis and experience indicate that the explanations for levels of employee performance are likely to be much more complicated than either management or the employee realize. For example, performance issues which appear to revolve around processes may actually revolve around expertise and motivation, and issues appearing to be about environment could actually be about communication and corporate culture.

   In determining what influencers are affecting performance, banks need to be aware that the influencers themselves may affect the fact-finding process. For example, in banks where the corporate culture discourages certain forms of communication, it may be harder to find out exactly what is affecting performance. This is particularly true where the values in the corporate culture are not the same as employee personal goals and management motivations. In such cases, the bank or its consultants will have to use sophisticated hypothesis-testing methods to ferret out the real influencers.

2. *Banks need to be cognizant of the need to address influencers as either more individual or enterprise-wide in nature, depending on where they sit on the*

wheel. My analysis makes it clear that some influencers are decidedly individual in nature, while others are decidedly enterprise-wide, and some are in between. However, most banks do not take that into account when they institute and administer employee-enhancement programs.

Enterprise-wide incentive systems which do not address individual motivations are the most prevalent example of this kind of problem. Another less well-known problem is attempting to change the corporate culture or environment one person at a time. Most of the influencers on the right side of the wheel require a "critical mass" to be achieved before the enterprise adopts them. Therefore, large group interventions instead of individually focused programs are needed. Important in achieving critical mass is enlisting certain opinion leaders within the bank, particularly those who do not occupy positions of authority, and gaining their public support for the new paradigm.

3. *Banks need to understand the causal relationships between influencers on each side of the wheel, and intervene at the right level.* In many instances, corporate intervention for the purpose of improving performance doesn't work because the influencer addressed is lower on the wheel than the influencer responsible for the performance shortfall. For example, attempting to change tools or processes without changing expertise or motivations is one of the most common reasons for the 70 percent failure rate in corporate process-reengineering programs.

Another common problem is attempting to change the environmental or communication influencers without the underlying changes in corporate culture or leadership. This disconnect is responsible for the situation in which everyone in a bank echoes the management's calls for cultural, environmental, and communications changes, but nothing of significance happens until there is a change in leadership, whereupon the changes cascade all the way around the wheel to individual motivations.

4. *In order for employee enhancement to become a permanent part of the corporate culture, the bank must establish a methodology for making it so.* Banks and nonbank financial institutions which have been able to maintain a tradition of employee development and performance improvement have done so by making, and sticking to, a long-term commitment of both attention and resources. Hit-or-miss, one-time efforts to enhance performance sometimes have a temporary impact, and sometimes do not, but they never have an extensive, long-term effect.

What is needed is a methodology for integrating performance enhancement into the everyday fabric of the bank's activities. Such a methodology must address the following questions:

❑   What is the appropriate performance level for each employee, and how is that determined?

❑   What is the current performance level for each employee, and how is that determined?

❑   How big is the performance gap, and what impact does it have on the bank's success?

❑   What influencer(s) is causing the gap?

❑   What forms of intervention are necessary to close the gap?

❑   How does the bank implement the intervention and manage the resulting change?

❑   Has the intervention had the expected impact, and how do we measure the improvement?

❑   How does the bank cycle back to step one in order to keep the process perpetual?

Developing a methodology to address these questions will be one of the most important tasks of senior management.

17 | Making a Merger Work

In the first edition of this book, I said, "The simple fact is that the financial services industry must consolidate. The number of banks will have to drop to between one-fifth and one-tenth of the current number." Today, three years later, the statement is still true. That consolidation can occur in several ways. Institutions can simply disappear, but the federally-insured nature of the business makes that an unlikely possibility.

A more likely possibility is the predatory process by which the stronger institutions acquire pieces of the weaker ones. We have already seen that occur in the sale of profitable businesses by some of the more troubled banks. Whether it is a portfolio management business or a portfolio of credit-card assets, some banks have been getting out of good businesses to concentrate on unprofitable ones for several years. However, banks which make a habit of doing that aren't long for this world.

Clearly, another avenue in the consolidation process is the merger. As discussed in Chapter 1, a wave of mergers in the banking industry has been foretold for some time, but the wave has yet to materialize. There are many reasons why merger mania has been slow to develop, but the fact is that mergers are an important and integral part of the banking scene.

However, the kinds of mergers which dotted the banking map in the 1980s gave way to another kind of merger in the early 1990s, and that shift was accentuated by the passage of banking legislation in 1991. The 1980s was the decade of *cross-market mergers* in the banking industry. Cross-market mergers are ones in which banks in different markets merge. Because of the interstate banking restrictions which the United States currently has, cross-market mergers are almost always interstate mergers.

Cross-market mergers are essentially expansionary in intent. The purpose for instituting a cross-market merger is to expand the institution's marketplace: to obtain new customers, to expand the geographical coverage, to do more business. To be sure, some contraction results from a cross-market merger. Most often, computer centers are consolidated, and some headquarters' functions are consolidated, but the primary thrust of a cross-market merger is to grow the business. Most of the superregional banks in this country were formed from a series of cross-market mergers.

The inability of Congress to remove interstate banking restrictions at the end of the 1980s forced banks to turn their consolidation efforts toward institutions in the same markets, resulting in a series of *in-market mergers.* The passage of the 1991 banking legislation without any provision for interstate banking virtually assured that most of the banking mergers over the first half of the 1990s were of the in-market kind.

In-market mergers are distinctly different from cross-markets. Where the primary purpose of a cross-market is to expand into new territory, the main purpose of an in-market is to reduce competition and capacity. Where the cross-market is designed to add branches to the bank's network, the in-market is designed to close duplicate branches. While the cross-market is designed to increase the customer base, the in-market is designed to reduce the work force. Some recent examples of in-market mergers are Manufacturers Hanover/Chemical, BankAmerica/Security Pacific, and NCNB/C & S Sovran.

Those recent in-market mergers were announced with a great deal of fanfare about the savings that would be wrung out of the combinations. In fact, regulatory approval appears to have been contigent on the achievement of a promised level of savings and the subsequent raising of equity capital. However, based on results shown as of the end of 1994, it does not seem certain that these mega-mergers did what they were predicted to do.

In fact, the January 9, 1995 issue of the *American Banker* carried an article by Daniel Kaplan referring to a study by Standard & Poors which showed that mergers of all kinds, but particularly in-market ones, have not improved efficiency. According to the article, "banks involved in mergers in the past four years have operated less efficiently by some measures than those that stayed out of the merger boom." In particular, the article points out that, "the study showed revenue dilution at banks that did merge, attributable to the dislocations associated with melding two institutions." The article quotes Tanya Azarchs, the S&P analyst who authored the study, as saying, "Most of the in-market mergers lost revenue momentum and underperformed the industry in the years after the merger." According to the article, the revenue growth for in-market merged banks in 1994 was 2.5 percent, while the expense growth for the same period was 3.9 percent. For banks which had not merged, revenue growth for 1994 was 5.7 percent, and expense growth was 5.9 percent.

What Makes a Good Merger?

Which brings up the question, how could these results have been avoided, and what constitutes a successful merger? If you were to ask the CEOs of some of the above banks how they would know if the mergers had been a success, the consensus would probably be *if the market capitalization of the combined bank was higher than the market caps of the separate banks before the merger.* That measure says that the investing public would value the combination more highly than the separate components, which is the definition of any successful merger.

By that definition, it is not clear that the mega-mergers of the early 1990s were all successful. In fact, by that measure a good portion of the recent bank mergers weren't a success. It is certainly true that mergers in general are a chancy business, and mergers were especially suspect at the end of the 1980s, but our goal is to ensure, as much as possible, that your merger is successful, so we need to determine the components that go into a successful merger.

We can begin with the requirement that the merger must maximize market capitalization, and that means that it must maximize two things: price/earnings ratio and return on equity (ROE). Price/earnings ratio is determined by the stock market, but ROE is up to the bank itself, so, there are three components to a successful merger, and they are set out in Figure 17.1. Most mergers are initiated to accomplish one, or at most two, of these components, but all three must be accomplished in order to ensure that the objective of maximizing market capitalization is reached. Let's look at each component in detail.

Figure 17.1

Capturing the best of both institutions
+   Eliminating excess capacity
+   Increasing market presence
=   Maximizing return on equity and market capitalization

Capturing the Best of Both Institutions

This component is listed first because it is the most important. It is sometimes expressed as a goal by the participants in a merger, particularly by the senior management, but it is much less frequently attained in reality. However, merging institutions can wring out excess capacity and even increase market presence without accomplishing much along the lines of capturing the best of both institutions, and it would be difficult to judge such a merger a success. So how does one capture the best?

Defining "Best"

The first step is defining "best." A simple process, right? Not really. The first problem that arises in defining best is *objectivity.* All mergers are fraught with corporate politics, and in-market mergers are among the worst in that regard. People stand to lose their jobs, departments stand to disappear, executives stand to be shifted or demoted, so it is no wonder that objectivity is difficult to achieve under such conditions.

The most common kind of subjectivity seen in a merger is the assumption that the acquiring institution's components are best. Often, the logic is expressed this way: "If we weren't better than they are, they would be acquiring us instead of us acquiring them." However, you have to remember that if there is no "best" to capture from the acquired institution, the merger may not make sense in the first place. There are plenty of efficient ways to capture customers and franchises besides a merger, so the only reason to undertake a merger is because there is something good in the acquired organization to capture.

In that respect, outside input might be essential in defining "best." Customers are often a good source of input regarding the quality of an institution. If you hear them complaining about your plans to do away with some part of an acquired institution, they may be telling you that you have missed the target in defining "best." Other outside sources, such as consultants, can assist you in defining "best."

Identifying "Bests"

There are four distinct categories for which you must identify the bests:

People
Products
Infrastructure
Processes

People are the most important, and the most difficult. Senior managers usually pride themselves on being a good judge of people, and they usually are, but this kind of judgment requires some period of exposure to the people. When an entire organization arrives at your front door, complete with its cultural and interpersonal relationships, it can be almost impossible to make objective judgments about its people.

It can be especially difficult to make objective judgments when the two organizations have been highly competitive. When your people have been struggling to convince customers not to switch their accounts to a competitor, when your branch managers have been toe to toe with theirs for years, it can be hard to make the mental adjustment from being enemies to being colleagues. This is particularly true when the people who aren't chosen are likely to be terminated. Choosing someone who has tried to take business away from you over someone who has been a loyal lieutenant requires an almost superhuman objectivity, but that is what is required.

The same kind of difficulty can arise in choosing the best *products.* The primary reason the problems are parallel is that the real product in many financial services is people. Another reason, oddly enough, is the basic similarity of many financial products. Checking accounts are just checking accounts, except for such things as balance requirements for fee waivers. Loans are just loans, except for such wrinkles as "one month a year interest-free." And even such services as portfolio management compete in a fairly rigorous world of past performance measurement, except that every trust department measures its past performance a little differently.

What becomes obvious is that institutions strive mightily to differentiate products that are essentially commodities. When they are two separate institutions, such differentiation serves a selfish purpose, but it takes on a different visage when a merger has been announced. Customers who previously were convinced that the products were so different must now be convinced to switch from one set to another. After years of being told, "You wouldn't want to use any of their services," now they have to be told, "It's in your best interests to switch."

The first step in selecting the best products is to determine whether best is defined in terms of customer acceptance or profitability. In many cases, institutions use certain products as loss leaders to gain access to a market segment, either geographical or functional. Those products often gain wide market acceptance without generating much in the way of profits. Such high customer loyalty can be a barrier to switching customers into a "better" product, from the point of view of profitability.

The solution is often to perpetuate the good parts of both product sets, as long as this doesn't present an insurmountable systems problem. As I will discuss later in this chapter, retaining customers is crucial in the early stages of a merger, and the only way to do that might be to retain their favorite products. Once the turmoil of the merger is a memory, the product sets can be melded. The flexibility in the software architecture of the institution is important as it may require maintenance of duplicate systems; however, that is often unacceptable to senior management.

It is unacceptable because one of the first jobs after the merger is agreed to is the consolidation of the *infrastructure,* or the physical plant and systems. Most in-market mergers are accomplished with a specific level of savings in mind, and the lion's share of the savings is expected to come from three sources: layoffs, branch closings, and data center consolidations. Two of those three involve infrastructure.

Branch closings are usually accomplished on a purely financial basis, but one which has two aspects. The first is the rental expense which includes the cost of breaking a lease. The second is the value of the leasehold improvements, which might have to be written off if the branch is closed. In more enlightened mergers, branches are looked at as independent business units, with their own operating statements, and the choice might be to retain the one with the healthiest operating results.

Technology, or systems, choices are more difficult. Since a bank's real product is information, changing the information-processing function would be akin to changing the assembly line at Ford. With something that central to survival, every choice must be made with the greatest care.

Except that it is usually done in a hurry. Everyone, no matter what his or her level of expertise, can see that running duplicate processing operations is inefficient, so collapsing the technology into one system is often the first order of business after the closing of the merger. Everyone who works in the systems area for both banks knows that job security is totally dependent on the choice of technology, so there is often fierce infighting from the day the merger is announced until the day the technology decision is announced.

Too many times, the decision is based on which bank wins the merger negotiations. Which chairman becomes the CEO of the merged bank? Which bank's name survives? Which bank's products survive? Of course, those factors are relevant, but not necessarily the most important. Instead, the questions should be: Which system has the best ability to carry the bank into the future? Which system better allows different business units within the bank to share data and function? Which system better allows the bank to connect electronically with other entities, including customers?

In many cases, the best solution is a combination of systems, or perhaps an entirely new one. This may be one of those cases where outsourcing is an ideal answer, if it is structured to give the merged bank a head start on bringing together its products, its people, and its customers. Doing this during a merger takes great courage, but it might eliminate much of the infighting and that could make it the best answer of all.

One reason it could make sense is that the merged institution must also select the best *processes* among those in effect in both partners. With all the selecting going on at this time, it is easy to overlook the selection of processes, but they might be the key to profitability in the future.

Given the turmoil attendant to a merger, and the demands on management's time, it is a safe bet that only a fraction of the processes will be reviewed and compared. In that case, it is mandatory that the processes be prioritized by their impact on profitability and customer satisfaction. Those two criteria will allow the bank to focus scarce management resources on selecting processes which will have the biggest short-term impact on the success of the merger.

For those with courage, the merger and its aftermath can present an opportunity to do some judicious process reengineering. If one of the purposes of an in-market merger is to reduce head count, then the merged bank will probably be faced with the same issue we discussed in Chapter 12, trying to execute the same processes with a lot fewer people. Because morale is often a problem in a newly-merged bank, process reengineering can play an additional role, in showing the surviving employees that the merger will have beneficial results for them. A properly executed reengineering effort can make a tremendous difference in bringing together the merged banks and their employees.

Integrating "Bests"

Bringing everything together, or integration, is the crowning achievement of the first component—capturing the best of both institutions. If you just capture the best of the institutions, the whole will equal the sum of the parts, but by integrating the bests, you can make the whole exceed the sum of the parts. Like capturing, integration applies to all four pieces: people, products, infrastructure, and processes.

Just as integration results in a higher level of value, it requires a higher level of effort. It also requires a unique way of thinking about a merger. The most common description of an in-market merger is "smashing the two organizations together," and that is how many people think of it, and how bank managements often approach it. I call it the "train wreck" theory of mergers, where the survivors are the ones left standing after the smoke clears.

But the premise of maximizing market capitalization requires abandoning the train-wreck approach. Not only must the two organizations be fitted together, a part at a time, the resulting engine must run as if the parts were made to work together. The fitting together begins with the people. Integrating people, in this case, means integrating corporate cultures. Once you have selected the best people from each bank, you will find that they come to the job with a set of approaches that is a result of their corporate culture, some of which is good, and some of which is indifferent. Senior management will have to set an example by absorbing the good parts of the culture of a formerly competing organization.

Another requirement is that the management pay homage to the histories of the two separate organizations which no longer exist. In some ways, going through a merger is like selling a business you have built for years. A large portion of people's egos are tied up in the businesses that they have been a part of, so burying the former organizations without a ceremony will be extraordinarily damaging, to customer perceptions as well as to employee morale.

Products are easier to integrate, except that they are dependent upon technology. Many merged institutions have dropped good, profitable, well-received products from an acquired institution because they were collapsing the technology investment and couldn't find a way to migrate the products from one technology to another. But customers become attached to products, so dropping them after a merger can telegraph the message to those customers that you don't value their business very much. Keeping the products, even temporarily, sends a different message, one which both customers and employees find more positive.

But truly integrating products requires a parallel integration of technology. The difficulty is that much of technology is an either/or proposition—software is not often written to share data and function with other software. Technological architecture normally requires one set of data instead of multiple sets, and one program, often designed to run on one kind of machine, to perform the functions. The idea of sharing functions across multiple programs, perhaps running on different operating systems, is one whose time is still a little way into the future.

However, new functions, designed to incorporate the features of newly integrated products, can be built into current technology. DDA accounting programs may be able to accept different balance-requirement levels in calculating fees. Host systems may be able to communicate with new ATMs and new networks, having different capabilities, which come along with a new acquisition.

The time to find out whether this is possible is before the merger. However, because of legal disclosure requirements, much of the necessary information may not be available from the potential merger partner, so you might have to learn as much as possible from vendors to the potential partner. Here is where a network of good contacts in the technology business can be a big help, as well as people with a good understanding of competitors' technology within your own organization.

Integrating processes can be the easiest of the jobs, provided the other integrations have been accomplished. If the people have come together and the cultures have been integrated, if the product line is an amalgam of the merged product lines, and if the best of both technologies has been integrated, then the processes will largely have been integrated.

But there are plenty of times when the processes must lead the way. In those cases, the approach is much the same as it is in reengineering. Management must determine what aspects of each process conform the best to the merged bank's objectives and strategies, and must combine those aspects into what becomes a new process. In fact, the requirement to integrate processes is often an ideal opportunity to do judicious reengineering under the cover of a merger.

Eliminating Excess Capacity

This is the exact opposite of capturing the best of both institutions, and it has a more negative connotation. Excess capacity has been the driving force in the entire consolidation process that has gripped the finance industry for the last several years, so one might expect that its elimination would be a fairly exact science. However, recent history has shown that eliminating excess capacity is an inexact science at best.

Identifying Excess Capacity

Excess capacity is elusive, so the first step in eliminating it is identifying it. Once again, let's use the four categories we have used before in this chapter: people, products, infrastructure, and processes.

People

People are the component of a financial institution most observers think of when the concept of excess capacity is introduced. According to conventional wisdom, there are too many tellers, account officers, credit officers, accountants, and programmers. Additional wisdom says that there are too many department heads, too many directors, and too many managers.

The question is, how do we pare down? Which of all these people constitute "too many?" How do we make the hard choices of who stays and who goes? Do we begin cutting at the top or at the bottom?

The last question is the key to the others. In many cases, personnel cuts have appeared to run from the top down, as heads of business units, and then departments, have been named first, with the population of the organization filled out as it moved down the pyramid. Unfortunately, this process often leaves the organization top-heavy, as managers preserve the positions of too many other managers. The real effect of a top-down approach to personnel has often been to concentrate the cuts at the lower levels of the organization.

This process can have two negative effects. First, the extent to which the personnel cuts affect the doers instead of the overseers will determine the organization's ability to deliver quality service. There is a business adage which says that a boat with eight rowers and one coxswain will beat a boat with eight coxswains and one rower every time. If you look with an unbiased eye at the productivity of people at all levels of an institution, you will probably find that a lot of the excess capacity is concentrated at higher levels of the organization. Think for a minute about the concept of cutting 10 percent of the lowest-level employees, 20 percent of the first-level managers, 30 percent of the department managers, 40 percent of the business-unit managers, and 50 percent of the top-level managers. That approach, while a difficult sell in the boardroom, might generate real productivity gains.

The second negative comes from the bugaboo which surfaced in the last chapter, reducing the work force without reengineering the job. Making across-the-board cuts of 15 or 20 percent without reengineering the processes practically ensures that service quality and employee morale will fall. But reengineering seldom works when it is imposed from the top. The best approach is probably the one embodied by General Electric's work-outs, where the employees themselves reengineer the process, often without the direct involvement of their managers. Work-outs were a daring gamble by GE, as they would be for a bank, but they have been shown to work. Bringing in outside experts in reengineering, and teaming them up with the employees, will often result in the employees self-selecting the ones who stay and those who go.

Products

Here the decision criteria are essentially the same as they were for capturing the best. Which products have both low profitability and low customer acceptance? These should be the first to be declared excess. Then, which products have either low-profitability or low-customer acceptance? These products need to be compared with competing products within the merged institution, as well as outside the institution. Are there obvious design flaws in some of these products which could make them winners if fixed? Will there be severe market reactions if customers are required to switch from one product to another? In dealing with products that have differing levels of profitability and customer acceptance, you can use the following matrix to prioritize your strategies:

Figure 17.2

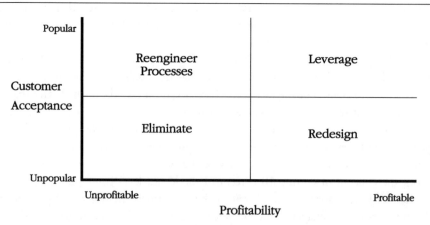

Another criterion for choosing is the relationship of the product to the underlying technology. In some recent cases, this relationship has been the overriding determinant of which products lived and which died. Decisions were made to eliminate one set of technologies, and the products dependent on that technology were eliminated as a result, almost without regard for profitability and market acceptance. To be sure, the profitability of a product may be affected by the technology's ease of use, or ability to grow, or its flexibility, but there is a fatal flaw in eliminating a good product because it depends on bad technology.

Infrastructure

The biggest problem with identifying excess capacity in infrastructure is that infrastructure, by its definition, supports the rest of the business. As a result, infrastructure decisions affect every other part of the business, sometimes in ways that are both damaging and unexpected. This is compounded by the fact that management is usually under pressure to eliminate this excess capacity in a hurry.

Sometimes the effects of infrastructure contractions are visible immediately, in the form of breakdowns in the processing of business. A few years ago, there was a wonderful comedy routine done by the radio team of Bob and Ray about the consolidation of a bunch of bank branches. After announcing all the closings and relocations, Bob and Ray revealed that, "In the turmoil, the bank lost the account records of all these branches. So, if you will drop by your new, relocated branch, and tell us how much money you had in your account, we'll get everything straightened out in no time." We all laugh, but the specter of this kind of disaster is never far from the surface. One real life example that has been repeated several times both in the United States and Europe is the specter of lines of customers standing outside recently-closed branches because the bank failed to inform them of the closing.

Sometimes the effects of the contractions are felt later, after business returns to normal. People who can't get to information they need, processes that can't handle growth in volume, and the inability to respond to moves by competitors are a few of the problems that surface after everything was supposed to be going smoothly again. Paying attention to the implications of the infrastructure decisions at the time they are made, even if time pressures are intense, can pay tremendous dividends later.

Processes

Just as there is duplication in all the components, there is inevitably duplication in processes. Once again, the question is which processes to keep and which to discard. This is where the kind of assessment implied by reengineering is so important.

In particular, a financial analysis of each process can point out which one of the duplicates is more expensive or has less of a positive impact on revenue generation.

A financial analysis is a start, but it doesn't cover all the bases. It doesn't, for example, cover processes which "set the table" for other lines of businesses, but which might not generate significant revenue on their own. In this category would be processes which put the customers in contact with the institution and expose them to other products and services. Another aspect that a pure financial analysis might overlook is the quality incorporated in the product. More businesses are coming to realize that quality is a very important component of products, services, and processes, but unless the evaluation specifically takes quality into account, it is easy to declare a high-quality process excess.

There is always the possibility that an objective analysis will conclude that neither of the processes used by the merging banks for a specific purpose is good enough, and they are both considered excess. In that case, a new and better process will have to be designed. New processes can be the foundations of a real increase in profits, but they will never happen if the merged bank simply chooses a process from one of the predecessors. Once again, it is a matter of having the courage to undertake this kind of change in the midst of a merger, but that is often the best time to do it.

Measuring Excess Capacity

The second prerequisite to eliminating excess capacity is measuring it, because there is no other way to be sure you aren't cutting into useful capacity. There are three ways in which excess capacity can be measured: *based on volume, based on function, and based on market coverage.* By making all three measurements, the institution can be fairly certain that it has the right measurement.

Based on Volume

This is a measure based on the volume of business done. Business can be measured in dollars: of assets, loans, trades, withdrawals, or it can be measured in transactions volumes: at ATMs, in custody accounts, or at teller windows. However it is measured, volume is an important, but fluid, criterion.

Its importance is obvious, but its fluidity might not be. The fact is that, however you measure it, volume is always changing. Some of that change is under the institution's control, but some is not. Institutions might have low volume in one kind of loan, for example, because they haven't marketed that kind of loan aggressively. If they determine that, with a new process, volumes will pick up significantly, eliminating capacity based on past volume figures could leave the bank in the position of having to replace that capacity within a short time.

Change that is not within the institution's control is also a factor. An economic downturn, for example, will reduce the institution's requirement for new loan-application capacity, but will likely increase its requirement for loan monitoring and refinancing capacity. Population shifts may require rural banks to reduce, or at best maintain, transaction-processing capacity, while urban and suburban banks will have to plan for increases. The important thing to remember is that, although these changes may not be under the institution's control, they are not invisible. Trends in most of these areas are visible to those institutions that look for them, and those are the ones that will likely have planned for the right capacity.

Based on Function

This is the most obvious measure of excess, based on the fact that most banks do most things for themselves, and there is really no need for two sets of credit committees or two accounting systems or two branches across the street from each other. Performing the same function twice is an obvious inefficiency.

However, the institution must make sure that the functions are actually the same. Even subtle differences in function will complicate the decision of which to eliminate, or whether elimination is an alternative. The most obvious place where functional excess surfaces is in the bank's computer departments. On its face, it makes no sense to run two separate processing systems for one bank, but it may be harder than it first appears to determine how much computer capacity is functionally excess. It is clear that the programs which handle deposit and general accounting should be normalized as soon as possible, but it is often not so clear how that normalization will affect systems which use data and processes within those main programs. Depending on which systems are chosen as the survivors, and what their functionality is, eliminating one of the main programs might severely reduce the functionality of other systems that the bank depends on for profits.

For example, marketing systems which search deposit and loan systems for customers with certain characteristics might work with one accounting system which has a relational database, but not with another which has a hierarchical database. Depending on the importance of such ancillary systems, some of the functionality of the bank's main systems might not be excess after all. This issue, of determining what impacts and dependencies there are for each of the redundant processing systems, is sometimes skipped because of the time pressure to consolidate the technology, but skipping it always leads to trouble later.

Based on Market Coverage

Excess capacity based on market coverage is seldom an issue in cross-market mergers, where the objective is to increase market penetration, but it can be a significant issue with an in-market merger, where the primary goal is to reduce capacity.

In many cases, the weaker of the in-market banks has reached that condition by expanding into markets where it has little or no expertise. Whether those markets are geographic or product in nature, the acquiring bank might determine that exiting some of those markets is the best course of action.

In that case, the first choice is often to close down the department or subsidiary providing that market coverage. While that is an option, a better one might be selling the business, or forming an alliance with an entity better able to serve that market. This is a case where alliances can be an excellent alternative, because they allow the bank to stay in touch with its customers who may need other financial services besides the one covered by the alliance, and because they give the bank an opportunity to participate in growth, should the market take off. As usual, choosing the alliance partner and structuring the alliance are the keys to its success.

A capacity issue which is endemic to almost all in-market mergers, and many cross-market ones, is the coverage of corporate customers. Unless the two banks are completely dissimilar, it is likely that they service the same corporate customers in many of their functions. Unlike retail customers, corporate customers are likely to have duplicate banking relationships, so the bank will often be faced with eliminating excess coverage.

What is important to remember is that different parts of the bank may have different levels of relationship with the same customer. Thus the lending group from Bank A might have a better relationship with XYZ Corporation, while the corporate trust group from Bank B has a better relationship in their product line. Matching the best relationships with the corporate customer can result in a patchwork relationship that provides a way of eliminating excess capacity, and that approach might be the best one.

Eliminating the Capacity

So far, the work has been easy. Now comes the painful part, because eliminating capacity invariably means eliminating employees. Layoffs and downsizing are commonplace within the finance industry, but that doesn't make the process any easier. There are, however, several steps that can make it a success if not a pleasure.

1. *Have a downsizing strategy.* This sounds obvious but isn't. Having a strategy means having objectives, and knowing both how to achieve them and when to implement them. Armed with a strategy, managers can keep their eye on the target when the going gets rough. Senior management can keep track of progress and make the necessary adjustments.

    Downsizing strategies must focus on maintaining the necessary strength to build your business, not just on eliminating expenses. It is easy, during a difficult period, to concentrate entirely on trimming the work force, or consolidating data centers, or closing branches, but the downsizing strategy must have as its primary goal the emergence of an institution that is in fighting trim and able to serve its market.

2. *Communication is of the essence.* As management struggles with integration and capacity issues, it is easy to neglect informing those people, both inside and outside the institution, who are essentially in the dark. Both employees and customers have a vital interest in knowing what is happening.

   Will my department continue to exist? Will my branch be closed? Will I have to get new checks? What will happen to my loan application? What will happen to our alliance? All these questions and more are being discussed and considered by countless people who work for, or do business with, the merged banks. Keeping them in the dark will increase defections and in-fighting.

   Of course, management doesn't have all the answers right away, so there is a temptation not to say anything until everything has been worked out. Experience has shown that to be a bad idea. A better practice is the issuance of regular progress reports, containing as much information as can be released. People who are going to be let go can sense what is coming, and will appreciate as much time to prepare as possible. Not telling anyone anything only prompts the better people to send out their resumes, and they may be gone by the time all the pieces are in place to be communicated. The same policy applies to customers and business partners. People will want to know who they will be doing business with, and not informing them will prompt them to make other plans. Whatever information you can release, you should, perhaps at regularly scheduled times. It may make you feel like you are operating in a fishbowl, but the fact is, you are, and clamming up doesn't change that at all.

3. *Think beyond the negatives.* The downsizing that follows an in-market merger is often portrayed by everyone involved, including the press, as a negative time. People are losing their jobs, branches are being closed, customer relationships are being disrupted, so it is easy for everyone to be feeling down.

   But the postmerger period is also an opportunity to generate positives. Reengineering the jobs of the remaining employees is one example. People whose jobs are more meaningful and productive will be quicker to put the consolidation process behind them than those who are simply doing the old jobs with fewer staff.

It is also a time to enhance products and marketing. If you have truly captured the best of both institutions, then you will have better products and services to offer. You will be better able to assist your business partners, and better able to serve your customers.

Increase Market Presence

Although it is not usually expressed as a specific goal, increasing market presence should be the underlying reason for entering into an in-market merger. But the opposite often happens. Caught up in the immediacy of reducing head count, closing branches, and consolidating data centers, managements are often surprised to discover that they have lost up to 20 percent of their customer base in the postmerger period.

The Risks of a Merger

In fact, the period between the announcement of an in-market merger and the completion of the consolidation process is fraught with marketing risks. During this period, in the minds of many employees, customers occupy last place, and customers often react by shifting their focus to other institutions. Amidst all the turmoil is an ideal time for competitors to poach the best customers and business partners.

In the marketing area, there are three major risks to be dealt with.

Loss of customer focus occurs because many employees are concerned with their jobs, and middle management is absorbed with the political maneuvering that accompanies high-level consolidations. When the merging banks announce that they will close 25 percent of their branches, branch managers and employees spend a lot of time thinking about whether it will be their branch that is closed, and do not spend much time thinking about what their customers need. Employees who are typing up resumes aren't expediting customer requests, and, when a customer calls up and says, "I'm having a problem with my account," the employee's reaction might just be, "You've got a problem! I may not have a job tomorrow—now that's a real problem."

Degradation of products occurs because institutions are in a hurry to combine systems. When good products depend on not-so-good systems and when there is a rush to consolidate data centers, it is easy to bury a good product. In many cases, management never notices that a good product just went by the boards; their attention is focused elsewhere. But the customers notice. When they have to accept a checking account with a higher average-balance requirement, when loan payments are misposted, when they get worse prices and service from a trading desk, or when they receive an unfamiliar and confusing statement in the mail, customers realize right away that the product has been degraded. And that leads to . . .

Customer confusion, where customers don't know what is happening to their bank, or to their account. When the bank you do business with has been taken over, your first question is, "Who am I doing business with now?" As a customer, if your service was good with the old bank, and it is noticeably worse with the new one, or if there are glitches in transferring accounts, it is easy to develop negative feelings about the bank. Predatory competitors will be aware of that possibility, and they will target your unsatisfied customers. Smart bankers know it is hard to switch a customer from one bank to another, but once it is done, it is also hard to switch them back.

Increasing Market Presence

Dealing with the risks of increasing market presence requires three major efforts:

Enhancing customer contact
Boosting employee morale
Achieving product synergy

Enhancing Customer Contact

During a merger is the time when you most need to stay in contact with your customers. The fact that your institution is undergoing tremendous changes, that people have to be terminated, is not really your customers' concern, and they will be thinking of themselves first. Giving them a rich flow of information, and giving them an opportunity to voice their concerns, will greatly enhance your chances of retaining them.

All this is hard to do when your employees are concerned with their own problems. In addition, many bank customers go for extended periods without entering a branch or talking to a bank employee. That is why it is important to maintain as much of this contact outside the branch arena as possible. Statement mailings, special mailings, ATM messages, and advertising are some of the ways banks can enhance their customer contacts.

Not only should contacts be more frequent, they need to be high quality. Customers will be sensitive to signs that your interest in them has declined, so you need to make your messages as personal and meaningful as possible. For example, ATM sign-on messages can contain the customer's name, so that their first contact with the bank through that medium can be a positive experience. Their first statement from the new bank can contain stuffers, like a coupon they can use to enter a "branch party" contest by bringing it into their new branch. Sophisticated marketing techniques can identify customers who are ideally suited for products or services, and those customers can be given introductory discounts to get them started. The point is, good marketing can turn a negative into a positive.

Boosting Employee Morale

Marketing doesn't just apply to customers; you have to market to your employees as well. In order to counteract the negative psychology of the inevitable downsizing, you will have to work extra hard to give your employees something good to strive for. Most managers don't realize that it can be a very negative experience being a survivor in a corporate thinning out. There is an axiom about managing during a retrenchment which says that keeping your job isn't really enough incentive to produce extra effort.

As a result, you need a constant stream of information and incentives for your employees, and that stream must reach all the way down into the organization. We have already discussed information about the personnel reductions, but employees also need information about changes in their job descriptions or changes in strategies. Incentives can be part of the pay packages, but there are also ample opportunities for contests, special recognitions, and letters of commendation. It is amazing what special recognition of one employee in a branch or department can do for the morale of the whole operation.

Achieving Product Synergy

Previously I discussed the risks of product degradation, and synergy is the opposite side of that. Bringing together two institutions, with two corporate cultures and two sets of products, can be a positive instead of a negative. Instead of cancelling each other out, the institutions can achieve synergy. Instead of wiping out one set of products, the institution can strive to use the best of each set.

As I have pointed out, that depends a great deal on the flexibility of the processing systems that support the products. Inflexible, closed systems will make it hard to incorporate the best of both products, and even harder to flow success from one product to another. So, in many ways, this part of making a merger work could be heavily dependent on those folks in the data center who represent a big part of the downsizing effort.

Who Wins When a Merger Works

Making all this happen requires a tremendous effort on the part of everyone in the organization. The institution will have to achieve economies of scale, moving ever closer to the goal of doing twice the business through the same size balance sheet with half the employees. The institution will have to achieve synergy and cross-pollination, resulting in better products and happier customers. And the institution will have to achieve cooperation with employees, from both merged banks, who will work together toward a common goal.

If you can achieve all that, who wins?

- ❑ *Your stockholders* will win, because your earnings will be maximized, the price/earnings ratio will go up, and their stock price will rise.

- ❑ *Your customers* will win, because their financial service will improve and, as a result, their financial well-being will improve.

- ❑ *Your employees* will win, because they will become more productive and, as a result, will be more satisfied and better paid.

- ❑ And *you* will win, because management always reaps the rewards of running a successful business.

Not every institution will win, but, if you can make yours a winner, you will have earned both respect and riches.

Good luck!

Index